# A SENSE OF HUMUS

Mum.

Happy Xmas —

Dec '97

# A SENSE OF HUMUS

## A Bedside Book of Garden Humour

### DIANA
### ANTHONY

SHOAL BAY PRESS

## DEDICATION

for Brian
who listens to
the gardener's Grand Tantrums
and for my daughter Sarah,
to both with love.

First published in 1997 by
Shoal Bay Press Ltd
Box 2151, Christchurch, New Zealand

Reprinted September 1997

ISBN 0 908704 49 6

Printed by G.P. Print Ltd, Wellington

# CONTENTS

## THE GARDENER'S PRAYER

*Lord, grant in some way it may rain every day, say from about midnight until three o'clock in the morning, but you see, it must be gentle and warm so it can soak in ... Grant at the same time it would not rain on the campion, alyssum, helianthemum, lavender, and others which You in Your infinite wisdom know are drought-loving plants – I will write their names on a bit of paper for you if you like ...*

*And grant that the sun may shine the whole day through, but not everywhere (not, for instance, on the spiraea or gentian, plantain lily and rhododendron) and not too much ...*

*That there may be plenty of dew and very little wind, enough worms, no mealy bugs, slugs and snails, no mildew or fungus, and that once a week thin liquid manure may fall from heaven. Amen.*

Karel Capek, *The Gardener's Year*, 1929

# INTRODUCTION

The trouble with most gardening books is that they are always commanding you to do something – prune, plant, hoe, sow, spray, weed etc. They forget that there are times when gardeners simply need to throw themselves into the depths of a favourite chair and read something entertaining about their passion; to learn how horticulturists of ancient times did things; to smile at the foibles, fancies and fads of other gardeners; to be amused by their eccentricities; to share their tears and triumphs ... and not to be overwhelmed with advice.

Garden literature contains some of the most entertaining writing in the world and, like gardening, it is often controversial, ironic, perverse, passionate and sometimes downright desperate. Gardening is an infinite source of comedy and semi-tragedy, furnishing scope for the full range of human emotions. Down-to-earth garden writers are scathingly satirical in the face of horticultural pretensions. Their waspishly witty pens take the reader on an exploration of gardens of love, hate, mishap, jealously and even absurdity.

The collection of wit and wisdom offered in this volume is a somewhat kaleidoscopic affair; but no matter how the pieces are shaken or dipped into, the vibrant pattern that emerges reflects the humour, the colour and vitality of the vagaries and vicissitudes attendant upon the garden and its maker.

Gardeners have been accused of being preposterous, full of ruthless cunning, guile, greed, conceit and self-pity. We explore these astonishing charges, finding perchance that there is a little of each and every one of us in the great green-fingered (or otherwise) between these pages. In so doing we make the most important discovery of all – that gardeners have a finely developed penchant for laughing at themselves and are possessed of a magnificent sense of humus. This shall be both our conclusion and our defence.

If we are to be on trial, we shall conduct that defence with razored repartée – with wisdom and witticisms ancient and modern – from the wags and wits of gardendom.

Diana Anthony

## THE GARDENER

*I find that the real gardener is not a man who cultivates flowers; he is a man who cultivates the soil ... If he came into the Garden of Eden he would sniff excitedly and say: 'Good Lord, what humus!' I think he would forget to eat the fruit of the tree of knowledge of good and evil; he would rather look round to see how he could manage to take away from the Lord some barrow-loads of the paradisaic soil. Or he would discover that the tree of knowledge of good and evil has not around it a nice dishlike bed, and he would begin to mess about with the soil, innocent of what is hanging over his head. 'Where are you, Adam?' the Lord would say. 'In a moment,' the gardener would shout over his shoulder; 'I am busy now.' And he would go on making his little bed.*

Karel Capek, *The Gardener's Year*, 1929

# 1

# THE GARDENER

*Every man reaps what he sows in this life*
*except the amateur gardener.* —Anon

The *Oxford Dictionary* defines a gardener as one who gardens, is skilled in the art of gardening. This description implies some degree of competence and knowledge and hints at expertise in things horticultural.

This does not accord with the way in which my family regard me in my capacity as a gardener. 'A sort of green-fingered lunatic' they say, and of my gardening: 'a disease poor mother suffers from – it makes us suffer too'.

If my family suffers only from impoliteness, my best friend, who is every bit as keen a gardener as I, shows even less respect. She tells me in some kind of variation on the 'you'll die with your boots on' theme: 'I'll know when it's your coffin on the hearse because the lid will open and a hand holding secateurs will come out and take cuttings off the wreaths … '

She is still my friend because, in spite of the eccentricities attributed to us by 'normal' people (non-horticulturists), we gardeners are blessed with great good humour and the ability to recognise our foibles and to laugh at ourselves. So just how *do* these 'normal' people see us? How have wags and wits ancient and modern perceived us?

Karel Capek, an early twentieth-century Czech playwright and gardener, discerns a certain acquisitiveness in our breed:

> The gardener is a man who, with a fading plant in his hand, runs round his little garden twenty times looking for an inch of soil where nothing is growing. 'No, it's not possible here,' he mutters in a low voice; 'here I have those damned chrysanthemums; phlox would smother it here; and here is campion, may the devil take it! Hum, here campanulas have run loose, and near this achillea there is no room either – where shall I put it? Wait a little – here – no, here is monk's-hood; or here – but here is cinquefoil. It might do here, but it

9

is full of tradescantias; and here – what is coming up here? I wish I knew. Ha, here is a bit of space; wait, my seedling, in a moment I will make your bed. So, there you are, and now grow in peace.'[1]

Yes, but in two days the gardener will discover that he has planted it right on top of the scarlet shoots of the evening primrose.

In addition to acquisitiveness, the gardener is often accused of peculiarity of habit. The arch-priestess of English gardeners, Vita Sackville-West, writes with affectionate good humour of her green-fingered neighbour:

> My neighbour … does the oddest things … she has not many real wooden seed boxes. There are cardboard dress boxes tied round with string to stop them from disintegrating, and old Golden Syrup tins, and even some of those tall tins that contained Slug-death, and some of those little square chip baskets called punnets. I verily believe that she would use an old shoe if it came in handy. In this curious assortment of receptacles an equally curious assortment of seedlings are coming up, green as a lawn, prolific as mustard-and-cress on a child's piece of flannel. There are cabbages and lettuces in some of them; rare lilies in others; and I noted a terrified little crop of auriculas scurrying up, as though afraid they might be late for a pricking-out into the warm earth of May.[2]

Well-known modern British gardening guru Christopher Lloyd has a deliciously eccentric approach to fertilising his favourite plants:

> We are probably all a little cranky in our ideas on manuring. The young man who used to collect the contents of his friends' ashtrays for later application to his roses is a case in point. Tea leaves get saved exclusively as a mulch for camellias, simply because the tea plant is a camellia species. For my part, I cast all my nail parings out of the bathroom window so as to feed the ceanothus below with hoof-and-horn. Since, at twenty-four years, this is the oldest ceanothus in my garden, and it is still flourishing, I naturally congratulate myself on a sagacious policy.[3]

We all, at some time or other, own up to the odd horticultural aberration, but none of us, surely, would exhibit eccentricities quite as dreadful as the gardener described by Sir Frederick Moore, recounting the visit to the Royal

---

*A gardener knows all there is to be done. And why.*
*And yet is still astounded by the miracle.* — Pam Brown

10

Botanic Gardens at Glasnevin, in Ireland, of Mr W.E. Gumbleton, a talented Victorian horticulturist:

> In the Aquatic House, Mr Gumbleton took me to task severely for my pro-
> nunciation of the name of a plant, emphasising his remarks by banging his
> umbrella on the flags (irises) ... Mr Gumbleton wanted to see the florists'
> flowers out of doors ... Mr Gumbleton denounced a plant as a 'tush plant',
> his term for any plant he did not like, and proceeded to beat it to bits with his
> umbrella, a habit of which he gave evidence in other gardens, where the own-
> ers had the courage to rate him soundly. I was too timid to do more than
> mildly remonstrate and bemoan the loss of a recently arrived plant. In 1907,
> in company with the late Mr William Watson of Kew, I visited Mr Gumbleton
> at Belgrove, and there Mr Watson was able to witness a similar atrocity per-
> formed by Mr Gumbleton with, I believe, the same umbrella, on one of his
> own plants amidst loud ejaculations of 'Tush! Tush!'[4]

Like Mr Gumbleton, some gardeners are less sweet-tempered than others. Victorian writer and horticulturist Walter Savage Landor was eccentric, irasci- ble and even violent at times. He lived for many years on the heights of Fiesole, above Florence, where he had a beautiful garden. His pride and joy was an extensive violet bed, about which his friend Lord Houghton records the fol- lowing incident:

> Landor, after a less than perfect dinner, picked his cook up and hurled him
> bodily out of the window, and while the man was writhing in pain with a
> broken limb, ejaculated 'Good God! I forgot the violets.'[5]

Understandably, non-horticulturists are (occasionally) bemused by our green- fingered eccentricities. A butler employed by a keen British gardener remarked recently that he didn't know what things were coming to.

'At one time,' he said, 'if you kept your ears open at a dinner party you could pick up good racing tips. But all you hear now is about the best perennials to buy and the best manure to give them.'

It is a well-known fact that although a couple of gardeners may be the very best of friends, intense horticultural rivalry often exists between them. English gardener-writer Beverley Nichols describes with a certain malicious humour besting his superior gardening neighbour:

> Mrs M is the only gardener I know who never walks down a border and says,
> 'You should have seen this six weeks ago ... the wallflowers were a mass ...

weren't they a *mass* Ada? ... a positive mass.' Nor does she pause in front of a collection of feeble shoots and say, 'Of course, if you'd only come next month, I don't know what you would have said about these dahlias ... what could he have said about these dahlias, Ada? ... Nobody knows what to say about them.' Mrs M is not like that. I have tried to catch her garden off its guard without success. I always seem to arrive at the crowning hour of something or other. I have a feeling that as my car draws up at the door, the stocks blaze into their ultimate, purple flames, the last of the lilies open their scented lips, the final rosebud sheds its virginity and flaunts itself in a southern breeze. Things are always at their very best when I visit Mrs M. Perhaps if I stayed longer ... but I can never stay long at Mrs M's, she annoys me too much.

She is damnably efficient. She spends up to nothing on her garden and gets astonishing results. She shows you a blaze of delphiniums. 'All out of a penny packet,' she croons. You pass a bank flaming with golden broom. 'All from seed,' she declares. 'A shilling packet I bought years ago.' In the rockery is a sheet of purple cyclamen. 'Just a few roots I stuffed into my suitcase after my visit to Italy last year.'

She bullies one. The first time she came to see me she cried, 'Oh, but you must have a lavender hedge ... and I can't see any scarlet lupins. You *must* have scarlet lupins ... so easy to grow ... have masses. I'll send you some seeds.'

If she does, they will go down the drain, damn her.

'And your rock roses ... where did you get them?'

Scenting a compliment, I told her.

'How much did you pay for them?'

Again I told her.

'But that's *monstrous!*' She poked her umbrella contemptuously into the middle of my best clump: 'It's daylight robbery. You shouldn't pay a quarter of that.'

Mrs M's most irritating trait is that she is always right. When I was beginning my little winter garden she went round it shaking her head, and saying in tones of utmost relish, 'Oh, I'm afraid this will never *do* here.' Of course, the things which she had indicated didn't 'do'. But I feel that at least part of their failure was due to the fact that Mrs M had cast an evil spell on them. Her spirit was like a chill breath, withering everything it touched.

Mrs M was, in short, a witch. We had better leave it at that.

I have just remembered the episode of the red-hot pokers. And if you are inclined to tell me that some of my opinions on women gardeners are unduly harsh, you may feel that I have an excuse for thinking as I do, in view of the constant proximity of Mrs M. For a long time I had been irritated by her claim that she grew everything from seed. If you walked through her garden with her you were gradually driven into a frenzy by that monotonous intonation – 'just a penny packet ... only a penny packet ...'

One autumn this penny packet business drove me to desperation. I had procured, at considerable expense, a collection of red-hot pokers (i.e. *Kniphofia*) … they had done very badly. When they flowered they did not even look luke-warm. It would have been possible to bear this blow with resignation had I not happened to visit Mrs M and discover in her garden a whole bed of magnificent red-hot pokers.

They blazed with arrogance … their stems were tall and sturdy. Their leaves were bursting with rude health. They really did look red-hot, and it made me red-hot to look at them.

Mrs M was chortling beside me. She said: 'Very fine, aren't they?'

I turned to her. 'You don't mean to say that these came out of a penny packet?'

'But certainly,' said Mrs M. Then – as though she suddenly saw the gates of hell opening before her, in answer to this fearful lie – 'at least, from a *packet*. From seed, I mean. Whether it was a penny, or twopence, or fourpence I really don't know.'

These last two phrases seemed rather funny to me, since I knew, from ulterior sources, that Mrs M always crosses the halfpennies off her accounts.

However, the sense of amusement did not last long. For when I left her the red-hot pokers began to proclaim themselves. They stung me to a sullen fury. They seared themselves into my brain. I could not sleep at night because of those red-hot pokers, which pursued me as vehemently as if I had been a religious person in the Middle Ages whipped by a fiery demon's tail.

The weeks passed by … again I went to see Mrs M … a purple flood of Michaelmas daisies swam into my heated vision. Then there were other daisies, tawny and grand, and a quantity of chrysanthemums, and a lot of things which I could not grow at all. I walked on. The red-hot pokers, of course, would be finished now, so that no maddening blaze could assail me. However, their memory was fresh enough to be bitter.

And then I saw it. I mean, her. What I am really trying to say is that Mrs M was presenting to me a substantial portion of herself which can only be presented when a lady in a thick tweed skirt is bending down with her head towards the north, while one is approaching from the south.

However, it was not this unconventional glimpse of Mrs M which caused my heart to beat with sudden rapture. No, it was something else. Mrs M's gardener was burning a bonfire. Bright red berries glimmering, like sparks … in the foreground a stretch of dark earth, a bundle of browny-green stalks that were once red-hot pokers – and – AND – a large row of earthenware pots, still earthy from their recent upheaval, containing in more than one instance, the authentic plant of a red-hot poker!

With glazed eyes I regarded these pots. At first the full significance of the occasion did not strike me. It was not until Mrs M had turned round, and flushed as deep as any of her pokers, that I realised the blackness of her sin.

For here was Mrs M, whose lips had paid lying service to the lore of seeds, detected in the comtemptible act of removing potted plants from her border. Plants which she had actually bought in pots! No, more ... which, having bought, she had failed to remove from their pots!

I smacked my lips. This indeed was a moment to remember. The whole thing was revealed before me. I saw on one ... on two, three ... yes on four of the pots a little label. True, the labels were faded and worn, but I managed, with the unusual clarity of vision which great passion engenders, to detect the Latin name for red-hot poker. Then exaltation was usurped by horror as the appalling nature of Mrs M's felony burst upon me. It was as though one had found a criminal, who for weeks had been protesting violently protesting his innocence, in the very act of dismembering the body.[6]

Leaving Mr Nichols and Mrs M to their altercations, we turn to one of the alternative definitions offered by the dictionary.

Gardener: A servant employed to tend the garden.

Little doubt who is servant and who is master here. This particular master offers no defined 40-hour week, no long weekends, no sick leave, salary or bonuses, but infinite scope for unlimited overtime – all of it *unpaid*.

Any 'leisure' time is measured in spans of labour given to the garden. If we tear ourselves away for a holiday, we must indulge in a frenzy of manic panic preparing for our absence. We fret all the time we are away – is it too hot, too dry? Are tender plants wilting? When we return there is a body-abusing reclamation job at hand.

At the end of each day, as we lob our tools wearily into the shed, our eyes light on all the chores that will make our tomorrow – the vast eternal labour of the gardener and his garden – the half acre that demands everything we have to offer and more. When it hungers we bestow food, when it thirsts water; when it ails we dispense medicine, and when inclement weather threatens we protect. Who else would be *happy* to administer these services for 365 days of the year – in all weathers and for no pay?

I can almost feel the stern eye of that 19th-century doyenne of English gardening, Miss Gertrude Jekyll, gazing in my direction as she advises:

I do not envy the owners of very large gardens. The garden should fit its master or his tastes, just as his clothes do; it should be neither too large nor too small, but just comfortable ... If the garden is larger than he can individually garden and plan and look after, then he is no longer its master but its slave, just as surely as the too rich man is the slave and not the master of his superfluous wealth.[7]

Pig-headed and stubborn we might be, but every gardener will admit to times when exasperation gets the upper hand. One is invariably daunted by the amount of labour directed by the 'now is the time to' lists in the various worthy gardening publications, but it is reassuring to know that the degree of labour demanded by our passion was much the same many centuries ago. Medieval gentleman John Evelyn sets out a day's tasks for his head gardener:

> Every Monday morning, he must walk about the whole place to observe what needs doing, and what is amiss, before he does any other work ... Make regular checks on beehives, seed and root boxes; clean, sharpen and repair tools in wett weather and put away every night. Stir heaps of dung and mould; clip hedges, mow lawns, prune fruit and murral trees and vines when stated. Ask every night what rootes, salading, garnishing will be needed next day, and bring it to cook in the morning and informe her from time to time what garden provision and fruite is ripe and in season to be spent ... gather and bring in all fruit ... He may not dispose of any fruit or sell any vegetables, flowers or plants without first asking leave of master or mistress. He must show broken and worn out tools to the master before before buying new ones.[8]

It seems we are infected with the gardener's disease in mid to later life and there is little doubt that it is terminal. Karel Capek observes:

> While one is in the prime of life, one thinks that a flower is something that one carries in a buttonhole or presents to a girl; one does not understand that it is something that hibernates, which is dug round and manured, watered and transplanted, divided and trimmed, tied up, freed of weeds, and cleaned of seeds, aphis and mildew; instead of digging the garden one runs after girls ... eats the fruit of life which one has not produced oneself, and on the whole behaves destructively.
>
> A certain maturity is necessary for a man to become an amateur gardener ... you must have your own garden. You have it laid out by an expert, and you think you will go and look at it when the day's work is over, enjoy the flowers and listen to the chirping of the birds. One day you may plant one little flower with your own hands ... perhaps a bit of soil will get into your body through the quick ... one claw and the whole bird is caught.[9]

On the progression of the dread disease, Capek continues:

---

*An optimistic gardener is one who believes that what goes down must come up.*
—Lesley Hall

15

The new gardener yields more and more to this newly awakened passion, which is nourished by repeated success and spurred on by each new failure; the passion of the collector breaks out in him, driving him to raise everything according to the alphabet from *Acaena* to *Zauschneria*; a craze for specialisation breaks out in him, which makes of a hitherto human being a rose, dahlia, or some other sort of exalted maniac. Others fall victim to artistic passions and continually alter and arrange their beds, devise colour schemes, move shrubs, and change whatever stands or grows.[10]

Thus the gardener is born, the behaviour pattern emerging together with a peculiar change in speech. As we will observe in a crash course in Hortus Botanicus Latinicus, the horticulturist's speech becomes peppered with plant names in Latin. British writer, Margery Fish, well-known advocate of the English cottage garden, though a dedicated gardener herself, did not wholly approve. When her favourite *Olearia gunniana* was identified by garden visitors as 'a nice clump of Michaelmas daisies', she observed:

> I like people to enjoy the garden in their own way and don't bother them with information unless they want it. I feel that gardeners can be very tiresome with their long names; in fact I wonder how ordinary people put up with it. We shouldn't think much of it if doctors peppered their light conversation with the longest medical terms they could think of.[11]

Returning to the ascerbic pen of Beverley Nichols, we find him quite merciless in his exposure of gardeners as non-gardeners see us. He perceives that we:

> ... must be like parents. No parents want to talk about anybody else's child.[12]

Nichols cautions us to heed our conversation when in the company of another gardener, in case it should go like this:

Myself: (showing the herbaceous border): 'There's nothing like this cosmos for September is there? I mean for a real show?'

Real Gardener: 'You *must* see my pink larkspur. Heavenly. Do come down one day ... '

Myself: 'I'd love to. These Japanese iris are rather fine, I always think. I divided them from one root two years ago.'

Real Gardener: 'Yes. And if you come down next weekend you'd be in time for the coreopsis.'

Myself: 'My own coreopsis is ...'

Real Gardener: 'Oh, yes … I see … over there. You really must come. You change at Dorking.'

Myself (harshly) 'All these dahlias were grown from seed.'

Real Gardener: 'Yes … yes … You must see the amazing dahlia I've grown … after you've changed at Dorking I can meet you in the car …'[13]

Nichols continues on the theme of women gardeners – with a discriminatory perception that would see him hounded out of town today:

The main complaint I have to make about women gardeners is that they are such appalling liars. A woman hates you for criticising her herbaceous border as much as she would hate you for criticising her profligate son … she always has some excuse to make for his behaviour … So she will make excuses for her weedy, straggly border by saying:

'Of course, you wouldn't *believe* the display we have … of course you've come at the wrong time … last week the cosmos was ablaze … Quite ablaze … not that we put much work in … flowers grow well for people that love them … I think you said that cosmos didn't do very well for you … no? How strange! And of course if you'd only come next month the chrysanthemums … yes … they look like that because they are a dwarf variety. Oh, do you? Like them a little taller? How interesting …'[14]

Could it be that we all recognise a little of ourselves?

Poet Laurie Lee has a kinder perception of the female gardener, perhaps because this one was his mother. He describes her as having:

… a touch with flowers … she could grow them anywhere, at any time, and they seemed to live longer for her. She grew them with rough, almost slapdash love, but her hands possessed such an understanding of their needs they seemed to turn to her like another sun. She would snatch a dry root from a field or hedgerow, dab it into the garden, give it a shake – and almost immediately it flowered. One felt that she could grow roses from a stick or chair leg, so remarkable was this gift.[15]

As modern gardeners we enjoy the delicious freedom of being whatever sort of gardener we wish to be, and of creating any type of garden we wish. This freedom, which we take lightly, was not enjoyed by all gardeners of the past – especially if they were female. For Elizabeth von Arnhim, married to a German count, gardening in Victorian Pomerania was so frustrating she yearned with all her heart to be male. Rigid social convention dictated that upper-class women did not actually *work* in their gardens. At Nassenheide, on her husband's country estate, Elizabeth, with true gardener grit, determined to create her garden in the face of severe opposition from her husband and his gardeners:

I am ignorant, and the gardener is, I do believe, more so, for he was forcing some tulips, and they have all shrivelled up and died, he says he cannot imagine why. Besides he is in love with the cook, and is going to marry her and refuses to enter into any of my plans with the enthusiasm they deserve, but sits with a vacant eye dreamily chopping wood to keep the loved one's kitchen fire well supplied. I cannot understand anyone preferring cooks to marigolds; those future marigolds, shadowy though they are, and whose seeds are still sleeping at the seedsmen's, have shone through my winter days like golden lamps.

I wish with all my heart I were a man, for of course the first thing I should do would be to buy a spade and go and garden, and then I should have the delight of doing everything for my flowers with my own hands and not have to waste time explaining what I want done to somebody else. It is dull work giving orders to and trying to describe the brightest visions of one's brain to a person who has no vision and no brain.[16]

Finally overcome with frustration and temptation, Elizabeth confides:

In all the first ecstasy of having a garden all my own, and in my burning ambition to make the waste places blossom like a rose, I did one warm Sunday afternoon during the servants' dinner hour slink out with a spade and rake, feverishly dig a little piece of ground, break it up surreptitiously, run back into the house and get into a chair behind a book and look languid just in time to save my reputation.[17]

Despite of the rigid code of behaviour imposed upon the women of her era, Elizabeth did find some measure of personal freedom at Nassenheide:

May 7th: There were days last winter when I danced for joy out in the frostbound garden in spite of my years and children. But I did it behind a bush, having due regard for the decencies.[18]

Karel Capek, writing 30 years later, describes the gardener's absorption with his or her garden with cheeky irreverence:

While I was only a remote and distracted onlooker of the accomplished work of gardens, I considered gardeners to be beings of a particularly poetic and gentle mind, who cultivate perfumes of flowers while listening to the birds singing … I will now tell you how to recognise the real gardener. 'You must come to see me,' he says: I will show you my garden.' Then when you go just to please him, you will find him with his rump sticking up somewhere among the perennials. 'I will come in a moment,' he shouts to you over his shoulder. 'Just wait till I have planted this rose.'
'Please, don't worry,' you say kindly to him.

After a while he must have planted it: for he gets up, makes your hand dirty, and beaming with hospitality he says: 'Come and have a look; it's a small garden, but – wait a moment,' and he bends over a bed to weed some tiny grass. 'Come along. I will show you *Dianthus musalae*; it will open your eyes. Great Scott, I forgot to loosen it here!' he says, and begins to poke in the soil. A quarter of an hour later he straightens up again. 'Ah,' he says, 'I wanted to show you that bell flower, *Campanula wilsonae*. That is the best campanula, which – wait a moment, I must tie up this delphinium.'

After he has tied it up he remembers: 'Oh, I see, you have come to see that erodium. A moment,' he murmurs, 'I must just transplant this aster, it hasn't enough room here.'

After that you go away on tiptoe, leaving his behind sticking up among the perennials.[19]

Which is, perhaps, the best description of the gardener I have ever found.

I dug
I levelled
I weeded
I seeded
I planted
I waited
I weeded
I pleaded
I mulched
I gulched
I watered
I waited
I fumbled
I grumbled
I poked
I hoped

so GROW ... Dammit
—Marion French

# 2

# 'TOUGH COOKIES, YOU LADY GARDENERS'

*[Gardening] is not graceful, and it makes one hot; but it is a blessed sort of work,
and if Eve had had a spade in Paradise and known what to do with it, we should
not have had all that sad business with the apple.* —Elizabeth von Arnhim

The brief history of gardening we explore in this chapter leaves no doubt
that women have been passionate, if frustrated, gardeners since the days
of ancient Rome and Egypt. Even then, society decreed that only women of
the poorer classes actually worked the land for subsistence or food production
purposes. We observe later that in medieval times women were expected to
have a comprehensive knowledge of the cultivation of herbs and their uses; by
the 17th and 18th centuries men were writing simple instruction booklets for
them, guiding them in their responsibilities. But the creation and maintenance
of flower and pleasure gardens was to remain largely a male affair for several
centuries to come.

The rigid social structure of the 18th and 19th centuries kept women firmly
in the home, their physical and intellectual capacities submerged in a stifling
round of social and domestic trivia. Though educated women were encouraged
in the study of botany and in drawing and painting their specimens, few would
have had anything to do with plant care or cultivation at source. Their lives
were often full of the frustration and boredom described by Elizabeth von
Arnhim in 1896, as she watched her husband's gardeners working the gardens
she was struggling to create in the purely supervisory capacity society dictated:

> I sometimes literally ache with envy as I watch the men going about their
> pleasant work in the sunshine, turning up the luscious damp earth, raking,
> weeding, watering, planting, cutting the grass, pruning the trees – not a thing
> they do from the first uncovering of the roses in spring to the November
> bonfires but fills my soul with longing to be up and doing too.[1]

Perhaps more than anything else, the two world wars were the catalyst that
brought about the emancipation of women as 'hands on' gardeners. Women of

all classes were desperately needed to work the land – and we've never looked back! Many of the great gardens of the twentieth century have been created by women gardeners, and as we approach the new millennium, statistics show that a staggering 75 per cent of garden labour is performed by women. (I can relate very well to this ...) In the most brutal of my gardening toil I am spurred on, as I think with sympathy of poor Elizabeth and her sisters.

Today I romped through a barrow and boulder job (lifting, loading, heaving) to repair a stone wall; wielded pick and crowbar to dig extra large holes in un-yielding clay for saplings; filled the pits with requisite (heavy) drainage materi-als; dug up, divided and replanted equally unyielding clumps of perennials; and took pruning saw – since the chainsaw is forbidden me – to the sturdy limbs of 'Madame Alfred Carriere'.

The lusty lady was threatening to engulf the outhouses forever. 'I'm sure we had a garage when we bought this house,' the family say by way of hint, or 'She'll need a logging truck in there soon.' Finding that Madame's more tena-cious tendrils had galloped across the roof, from atop a high ladder I risked life and limb crawling across hair-raisingly slippery tin slopes, hanging on with one hand and clutching loppers and saw with the other.

On this day of rose abuse a builder and his apprentice were working on the verandahs; they watched my day's work with as much interest as I watched theirs.

When I descended to *terra firma*, wild, torn and bleeding, the dishy young apprentice grinned, rearranged his lounging position and said: 'Tough cookies, you lady gardeners.'

Leaping onto the ride-on mower for a restful cruise round the lawns as a reward for my diligence, engaging the gears and letting the mind go into neutral, I pondered. Are we really such tough cookies, and if so, where did we begin?

Probably with Queen Hatshepsut of ancient Egypt. Undergardeners summoned to her presence had to get her tongue-twisting name right or it was instant execution. But this was only for minor transgressions; planting the wrong perennials, for example, could get one long-term employment carving floral murals inside her tomb – after it had been sealed. Queen H was an avid plant collector, and a gardener's best hope of survival was to find her a really interest-ing specimen. She'd be so pleased, she'd send you off to far-flung places to find better exotics still. Undergarden persons could hedge their bets this way as finding choice plants could take years, and should one have the misfortune *not* to find another little treasure you'd have to go into exile, but at least your head went with you.

Queen Hatshepsut lived in a very arid area of Egypt but she didn't let that interfere with her plans. She organised veritable armies of serfs to pot pots and created the world's first container gardens – acres and acres of them. Roses and rhododendrons, she had the lot.

Queen Hat was a tyrannical master gardener all right, but she left the world a legacy of exquisitely carved, highly detailed murals, teaching us what plants were in existence and under cultivation as far back as 1500BC.

History does not record further lady horticulturists of note until Josephine, Empress of France and Queen of the Rose, took the world by storm around 1799. Widowed, wilful and extravagant, Josephine pursued and married the brilliant military tactician Napoleon Bonaparte. As soon as he was away routing the enemy, she ran up enormous debts and indulged in an impressive series of love affairs, leaving her new spouse's throbbing love letters unanswered.

When the conquering hero returned, still extraordinarily smitten, he forgave her, carrying her off to the vast estates of his Château de Malmaison just outside Paris. Josephine settled down, her wildness forgotten as she indulged her life-long passion for flowers.

She had a dream that was as ambitious as it was bold: she would obtain every rose species and every rose variety growing anywhere in the world and create with them the greatest rose garden ever known. To contemplate creating such a garden today with all the miracles of modern communication and travel would be pretty mindbending, but for Josephine to have undertaken her scheme with no telephone, no fast ships, or aeroplanes at her disposal was like reaching for the stars.

Great botanists and horticulturists were summoned to Malmaison, the eminent Thomas Blaikie was despatched to landscape the entire estate, and André Dupont was informed that his mission in life henceforth was to organise a world-wide search for new roses. Pierre-Joseph Redoubte was ordered to record each new acquisition for prosperity, and exquisite pictures poured forth from his brush.

Locked in war across Europe, Napoleon's troops were ordered to spend any spare time between being brutal and licentious soldiers collecting unusual roses – which were transported on the general's battleships back to Malmaison!

Josephine had her roses but she remained childless; the sorrow that was to permeate her tempestuous relationship with Napoleon until the end of their lives. His consuming need to father a son for France drove him, loving her still, to annul the marriage.

Though the ex-Empress moved permanently to Malmaison to devote her life to her roses, and Napoleon remarried, their grand passion for each other endured. Defeated and exiled to Elba, Napoleon sent Josephine devoted love letters accompanied by violets, which she had always adored. Josephine died in 1814, and when Napoleon was captured and due to be exiled to St Helena, his last request was to visit her grave. He picked some of the violets he had ordered planted there, and after his death the blooms were found in a locket over his heart.

The gardens at Malmaison suffered badly at the hands of the Prussians in the 1870-71 war, but Josephine's dream, like the love story, has endured – her inspiration passed down through the centuries to other rose lovers and gardeners. The Malmaison rose collection, one of the world's finest, has been recreated at La Roseraie de l'Hay-les-Roses in Paris, a tribute to the Empress's indomitable spirit.

The late 19th century brought a duo of female master gardeners – Gertrude Jekyll and Vita Sackville-West. Their vision was so awesome that their word is law even today.

Around 1875 Miss Jekyll came striding up the garden path in a pair of perfectly stunning black hobnailed boots, which so captivated the eminent Victorian artist William Nicholson that he immortalised them in a masterpiece.

Strictly a no-nonsense dame like Queen Hat, Gertrude insisted on her surname being pronounced correctly – Jekyll – as in 'treacle', and even in modern times she is still reverently referred to as 'Miss Jekyll'. Unlike Empress Josephine, she was no femme *fatale*, but a plain portly little soul with spectacles perched on the end of her nose and a severe, uncompromising hairdo. But Miss Jekyll, a confirmed spinster, skilled artist and needlewoman, was something of a feminist, counting as close friends and colleagues leading male artists and horticulturists of her day.

In her 50th year she was told that she was in grave danger of going blind, and must give up completely her sewing and painting. But no languishing on a chaise-longue for Miss Jekyll in the face of such devastating news. She made a decision which was to irrevocably change the face of gardening. She would paint her pictures using flowers in a garden, rather than on a canvas or with embroidery silks.

She met and was influenced by the fiery Irishman William Robinson, who was ranting against formality in the garden in his magazine *The Garden*. Possessed of a finely developed penchant for raising the ire of his readers, Robinson wrote in his book, *The English Flower Garden*, the most daringly impolite things about garden landscapers and architects, tawdry bedding displays and all artifice in the garden.

Miss Jekyll also met a young garden landscaper called Edward Lutyens, who had the temerity to refer to her as Miss Bumps. 'Come and plant up these gardens I've designed,' he invited her. 'Shan't!' said Miss Jekyll, eyeing his extraordinarily complicated formal designs. Then, realising they would set her the challenge of clothing severely geometric confines with the informal cottage garden look she loved, she was planting them up in no time, fondly referring to the young man as Ned. This seemingly odd couple formed a professional partnership that was to last for more than three decades, for the dynamic Miss Bumps was planting gardens in her 80th year.

She took inspiration for their joint designs from the cottagers' gardens in her village but did not allow the happy hotch-potch of plants and colours permitted there.

Her genius lay in her accurate judgment of which plants would complement each other, and her colour sense was unerring. The texture, form and colour of every plant was carefully considered in association with its neighbours. Nor was it only the exotic and costly plants she employed – she loved simple wild flowers equally and used them exclusively if they suited her purpose.

This no-nonsense approach extended to the famous Jekyll-Lutyens herbaceous borders. A true herbaceous border uses only perennial plants and can be stunningly dull in winter. Miss J did not give a darn whether the plants she employed were herbaceous or not as long as they fulfilled her purpose and gave good service. Herein lay her special magic – the magic which was to give her the title by which we know her today – the First Lady of Gardening.

Meanwhile, over at the castle at Sissinghurst, Miss J's contemporary, the dashing Vita Sackville-West, was compensating for any lack of sartorial elegance on the gardening front with a class and style uniquely her own. Her laced knee-high boots of soft leather made Gertrude's black hobnail jobs look like a labourer's cast-offs.

Vita's gardening gear consisted of jodpurs topped with silk shirts, snazzy waistcoats and pearl necklaces. She sported a long cigarette holder and a man's trilby hat. (Out, vile tattered singlet, shorts and sandshoes …)

There is little to choose between Jekyll and Sackville-West in terms of the influence they have exerted over the gardening scene of the last 150 years. Both were self-taught – Vita was an amateur when she began, reclaiming the gardens at Sissinghurst from total wilderness. Her husband, Harold Nicholson, and her sons thought her quite mad, but she 'did it her way'.

Harold ('persuaded' into submission) designed the garden layout in the most formal and classical of styles. Strict boundaries of buttressed yew hedges and paths at right angles crossed each other with geometric precision. Vita took one look and decreed 'plantings with the maximum informality, profusion, extravagance and exuberance'. She sallied forth to 'cram, cram, cram' the linear confines with romantic plants that tumbled in gay abandon over walls, pathways and hedges. With wry humour she records how Harold, 'after weeks of struggle on paper designing a symmetrical vista, would come home to find I had stuck some tree or shrub bang in the middle of it!' The fusion of their separate visions resulted in a garden to which visitors still make pilgrimage from all over the world to pay homage.

Vita was often reclusive and had an immensely private retreat in one of the castle towers; she wrote with quirky amusement of how she could 'see without being seen' when studying the gardens and visitors. Her son Nigel recalls having been invited into his mother's most private room only two or three times in 30 years. Vita would garden all day and write long into the night, sometimes leaving her desk in the tower to meditate or to garden again in the small hours.

She planted her world-famous white garden under the first snowflakes of winter, describing how barn owls swept across its pale ethereal face as she worked in the silvery silence of moonlight. Vita Sackville-West was an eccentric aristocrat, and an immensely talented writer and poet. A complex personality, she created scandals by indulging in tempestuous relationships with women friends despite her devotion to her husband. But above all, she was a gardener extraordinaire.

The passion, vision, and creativity of these gardeners of long ago has left us with a rich heritage of styles, inspiration and instruction from which we can draw as we shape our gardens in the late 20th century. But as we have already indicated, there is one fundamental difference between these doyennes and ourselves that cannot be left unspoken.

The Victorian and Edwardian eras with their extreme class-conciousness and rigid sex-role stereotypes decreed that none but working-class females should indulge in physical labour in their gardens. A 'lady' – i.e. a middle- or upper-class woman – did not 'work' her garden. Like Elizabeth von Arnhim, she planned, she directed, she supervised, but no way did she do the heavy labour.

This was not a huge problem: armies of skilled undergardeners could be employed for a few shillings a month, for which her husband paid, usually with money 'inherited' from his wife through marriage! This was a fairly convenient arrangement, since the grand herbaceous borders, sweeps of velvet turf, and

---

*The way to make your garden a success is never to plant more land than your wife can manage.* —Anon

shrubs and yews clipped into anything as long as they didn't resemble a shrub or yew – were pretty labour-intensive.

Miss Jekyll and Vita Sackville-West were the exceptions to this rule, of course, being pretty exceptional women. In fact through the medium of her weekly gardening column in the prestigious British newspaper *The Observer* Vita replied somewhat irascibly to a male correspondent:

> May I assure the gentleman who writes to me (quite often) from a Priory in Sussex that I am not the armchair, library-fireside gardener he evidently suspects, 'never having performed any single act of gardening' myself, and that for the last forty years of my life, I have broken my back, my fingernails and sometimes my heart in the practical pursuit of my favourite occupation.[2]

But they both had plenty of help on hand for the brutal, menial and boring bits. Many a time, tired and dirty at the end of a long day, I have daydreamed of being lady gardener, granting my head gardener audience first thing:

'I'll have purple petunias in the parterres this summer, and you can plant dwarf pink lavenders between.'

'Very good, Ma'am.'

'Go and tell Bert and Jim to get manure from the stables and mulch the new vegetable beds all over.'

'Yes, Ma'am.'

'Then there is the new rose walk. Have you written my order out yet?'

'Yes, Ma'am, it's all ready for you to sign, and enclose the cheque/despatch the gold pieces.'

'La! All this gardening has left me quite exhausted – my strength has quite gone. I'll do it this afternoon after my nap.'

'Very good, Ma'am.'

Returning briskly to reality I reflect upon how blessed we are in both northern and southern hemispheres with talented women gardeners and writers, who have picked up the torch lit by the doyennes of the last three centuries.

Here in New Zealand we have women such as Olive Dunn, florist, author, and creator of enchanting cottage gardens; Toni Sylvester, who pioneered the concept of opening private gardens to the public and then cast a spell over us with her old-fashioned roses; we have Bev McConnell at Ayrlies, who began her magnificent park-like garden from bare paddocks in 1964 and 10 acres, 15,000 trees and four ponds later it is one of the country's foremost; we have photographer Gil Hanly, whose extraordinary talent captures the essence and ephemeral magic of gardens within her camera lens.

World-famous New Zealand rosarian Nancy Steen, like Empress Josephine, devoted her life to collecting, cultivating and perpetuating old roses. She spent many years travelling the length and breadth of the country seeking the lonely cemeteries and long-forgotten homesteads of the pioneers. She piled her car with cuttings of treasured old roses – roses grown from cuttings the settlers had found room to tuck into their scant possessions as they travelled the longest emigration route in the world. Nancy died in 1986 and the wealth of heritage roses with which we enthusiastically cram our gardens today is the gift of her life's work.

From overseas, the wisdom and inspiration of great modern English gardeners such as Rosemary Verey, Penelope Hobhouse and Beth Chatto comes to us on television and through books written by their own (gnarled) gardening hands.

Travel companies arrange extended tours between northern and southern hemispheres so that we might visit and swoon over their visionary gardens. These are the women whose vision and inspiration will shape the gardens of the not-too-distant 21st century.

I hasten to add that we do not presume to forget that we have as many equally talented and visionary gentlemen gardeners on either side of the globe, and just as many generous and good-natured husbands who have lent more than a casual hand in the making of all these blessed plots.

Nevertheless, as I drove the ride-on back into its shed, the young man's words lingered. Tough cookies? To a woman!

I think I'll plant delphiniums
(Or should that be delphinia?)
To add some height and colour
And soften aspect linear.
—Diane Padmore

3

# THE TROUBLE WITH GARDENING

*The trouble with gardening is that it does not remain an avocation.*
*It becomes an obsession.* —Phyllis McGinley

During the writing of this volume I have watched a non-gardening friend become bitten by the bug. Moving into an historic homestead, she inherited a large rambling country garden, designed in the days when help was affordable and plentiful.

Laid out in a grand manner were neglected lawns, rose parterres, a jungle of shrubberies and a wild untamed orchard bound by vast macrocarpa hedges that desperately needed a grand massacre. The orchard was a rabbit and possum sanctuary. My friend was a young mother to whom the lore of gardening was a mystery and every morning she'd carry the baby outside to survey the wilderness, only to return indoors in despair.

She told me she felt like King Canute trying to halt the incoming tide. The very thought of pruning roses brought her out in a cold sweat and it simply wasn't fair that in order to get the home she wanted she'd had to have this huge land mass forced upon her too. She had no interest in gardening whatsoever.

She eventually decided that when the baby was having his morning sleep she'd at least try to tidy it. She was depressed by her predecessor's predilection for lashings of hot colours, and she resented the loneliness, manual labour, backache and fatigue that gardening obviously represented.

Only the most hard-hearted of gardening friends could have resisted such a *cri de coeur*. I helped her gain control of the overgrown lawns and performed carnage on rose bushes and shrubberies. We organised a contractor to come and reduce the huge macrocarpa hedges to a reasonable level, and light and sunshine flooded in.

She began a half-hearted race against weeds, rabbits, possums and a chronic

---

*It is utterly forbidden to be half-hearted about your gardening. You have got to love your garden whether you like it or not.* —W.C. Sellar & R.J. Yeatman

water shortage. This period of maintenance served as a sort of apprenticeship; I saw her timidly try to bestow a personal touch here and there. She removed the brighter of the two-tone roses and replaced them with those of softer colours. This was the period of true amateur gardener apprenticeship. The plants were bunged in hastily prepared holes, and watered only when water was available and the children's routines allowed. The combination of lack of regard for climate and position, soil impoverished by years of planting, and depradation by pests earned the inevitable heartbreaking results.

One morning after her small girl began school she rang me and said, 'I'm not going to let it beat me, you know.' She launched into daring experiments with sacks of compost and manure; experimented with weedkiller and learned what happens when it runs off into the roots of prized plants. Tackling small areas at a time she planted anything that she herself liked as long as it said 'hardy' on the label. The plants grew. She progressed to perceiving that the aggressively salmon-pink azalea she'd liked so much in the shop definitely was not a suitable companion for the purple rhododendron that was its neighbour. Her plants, like those of all novice gardeners (and those of the not-so-novice variety) soon became upwardly mobile, suffering long rides in the wheelbarrow. She progressed a step further and began to actually pause before firing in a new plant, to assess whether it would complement its neighbours or not.

She devoured whole shelves of tomes on garden style and the house became littered with scraps of paper covered with plans for vistas, foundation plantings and colour schemes. She agonised over style – formal or native, subtropical or cottage?

A year down the track, it must be admitted that the gardens around the homestead are pretty eclectic in style and content as its new owner potters happily trying everything and anything. She rings me once a week with progress reports and plans for the future. 'Gardening is so rewarding, so creative, I can't wait to finish the chores and get out there each day,' says she.

Getting hooked is oh, so easy.

The main trouble with gardening is that it requires discipline. Not only the discipline to spray, prune, mow, deadhead and so on when the plants require it (rather than when the gardener feels like it), but also the discipline to get out of the garden when the awful depths of the ironing basket must be plumbed, the house needs a major blitz, the family are pleading malnutrition, you have to get to work on time etc etc.

promtu dressage arena in the evenings when I would prance about chant-
: 'Enter A...' etc. I had not reckoned on Champagne's complete indiffer-
:e to the subject of dressage.

The judge's written comments on the test sheet, which caused me so much
grin at the time, are now a source of much amusement: 'No canter at E.
vy line between C. and D. Failed to halt before leaving the arena,' and so

n much the same way, garden plans that have been transformed into actu-
have cryptic comments scrawled across them: 'Frulingsgold' and wall-
ers bloomed weeks apart – hopeless, try again. Day lilies swamped
thing else in the border. 'Moonlight Mist' much better with 'Bredon' –

his provides a valuable record of failures and successes in black and white.
hich reminds me – I am currently struggling with a very demanding
for a black and white garden. In fact I am obsessed with black and white.
k that it is due to the fact that when I was Emily Brontë in another life,
was a parson.[1]

n writer Barbara Wenzel chronicles the pitfalls that befall every ama-
ener in the 'try everything' years as he or she negotiates the learning
n novice to expert.

ation of a garden from a wilderness is a daunting task for an amateur
I was; unfortunately, I wasn't daunted enough. The basic problem
much that I knew next to nothing, but that I didn't realise this at the
d I called in a professional then and there, many problems that have
us ever since would have been avoided. But having from time to time
a 'good show' in our first garden with some pots and annuals, I
considered myself something of an expert. Occasionally friends even
advice. I'm ashamed to say that I gave it, probably with an air of
hority. So I tackled the wilderness with all the confidence of that
gerous of species, the possessors of a little knowledge.

step was a detailed, and elaborate, plan …

that I knew what I wanted I briefed a firm of builders … splendid
d pavers they were; landscape gardeners they were not. My plan
ised beds around the fences (turf seats perhaps?) and a paved area
the lawn. This was to have a sundial in the centre surrounded by
beds arranged in a formal patter. The area was duly levelled ready
crete pour. Did anyone think of drainage?
y not me. I was into design and aesthetics, not workability. There

The trouble with gardening is the stealth with which it sneaks up on you. You go to peg the washing out and you just can't believe the number of weeds in the vege patch; you wanted to pick some salad for lunch anyway so a few minutes' weeding won't go amiss. The weeding leads on to trimming the hedges around the *potager*, and suddenly it's a wheelbarrow-and-spade job as you decide to dig the bean plot over for another sowing of a late summer crop.

Late is the operative word: the picked saladstuffs lie wilting in the hot afternoon sun; the washing is too dry for ironing; the *potager* is now looking eminently civilised but nothing in the house has been done and the family will be home not for lunch but for dinner in less than an hour.

At this point you rush indoors and fling a couple of lidded pans filled with water on the stove. While they bubble merrily away, convincing the starving that a meal is well under way, you calmly defrost some schnitzels to go with the (wilted) salad which you miraculously resurrect by casting it into a bowl of iced water.

The trouble with gardening is that it compels you to consort with other gardeners who are just as hooked as you are. They inspire and encourage you ('Just imagine a whole bed planted with those new David Austin roses', 'A water garden would look just divine there', 'With your soil you could grow the most incredible lilies/asparagus/alstromerias'.) Their hands are busy all the time they are chatting. Mouthing platitudes like 'The secret is to finish one area before you start on another' they generously load you down with cuttings to take home. You stop off at the garden centre for a David Austin rose catalogue en route.

These other gardeners all tell you also that gardening is so good for you – the exercise, keeping fit, the fresh air – and this is just as well because once you are hooked you can't afford to do anything else anyway.

The trouble with gardening is that it keeps you constantly teetering on the edge of financial ruin. You abuse your credit card to support your habit, and to oblige the garden centres which, while clasping you to their bosom, will relieve you of large amounts of cash. 'Always plant in groups of three for maximum visual impact,' they say, which means one comes home with a dozen plants instead of four. Then there are the punnets of annuals that will make the most divine underplanting, and of course a sack of blood and bone to give them a good start.

The trouble with gardening is that it is such a pleasant occupation. Once

---

*Gardening should be done in blinders. Its distractions are tempting and persistent, and only by stern exercise of will do I ever finish one job before being lured off to another.* —Richardson Wright

34

31

past the tedium of general maintenance one is (usually) rewarded by beds that are a symphony of colour and scent. Plants are very forgiving and, as my young friend discovered, one of the wonders of gardening is that despite our best efforts so many plants live.

But the other trouble with gardening is that not everything goes according to plan, as New Zealand horticulturist Jonathan Cox has discovered:

## ACCORDING TO PLAN

These days, everyone from Princess Di down is busy telling anyone who will listen, whom they were in a previous life. I refuse to be outdone: in another life I was Emily Brontë. (After all, Virginia Woolf changed Vita Sackville-West's gender with the stroke of a pen in Orlando, so when it comes to past lives, a change of sex is practically *de rigeur*.)

This helps to explain my predilection for galloping off across fields and up hillsides (sometimes even on horseback) and I have transferred the passion I once shared with Charlotte and Ann for the imaginary country of Gondal (see F.E. Ratchford's *The Brontës' Web of Childhood*) into a passion for garden plans. Because that's what a garden plan is, of course: an imaginary country in which, in the twinkling of an eye, we have the rose 'Birthday Present' intertwined with dark purple clematis, scrambling up a wall with bronze and inky-blue bearded irises cavorting at their feet while nearby apple trees blossom in a sea of late-flowering pink and white tulips.

Which is not to say that garden plans are easy, of course. Far from it! First, there is the difficulty of measuring up. This necessary manoeuvre may be fraught with danger. I use one of those retractable measures which, when one presses a little button on its side, whizzes back into its case with a wicked screech of flimsy steel and the speed of a Kenyan sprinter. It is no respecter of any fingers or fingernails it may encounter in its rapid bolt for home.

Not only that; it has distinct mind of its own, sometimes stubbornly refusing to extend more than a metre or so without dire threats being uttered against it, while at other times it will lie happily at full length across the lawn for several minutes until just that moment when measurements are due to be recorded, whereupon suddenly it disappears like some thin, silvery serpent darting back into its den.

Then there is the perplexing question of scale. I have never understood scale. If on a scale plan a cherry tree becomes a circle slightly bigger than one's thumbnail, what does a daffodil bulb become? Aha, answer me that if you can!

No, I pay scant attention to scale (although I do concede it can be fun arranging the shapes of flowerbeds on the lawn with a hose, while a friend is positioned here and there with arms aloft to simulate a tree). I prefer to get

straight down to one of those Impressionist-type waterc
portrays the colours to be used in a border. Even this, how
its difficulties.

One rapidly discovers what one found out as a child
do not dry the same shades as they were when they were
as a pleasing approximation of *Cynoglossum nervosum* drie
akin to *Tweedia caeruleum*. Anything plummy maroon, li
rose 'Charles de Mills', fares worst of all. This colour fad
apple brown, charming in its own way, but not exactly v

Not that it really matters all that much, because l
water has been spilt all over it (usually with the help
takes an avid interest in garden plans) the whole thing
tie-dyed T-shirts we used to wear in the seventies. Ir
would not have looked out of place at Woodstock.

Penelope Hobhouse and Rosemary Verey obvious
I don't – their watercolours always dry the same sha
went on.

Gertrude Jekyll's garden plans are a continuing
me. Miss Jekyll's admonitions to plant in drifts me
feature inter-locking sausage-shaped groups of p
easy to copy. One simply goes on adding group
adding segments to the form of a giant earthw
Jekyllesque colour harmonies or contrasts, as the

This helps to explain why the main border a
feet long and why Miss Jekyll regularly saw the
like *Yucca filamentosa* at the ends of the beds. In
odd yucca here and there, Munstead Wood may
County.

Miss Jekyll also had the right idea when it c
requirements of a specified plan.

If your partner objects to your rushing abou
obscure destinations in a search for plants, I s
Miss Jekyll on the subject of sourcing plants
be fervour on the part of the garden owner,
plant pilgrimage to all good nurseries withi
out of reach.'

I am an inveterate hoarder and keep all
everything. The other day I came across t
one of the first horses I ever owned. He w
and rejoiced in the expensive-sounding n

I committed the test to memory with
patience of everyone else in our househe

was much marking out of my patterns with stakes and string on the rock-hard clay that stood stripped of any vestige of topsoil. I was the overseer of a group of bewildered Italians. One finally begged me to answer one question: 'Lady, what *is* it?'

After many delays due to rain (why is it lying about in lakes like that?) the concrete was poured and inexorably set, precluding the possibility of ever doing anything adequate about the drainage. We waited six months for the bricklayer's back to heal and his mother's funeral to conclude. When he saw the paving pattern I wanted him to follow, his disc shot out again and his father's hold on life started to look shaky.

From plans to planting …

… I must lay some small blame at the august feet of that high priestess of the art, Vita Sackville-West. To a greedy gardener such as I, her advice to 'cram, cram, cram every chink and cranny' was a licence to do just that, to a degree she had never envisaged. Possibly it was not Miss Sackville-West's intention to encourage the planting of the entire contents of Sissinghurst in a quarter-acre patch – I'm not sure she'd ever seen one. Nevertheless, when her message reached inner-city Melbourne that was roughly the result, and the years since the first plantings have seen a more or less continuous process of removing, relocating, cutting back and wondering what on earth happened to all the things that disappeared without trace in the battle for survival.[2]

We conclude with some pragmatic advice:

Begin at the end. When starting a new garden always start at the furthest point from the house. By the time you have worked back you will have made most of your mistakes – and they won't scream at you as you sit on the patio (drinking in the garden).

Second thoughts. Thinking of increasing the size of your garden? Don't. Consider the costs involved in five years' time, the extra labour, your diminishing energy and increasing girth, favourite armchair, good book …

Lost in the wilderness? If your garden is too big, accept the fact. Mine is, and beyond the lawn is jungle, impassable, possibly the home of wild animals. Friends from whom we have not heard of late may be lost there. We call it 'the reservation', 'bird sanctuary', 'wild garden' or 'butterfly reserve' and are at peace.

When attempting to place a difficult plant, try it in three positions in the garden. First, where you think it will grow best. Second, where you wish it to grow. Third, the least suitable spot where no one will see it. It is here that it will do best.[3]

# 4

# GARDEN ATTIRE

*A Guide to Sartorial Elegance for the Busy Gardener*

Gardeners' families mutter constantly about being embarrassed because mother/father looks like a refugee from a Third World country. It would be less than truthful to deny that unless we affect the gardening gear recommended later for the avant-gardener, we are inordinately fond of terrible old gardening sweaters, weathered slacks and ancient baggy shorts, and that our favourite gardening hats and footwear defy description.

We are all agreed that it is essential to dress comfortably and warmly for gardening. Lee Bailey advises:

> Weeds have begun to show themselves ... When I decide to go at them in earnest, I try to make myself as comfortable as possible. That way, I'll stick to it longer. I put on a couple of layers of clothes, which I can shed if the sun warms me and the wind stops. I also have a pair of old wool gloves with holes in the fingers, which are perfect for weeding. And since my nose always seems to be running when I am out of doors at this time of year, a good pocketful of tissues. I paint a lovely picture, don't I? You wouldn't know it to look at me, but I am as happy as a clam.[1]

While a clam is not a mollusc with which I have had occasion to have intimate contact, I too favour a pair of fingerless mittens for weeding. The state of our hands (which only the most brazen among us would describe as anything but lamentable) brings severe censure.

The question of gardening gloves is a vexing subject that has pre-occupied gardeners from centuries past. Writing in 1897, Theresa Earle offers very right

---

*For those who have a drip on the end of their nose when gardening in cold weather – what gardener doesn't? – a tennis sweatband on the wrist is a perfect wiper.*

and proper advice. It seems the variety of gloves she recommends are more satisfactory than those on offer today, though those of 'old dogskin' carry slightly sinister undertones.

June 2nd. – It must be admitted that one of the great drawbacks to gardening and weeding is the state into which the hands and fingers get. Unfortunately one's hands belong not only to oneself, but to the family, who do not scruple to tell the gardening amateur that her appearance is 'revolting'. Constant washing and always keeping them smooth and soft by a never-failing use of vaseline – or, better still, a mixture of glycerine and starch, kept ready on the washstand to use after washing and before drying the hands – are the best remedies I know. Old dogskin or old kid gloves are better for weeding than the so-called gardening gloves; and for many purposes, the wash-leather house-maid's glove, sold at any village shop, is invaluable.[2]

(An interesting aside is that Mrs Earle's book, *Pot Pourri from a Surrey Garden*, was a runaway bestseller when it was published. Her husband had offered her £100 *not* to publish it!)

A present-day New Zealand gardener, Shirley Ernest, challenges glove manufacturers to come up with a more efficient product:

PLEA

I like to wear my gloves while gardening
They surely stop my hands from hardening
But has it e'er occurred to you
That a pack with two is one too few?
For while my right is thin and worn
My left is new and scarcely worn.
So what about a spare left or right
To overcome this gardener's plight?
Or failing this I hope to find
A South Paw with the same in mind![3]

Another New Zealand gardener, Valda Paddison adds:

I admire intensely those well-disciplined folk who don their gloves as readily as hat and sunscreen when beginning a spot of gardening.

I admire their soft skin and the absence of cracks, calluses and assorted scratches and I long for my hands to be as clean and smooth as theirs. I feel this especially when my mother asks: 'Why on earth don't you wear *gloves*?' as she surveys the broken nails and ingrained dirt.

The answer to this is a complex one. While none of us would be without our spade, trowel or secateurs there is one gardening accoutrement that appears to divide us down the middle. We become the gloved and ungloved and sadly, for the state of my hands, I belong to the latter.

It's hard to explain to Mum that gloves don't allow me to feel things properly. There is something about weed pulling that is extremely tactile; extracting a dandelion with a gloved hand is just not the same as using bare fingers.

Pausing in one's work to stroke the bark of a tree is futile in gloves, and scrambling begloved in the earth in search of dock roots loses much of its meaning. While these may be somewhat intangible reasons they are only part of the story.

Gloves are seldom a correct fit. (Ah yes, I can see many of you nodding your heads in agreement.) There is often no visible difference between small, medium and large sizes. I usually find there is half an inch or so dangling off the end of my fingers, which neither looks elegant nor is conducive to efficient gardening.

The materials gardening gloves are made from are another bone of contention. My gardening shed is littered with the corpses of failed gloves. There is a tough-looking leather pair that proved too inflexible and therefore very clumsy. There are rubber ones whose flexibility I admired for a good five minutes and then realised that my busy hands were creating an unbearable sauna-like environment.

Also there is a vast array of light-coloured ones, often patterned with stripes, spots or florals. A decent day's work can reduce them to tatters with fingers soon popping out of the end. While fingerless gloves may be fashionable, in this case they rather defeat the purpose.

Well, today I had a close encounter of the 'Mermaid' kind. No one, not even the most ungloved stalwart, would attempt to touch this particular rose without protection and so I searched the shed for two gloves less tattered than the rest and set to work.

I simply wanted to persuade an errant cane back into place. A little tying up was needed and it should have been a five-minute job but it took nearly half an hour because 'Mermaid' snared me by the shirt, shirt, shorts, hair and gumboots and as I gingerly tried to free myself she played her trump card and snared me by my gloves.

Somehow, after manoeuvrings that would make a contortionist proud, I managed to extricate myself but 'Mermaid' refused to part with one glove, which hung from a barb like a dismembered hand.

This little adventure caused me to wonder why, when we live in an age full of marvels like satellite TV, space exploration and McDonalds restaurants, someone can't produce the ideal gardening glove. It would be made of material that was strong, flexible and 'Mermaid' repellent. It would be well stitched, reasonably priced and, above all, fit like a glove![4]

Addressing the subject of the gardener's entire working outfit, English noble-woman Lady Seton, writing in 1927, advises:

> While about the subject of outfit, I think for a great part of the year an ideal gardening dress for women is a short tweed skirt, made very wide, so that one can step across plants without injuring them, a loose jumper made of khaki or brown flannel (for half an hour in wet weather will take the shine off a romantically becoming jumper in pale colours), a gardening apron all pock-ets, a pair of thick shoes or boots, and a light scarf tied over one's hair. Hats are dreadfully in the way, and if quite uncovered and unshingled, our hair catches in every twig, like Absolom's, and the result is very painful and un-tidy.[5]

In the mid-1840s at Warley Place in Essex, Lady Seton's predecessor, the eccentric Miss Ellen Willmott, was creating the most famous of her three gar-dens. She employed some 104 gardeners and took their sartorial elegance most seriously. They wore uniforms that comprised:

> ... boaters in green and natural straw with a green band around them, knitted green silk ties, and navy blue aprons which had to be removed, folded up and tucked under their arms when they went home or even when they crossed the road to get to the other part of the garden.[6]

The lady gardener pottering among her flowers is advised on protective foot-wear:

> ... an article I pronounce to be indispensable is a pair of Indian rubber shoes, or the wooden high-heeled shoes called 'sabots' by the French. In these pro-tections, a lady may indulge her passion for flowers at all seasons, without risk of rheumatism or chills, providing it does not actually rain or snow; and the cheering influence of the fresh air, combined with a favourite amuse-ment, must ever operate beneficially on the mind and body in every season of the year.[7]

The well-dressed horticulturist must have plenty of pockets upon his or her person. We modern gardeners have trendy belt pouches in which to carry our smaller implements, but they pale into insignificance compared with the pock-ets sported by earlier generations, as described by Eleanor Sinclair Rohde:

> In appearance great-aunt Lancilla was a very impressive old lady ... Under her skirt and fastened like an apron she wore a Pocket. Only a capital letter can give an idea of the size and importance of this curious garment, which consisted of a whole array of flat, envelope-like receptacles, into which she slipped anything and everything she needed. A trowel and a small hand-fork, for instance, disappeared easily into these capacious depths, to say nothing of

such trifles as stale bread for the ducks, corn for the pigeons, etc. Most people would find it difficult to walk gracefully with trowels and such knocking at their ankles, but these impedimenta never seemed to interfere with her quick, yet dignified movements.[8]

Jonathan Cox, New Zealand horticulturist and writer, offers the following reflections on practical and sartorially elegant outfits for the modern gardener:

Not everyone knows that Germaine Greer, world-famous author of *The Female Eunuch*, is a passionate gardener. In a slim volume, *The Revolting Garden*, written under the delightful pseudonym Rose Blight, Greer tells us that her mother used to 'garden semi-naked, with an old pair of knickers wrapped around her hair to keep the dust out. In colder weather, she would rope up a pair of father's old trousers and put on a cardigan back to front. Thus attired she felt ready for anything.'

She then hastens to add that, needless to say, her mother was not gardening in metropolitan London.

Neither was she gardening in these days of ozone depletion. Today only the terminally foolish would emulate Mrs Greer's semi-nude example. Indeed, by the time she has slathered every piece of skin likely to be exposed to the sun's deadly rays with Sun Protection Factor 15, the weeds have grown another four inches, it has begun to rain, and the inclination has passed anyway.

Vita Sackville-West used to garden wearing jodhpurs and riding boots, which has always seemed to me a particularly good idea. You look as though you have just dashed home from, or are about to dash off to, the hunt, and your friends never know if the mud and grass stains upon your person came from parting company with your mount at a jump or an excessively violent tussle with wandering jew.

I never attempt any serious gardening dressed in anything but my oldest clothes. I harbour vague nagging suspicions that I was in fact personally responsible for the craze for provocatively ripped jeans and had I had the sense to market them I could have been as rich and famous as some latter-day Mary Quant.

Usually, the minute I don my disreputable ensemble it is a signal for friends to arrive, or the neighbours to decide to have lunch outdoors on their back lawn and I garden on, resembling some cross between Fagan from *Oliver Twist* and Steptoe or son, keenly aware that four pairs of eyes are continually boring into my back and that their owners are no doubt thinking that I look like an escapee from some rag collection.

Once, thus attired, I abandoned the garden to pay a lightning visit to my local garden centre and was promptly cornered by an impeccably dressed customer who wanted to know why her rhododendron had died. She obviously thought that anyone so dirty and dishevelled could not be anything other than a garden centre assistant.

I'm surprised that some enterprising clothes designer has not developed the obvious answer to the shy suburban gardener's desire for privacy: camouflage. Imagine splashing about happily (and invisibly) on the margins of your bog garden tastefully attired in an all-over silkscreen of Monet's Waterlilies.

Those who favour the tropical look can potter unobserved among their bougainvillaea or hibiscus in a bold Hawaiian-print sarong and matching headscarf. The entire Sanderson range of furnishing fabrics awaits the devotees of old roses, paeonies and the like. (Imagine your neighbours signing the pledge as part of the herbaceous border disengages itself from its surroundings and wanders back to the house in search of a reviving cuppa.)

Nowadays, no matter what your basic garden outfit, it is possible to procure all kinds of accessories: knee pads, elbow pads, holsters for secateurs, canvas gauntlets, and detachable chaps of the kind favoured by rodeo riders. Decked out in this lot you will resemble some strange hybrid of an extra from a *Mad Max* movie and a national skate-boarding champion.

Vast gardening aprons, with a commodious pouch to hold all your lesser implements that would be the envy of any kangaroo, are also available. Beware, however, because secateurs, trowels and pruning knives have an unhappy knack of working themselves deep into the outer and innermost reaches of the pouch, and as you lower yourself exhausted onto the lawn for five minutes' respite you are likely to receive a vicious jab somewhere in the vicinity of the hip or some other tender nether region!

Footwear, too, has come a long way since the strictly utilitarian boots favoured by Gertrude Jekyll, which as Jared Sinclair tells us in his Barnhaven Primrose Seeds catalogue (one of the best pieces of gardening writing ever) 'had all the little things that live under stones slithering and scuttling home in terror'.

Trendy gardeners today all favour tall green wellies with the shape and fit of a traditional hunting boot. They blend wonderfully with the lawns and borders alike, giving the distinctly surreal effect that you are going about your tasks cut off from the knees down.

Unfortunately, if your calves swell from the heat you may well find your wellies next to impossible to remove and be forced to suffer the indignity of lying spread-eagled on the ground, holding firmly onto the clothesline or some other sturdy object, while someone else does their best to free you from their rubbery embrace.

For a long time my mother had very definite ideas about gardening footwear, particularly in wet weather. She simply appropriated a pair of my father's old shoes, removed the laces and wore them over her own high heels. Shod thus, she did not actually lift her feet to walk in the normal manner (Dad's shoes of course being much too large for her, and liable to be stepped out of) and used to glide laboriously across the lawns with great dignity, looking like some elderly ice-skater.

One damp spring day I watched her gliding at a snail's pace across the front lawn with a huge bunch of crabapple blossom held aloft in one hand, an old coal bucket overflowing with weeds wedged firmly under her other arm, while her skirt,which she had loosened for greater flexibility, descended slowly to her ankles. There it was immediately pounced on by Kanga the cat, who was convinced that this was some wonderful game put on solely for her benefit.

My personal vote for best-dressed gardener goes to an unidentified elderly lady whose photograph appears in a British photographic annual.

She is pictured on her allotment (a bewildering array of flowers, vegetables, garden gnomes, coloured bottles, rolls of wire netting and weathered bamboo stakes), sitting on an old canvas deckchair and beaming broadly at the camera, revealing very few teeth.

Over a bulky black fisherman's jersey she wears fluorescent lime-green dungarees rolled up to reveal knitted yellow socks and men's brogues.

A budgerigar is perched on her shoulder and upon her head she wears a tam-o-shanter to which a slogan-button bearing the legend 'Elvis Lives' has been pinned. Fastened to her jersey, just above her heart, is another button which reads 'The Answer Lies in the Soil'.[9]

# 5

# THE ANSWER LIES IN THE TOIL

*The soil conditioner which is
still unmatched
is a simple spouse with a
spade attached.*
—G. S. Galbraith

In my days as a novice gardener I regarded the owners of fine gardens as
poetic, tranquil souls who pottered about decking the earth with flowers
and listening to the birds singing. It never occurred to me that gardens such as
these were attained only by the gardener making himself the hard-working ally
of the soil that was his lot. I regarded the old adage 'the answer lies in the soil'
with impressive indifference.

It took several years of hard experience to reveal to me The Great Truth: that
the gardener gives his all, not to his plants, but to the soil in which he plants
them; that he dedicates to it continual rites of conditioning, mulching, enriching,
feeding and moisturising.

Karel Capek had no illusions about the gardener's preoccupation with the
quality of his soil, and was firmly in possession of The Great Truth:

> A real gardener is not a man who cultivates flowers; he is a man who culti-
> vates the soil … he is a creature who digs himself into the earth. He lives
> buried in the ground. He builds himself a monument in a heap of compost.[1]

The assimilation of Great Truths takes time. I continued to commit the ex-
otica that is the fancy of the novice into the funereal embrace of crude orange clay
– concrete or quagmire according to the season. When death by drowning, drought
or soil deprivation despatched my exotics, I felt this had little to do with the
quality of my husbandry. I would trot out the disgusting excuse of the ignorant
and lazy gardener with total lack of conscience: 'Mine is such poor soil.'

Sadly, failure and plant demise is the beginning of the education of the most
hard-bitten of gardeners. This is the path of bitter experience we must tread
before we comprehend the nature of our adversary – it is a gross and constant

feeder. We begin to think a little, to ponder the implications of the eternal preoccupation of the real gardener with his soil. His speech is peppered with the words such as humus, compost, organic materials, conditioners and fertilisers.

We realise that the experienced gardener *knows* he can fire in plants until he is bankrupt but they will continue to expire if the condition of his soil is poor.

The blissful (but costly) ignorance of our novice days is replaced by the creeping suspicion that the soil is not ours to dictate to and coerce at will; we grudgingly admit realisation that we must work with and for it if we are to have a happy garden. We accept the need to have a soil test done to assess the shortcomings of our plot. When the results come, we rant and rave that real estate agents should be compelled by law to provide the prospective buyer of every property with a complete soil analysis report. Then we get down to the hard labour required to reclaim the earth.

Further discipline is required to practise that concept that comes hardest to the gardener's soul – to plant in our soil only those species that enjoy its basic structure. In a word, to accept that blue Himalayan poppies and lilies will still keel over in quagmire clay, and roses and bog plants will expire on arid hillsides, no matter how Herculean our efforts to better them.

We move towards acceptance of the final truth – that cultivation of the soil must come first; yummy exotic specimen trees, shrubs, tender perennials and velvet lawns last.

The need to constantly work the soil becomes engraved on our hearts – humus, humus and more humus, to give body and substance to light, sandy soils, to break the brutish lumps of heavy clay and to nourish both.

So to the acquisition of this elixir of life – for a user of humus becomes an addict and craves it more and more.

We begin to construct bins and enormous compost corners for the composting of anything that converts into humus. Nothing escapes our attention: leaf mould, kitchen waste, sawdust, seaweed, sand, weeds, grass clippings, shredded newspaper and card, dollops of manure from any animal you care to name, peat, weathered clods – there is little we do not see as convertible material for the feeding of our habit.

Unfortunately the city gardener does not always have on hand rotten dung, guano, mountains of leaves, soot and wood ash, charcoal, pond mud, dead possums, rabbits and the other basic materials described by gardening oracles as nitrogenous, potassic, phosphatic and eminently desirable.

---

*Soil: a type of dark mud in short supply in the garden but readily found on paths, patios, verandahs, clothing, boots etc.*

Urban gardeners must practically plead for interest-free terms at garden centres to be able to afford the potions and powders, slags, salts and sulphates and other soil preparations that smack distastefully of ritualistic slaughter and sacrifice: ground bones, hoof and horn, dried blood and ground fish fertiliser. They collect cabbage stalks and the contents of the vacuum cleaner bag; they hoard egg shells, soot and every speck of ash from the wood-burning stove; they steal seaweed and sand from the beach and their children's sandpit; they lie in wait to ambush the contractor their sensible non-gardening neighbour has commissioned to mow his lawns and clip his hedges, hijacking the contents of his trailer.

Regardless of their soil type and location, gardeners jealously hoard such materials to feed and fuel the appetite of their insatiable adversary. No recipe for a gourmet banquet could be more elaborate than that for the preparation of garden compost.

The perfect soil, we are told, is composed of 'rich unctuous loam' – the very words have a fecund, fertile and productive ring about them. We now know that it may only be acquired by practising composting and manurial rites to the full, but even when we have spread the delicious loam all over the garden there is still no end to our servitude. We can never sit back and watch staggeringly healthy plants burgeon forth from the conditioned soil. The need for continual feeding and nourishing constitutes a gardener's life sentence.

It is possible to cheat with the ongoing need for organic matter. If we are wealthy we may have expensive rich dark compost (which looks good enough to eat) brought in by the truckload, but treading a well-beaten path to the home-made heap is the way for most of us.

We can buy proprietary compost activators, which contain bacteria to rot organic materials down more quickly. But this turns into a vicious circle – a kind of composting treadmill from which there is no escape. The compost rots down and is used more quickly and we are faced with the unthinkable – empty bins – so life becomes an endless frenzy of collecting materials and manufacturing more.

Gardeners in medieval times could not, even had they wanted to, have cheated and poured bags of instant compost onto their plots. They had to make do with what they could get in the way of fertiliser, and this was mostly dung.

The great Greek botanist and ecologist Theophrastus was advocating the use of 'dung waters' – liquid manure – as far back as 250BC. He was also aware of the soil-warming properties of dung, advising his readers that if they dug in fresh manure the harvesting of crops could be speeded up by a month. The pre-war gardener was well aware of the hot-bed technique, but gardeners today are not as aware of the soil-heating properties of dung. One up to Theophrastus.

By the early 16th century the ancients were recording advice on the acquisition and processing of manure to enrich their soil:

> Doves dung is best, because the same possesseth a mightie hoteness. The dung also of the hen and other foules greatly commended for the sournesse, except ye dung of geese, ducks and other waterfoules.
>
> A commendation next is attributed to the Asses dung, in that the same beast for his leisurely eating, digesteth easier, and causeth the better dung. The third place is the Goates dung, after this both ye Oxe and Cow dung; next the Swines dung ... The dung which men make ... is greatly misliked, for that by nature is hoter, and burneth the seedes sown in that earth.[2]

John Evelyn discloses:

> Pidgeons and sheepes dung infused in Water is excellent for Oranges, choice greenes, and indeed any Fruite. The scouring of muddy-pond, and where cattell drinke and stand, is good for all plants. The scouring of privies and sinkes so well dried and made sweete, well mixed with fresh earth so as to retain no heady scent, is above all other excellent for Oranges and the like choice fruits.[3]

Several centuries later the Reverend Samuel Reynolds Hole, Dean of Rochester and famous rosarian, admitted to a 'wild passionate affection' for animal manure and tells the following tale:

> Returning on a summer's afternoon from a parochial walk, I inferred from wheel-tracks on my carriage drive that callers had been and gone. I expected to find cards in the hall, and I saw that the horses had kindly left theirs on the gravel.
>
> At that moment one of those 'Grim spirits in the air, Who grin to see us mortals grieve, And dance at our despair' fiendishly suggested to my mind an economical desire to utilise the souvenir before me. I looked around and listened; no sight, no sound of humanity. I fetched the largest fire shovel I could find, and was carrying it bountifully laden through an archway towards a favourite tree of 'Charles Lefebvre', when I suddenly confronted three ladies, 'who had sent round the carriage, hearing that I should soon be at home, and were admiring my beautiful roses'. It may be said with the strictest regard for veracity, that they saw nothing that day which they admired, in the primary meaning of the word, so much as myself and fire shovel; and I am equally sure that no rose in my garden had a redder complexion than my own.[4]

Most people realise that odiferous manure is revolting but don't realise that

46

practically anything revolting is manure. Sellar and Yeatman give advice on the acquisition of noisome organic material for the compost heap:

> When you go to the seaside don't collect shells or peculiar postcards but large bunches of Seaweed, and hang it up in the spare room when you get home, till it is naught but fragrancy. If your guests object, remind them that Dried Blood is excellent for giving colour and texture to the soil – though between ourselves you are no longer allowed to kill people in order to get it.
>
> There is nothing in the whole realm of gardening which arouses so much pride and adoration or, if it belongs to your neighbour, so much envy as a really vast stack of crusty well-matured, asphyxiating, Vintage Dung.[5]

So we have with all diligence collected our organic materials, stacked, piled, turned, covered, drenched them with compost activator, and left them to mature as a connoisseur would lay down his vintage wines. But despite our labours we are persecuted by the fact that the soil also requires *dressing*. It requires frequent applications of lime to keep it friable and sweet-tempered.

We must also till the soil, which consists of endless diggings and turnings to various spade depths, hoeings, rakings, buryings, loosenings, firmings, pattings and smoothings. It is a wonder we ever have time to actually put any plants into it at all. But we have learned that humus and the soil are inseparable elements, and our education as gardeners is almost complete.

Now concrete clay disintegrates and crumbles with a sigh, thin sandy soils breathe body and substance, and each eagerly receives the plant life committed to its care. To have created soil that is warm and malleable, that receives your spade gladly to a couple of depths, that is dark and crumbly in texture, is your great victory. It lies there beneath your boots – deep, soft and beautiful.

From this time on you will never walk over soil without an appreciation of what you are treading on. You will be compelled to bend down and pick up a fistful, crumble it through your fingers to test its body, weight, fragrance, colour and texture.

We accept, finally, that there is no excuse in our gardeners' hearts for soil that is compacted, wet, cold, greasy, clayey and sterile. 'My soil is so poor' announces to the world that one is a slovenly gardener, that one's soil will remain just so until one has accepted that the answer lies in the *toil*.

---

*The ideal soil is a 'rich unctuous loam'. This, however, is never found, except in the gardens of rich unctuous people, or possibly in the garden of the frightful people next door.* —*W.C. Sellar & R.J. Yeatman*

## ADO

It grows too fast! I cannot keep pace with it!
While I mow the front lawns,
The drying green becomes impossible;
While I weed the east path,
From the west path spring dandelions;
What time I sort the borders, the orchard escapes me.
And then the interruptions! The interlopers!
While I clap my hands against the blackbird,
Michael, our cat, is rolling on a seedling;
While I chase Michael, a young rabbit is eyeing the lettuces.
And oh the orgies, to think of the orgies
When I am not present to preside over this microcosm!

—Ursula Bethell

# 6

# THE VAST ETERNAL LABOUR

*An experienced gardener knows that all he has to do*
*to get rid of weeds is nothing else.* —O.A. Battisa

A recent national survey by the Department of Statistics indicates that the gardener spends 40 per cent of his or her time weeding the garden, 35 per cent mowing it, and the remaining 25 per cent actually growing anything (like flowers, fruit and vegetables). A hefty seventy-five per cent of the garden, therefore, is composed of weeds and bolting grass, and other more desirable features must be crammed into the remaining 25 per cent. Small wonder that the greater part of all 'how to' garden books is devoted to the identification and eradication of weeds and to the cultivation and maintenance of lawns. As generations of gardeners have done before us before us, we ponder first the perennial problems of weeds.

The philosopher who said work well done never needs doing again obviously never pulled weeds in a garden. A 20th-century American philosopher, Stevenson, goes as far as to praise the tenacity and determination of weeds:

> Rome had virtue and knowledge; Rome perished. Some weeds have indigestible seeds – and they will flourish forever. I give my advice thus to a young plant – have a strong root and stem, and an indigestible seed; so you will outlast the eternal city, and your progeny will clothe the mountains, and the irascible planter will blaspheme in vain.

Stevenson was wasting his time trying to teach weeds. A weed is born wise. The gardener *becomes* wise; even as he blasphemes he *knows* the power of the adversary, and though he maligns it, he never underrates it. In more benevolent moods he may admit to deriving some sort of satisfaction from the process of weeding. It gives scope to the aggressive instinct, and there is satisfaction to be derived from yanking up the enemy by its very roots and hurling it into a heap.

---

*Give some weeds an inch and they'll take a yard.* —Anon

The French philosopher, Thoreau, obviously had no time for finicky hand weeding and advocates bearing down on the enemy with trusty hoe in hand:

Many a lusty crest-waving Hector, that towered a whole foot above his companions, fell before my weapon and rolled in the dust.

Pretty strong stuff, but such a doughty foe is not easily slain. Decapitation means little, since its most vital organ is its root; in infancy is the time to get it, when its hold on life is slender. There is no courage like weedly courage. Cut down or wrenched out in its prime in the morning, after a shower or in the cool of evening it is upstanding again; its rootlets have only to touch the soil and they are miraculously resurrected.

Most insidious of all are thugs such as sorrel, bindweed and ground elder, which, with metres and metres of indestructible roots, string together countless little plants above the ground, all looking so frail and innocent that less experienced gardeners are inclined to spare them. Yet when one finally tugs at a tiny two-leafed individual, out comes a tough horizontal thread strung with hundreds of plants. Sooner or later the root breaks and every scrap left in the earth is the starting point for bigger, busier and better specimens.

The gardener has little comfort but the fact that among tedious garden chores weeding does at least show instant results. It has, for example, none of the trauma and stress of transplanting, where a bed is filled with ridiculously small seedlings all fainting and flopping about everywhere. A bed that has been purged of weeds looks wonderful at once, and the gardener does not have to wait anxiously for a month to see whether his work has been successful or not. He just has to concentrate on the ordered roomy bed and forget that a month hence, it will probably be smothered in the selfsame weeds.

The $60 million question is what is a weed and what is not? As far back as the 15th century gardeners argued the point in the first handwritten manuals on horticulture. Epochs have passed and dynasties crumbled, but the anguish and advice of the ancients on weed management is as relevant today as it was nearly 600 years ago.

A typical 20th-century dictionary definition of a weed reads thus: 'Any useless plant of small growth: any plant growing where it is not wanted by man.'

---

*We sow with all the art we know and not a plant appears.*
*A single seed from any weed a thousand children rears.*
—Anon

A bit sweeping by most standards. Some weeds are handsome rampers and attain such size they may be mistaken for shrubs; many 'weeds' are often true wild flowers whether or not they settle themselves in the precise location man would have them. Some modern gardeners work themselves to the bone cultivating wild-flower meadows and orchards, while others live out their gardening lives, hoe in one hand and weedicide in the other, their mission to cut down in its prime anything that shows an unscheduled or unrecognised head.

Opinions on what constitutes a weed leaves gardeners ever divided. Many would say that that ghastly plant that rampages through your garden is a thing of beauty and a weed only in the eye of the beholder.

The ancients, however, were pretty specific about which plants were weeds, adopting the attitude that anything that grew like a weed was one, and were highly articulate on the subject of what to do about it. They insisted that one should not allow liberal-mindedness to lull one into a false sense of security.

John Evelyn's uncompromising advice from 1664 is succinct:

> In the garden ... have still an eye to the weeding and cleansing part; begin the work of haughing [hoeing] as soon as ever they begin to peep; you will rid more in a few hours, than afterwards in a whole day; whereas neglecting it until they are ready to sow themselves, you do but stir and prepare for a more numerous crop of these garden sinnes ...
>
> Above all, be careful not to suffer nettles, dandelion, groundsel (and all downy plants) to run to seed; for they will in a moment infect the whole ground: wherefore whatever work you neglect, ply weeding at the first peeping of ye spring ... Note that while the gardiner rolls or mows, the weeder is to sweep and cleanse, and never be taken from the work 'til she be finished. First the gravel walks and flower borders; then the kitchen gardens; to go over all this she is allowed one month every three months, with the gardiner's assistance of the haugh [hoe] and rough digging where hand weeding is less necessary.[1]

Like the philosophers discussed earlier, 19th-century American naturalist Nathaniel Hawthorne questions the sheer darned fortitude of a weed:

> What hidden virtue is in these things that it is granted to sow themselves with the wind and to grapple the earth with this immitigable stubborness, and to flourish in spite of obstacles, and never to suffer blight beneath any sun or shade, but always to mock their enemies with the same wicked luxuriance?

The despair of the ancients reinforces our growing perception that try as we might to see weeding in a positive light, it remains the vast eternal labour of the gardener. Vita Sackville-West sighs:

The thistle and the groundsel with their fluff;
The little cresses that in waste explode
Mistaken bounty at the slightest touch;
The couch grass throwing roots at every node,
With wicked nicknames like its wicked self,
Twitch, quitch, quack, scutch;
The gothic teazle, tall as any hollyhock,
The sheeny celandine that Wordsworth praised,
(He was no gardener, his eyes were raised;)
The dandelion, cheerful children's clock
Making a joke of minutes and of hours,
Ironical to us who wryly watch;
Oh why, we ask, reversing good intentions,
Was nature so ingenious in inventions,
And why did He who must make flowers, make weeds?[2]

Attempting to remain positive, we find there are a few – very few – lone gardeners who are prepared to champion the cause of weeds. Ralph Waldo Emerson comments charitably:

A weed is a plant whose virtues have not yet been discovered.

Mrs Gatty, the mother of author and gardener Juliana Horatia Ewing, also defines the weed with a measure of tolerance:

A weed is a plant out of place, or a plant which has the disposition to GET INTO THE WRONG PLACE. This is the very essence of weed character – in plants as in men. If you glance through your botanical books you will often see added to certain names 'a troublesome weed'. It is not its being venomous or ugly, but its being impertinent – thrusting itself where it has no business and hinders other people's business – and that makes a weed of it.

The present sovereignty of weeds in the author's garden while she strives to complete this volume results in her simple philosophy:

My weeds and I are very good friends.

Accepting that the unwanted plants in one's garden are indeed weeds no matter how glamorous they might be, we remain perplexed by the eternal question of how they got there in the first place. English gardener Reginald Arkell, horrified at the length of dock roots, quips of their origin:

# GEOGRAPHY

The gardener's boy had worked from dawn,
Pulling the plantains in the lawn.
Each root seemed longer than the last,
And one was saying as I passed:
'Orstralia! That's the country, Joe,
Where all these plantains start to grow.'[3]

Sir Edward Salisbury, latterly a learned director of Kew Gardens, came up with the intriguing theory that large numbers of so-called native plants were introduced in the British Isles by the legionaries of Caesar marching through the dust of Roman roads.

He explains that the Roman military sandal, which was studded with hobnails under the margin, toe and heel, would have formed a most effective temporary catchment in the dispersal of the seeds of weeds and aliens. As the conquering heroes went on to sail the seven seas, do we assume they carried weeds in embryo from ancient Rome to 'plant' in gardens around the world? What hope for us in the 20th century when the potential for such dispersal is ever-magnified: in the tread of aircraft tyres, for example, particularly if it has been obliged to make a forced landing in some foreign field?

Giving imagination a little scope, could weed seeds secrete themselves in chinks and crevices of spacecraft to populate the moon? Any gardener knows that no matter how wet, dry, hot, cold, bleak and inhospitable a garden situation might be, nature holds the trump card by ensuring that there are plants that will not only absolutely adore it there, but self-sow prodigiously.

Then there is the embryology of nature, whose ingenuity at reproducing herself knows no parallel. Seeds that have been exhumed in archaeological excavations have germinated after hundreds of years. Those from the huge pods of an Egyptian lotus dug up from peat beds in Manchuria were found to be viable after lying dormant for over 1000 years. It has also been proven that raspberry, blackberry and other berryfruit seeds thrown onto the compost heap as boiled jam pulp have germinated to form active healthy plants. The fainthearted among us may be tempted to eschew the unequal struggle when horticultural scientists also tell us that there are many seeds whose viability exceeds the normal life-span of human beings.

The kikuyu grass that afflicts Australasian lawns is the equivalent of the couch or twitch grass of the northern hemisphere. New Zealand gardener Joyce Beumelburg gets down to grass roots with an apt ode:

# GRASS ROOTS

A garden is a lovesome spot?
I've news for them – my garden's not
What one would term a lovesome spot –
Kikuyu's everywhere …
It'll creep and crawl and twist and twine,
And drive me to despair.
But *still* the pestilential weed does fine –
It comes from everywhere …
A lovesome place my garden's not,
My efforts are pure farce.
And I'm sure that when I've had my lot
The mantle on my humble plot
Will be kikuyu grass!

The eradication of weeds such as these is one of the great imponderables of good husbandry. They have driven me to chemical warfare, which is against my garden religion, causing me to spray poison from a backpack theatrically marked with a skull and crossbones. I have corrupted family young, offering financial reward for back-breaking hours spent unwinding tenacious spaghetti tresses. I have ignited the villainous stuff, stamped on it and verily cursed it – only to have it fight back every damned time.

So cunning are these unspeakables that they employ the defensive tactic of growing best and thickest at the base of choice plants, thereby cheating one of the satisfaction of an annihilating blast of toxic spray. But gardeners are full of guile and innovative in the extreme when it comes to plant treasures being strangulated by such low-downs. With Machiavellian fervour we pull on a pair of stout rubber gloves overlaid with a thick pair of woolly gloves. We mix a bucket of lethal weedicide, crooning witch-like incantations, then stroke and caress their tenacious tendrils with the brew. Precious plants remain untouched, and one does not have to risk neighbours' wrath since puffs of toxic potion don't waft over the fence.

The tragedy is that the weeds *still* have the last laugh. This hand-in-glove method does eradicate them above the ground, allowing us to fool ourselves that we've beaten them this time; until their vicious web of suffocating roots, spreading an ever-widening network below the beds, romp up with rude good health miles away from where they began … Common sense tells me there can be only one real release from their torment – move to another address that doesn't have any.

54

Care must be taken, however, that the gardener does not inadvertently turn his weapons of destruction upon himself. British journalist and gardener, Sir William Connor ('Cassandra'), offers a cautionary tale:

## A RAY OF SUNSHINE

It always surprises me how much joy people can get out of other people's mishaps. I have just given immense pleasure to many of my friends. I have brightened their lives. I have let sunshine into dark places.

I was in the tap room of a pub noted for the fierce conversations that go on about gardening, and a acquaintance of mine, with whom I have horticultural rivalry, said:

'Growing sweetpeas again this year?'

'Yes, I am – I mean, yes, I was.'

'Come again?'

'My sweetpeas are strictly in the past tense.'

'Frost?'

'No, they are in the greenhouse. Or rather they were in the greenhouse.'

'What happened to them?'

'I watered them with weed-killer.'

'Pray say that again?'

'I watered them with a can that contained weed-killer.'

A roar of pure delight shook the pub.

'Intentionally?'

'No, you great dolt.'

'The tomato plants ... I trust they are well?'

'They are dead. Burned to a frazzle. Withered. Finished.'

Thunderous laughter. Men with great dirty pints in their hands are choking with glee.

'May I enquire about your zinnias?'

'They look as though they have been nursed by a blow lamp.'

'And how are your dwarf dahlias?'

'Wiped out.'

People are crying with laughter. They are sobbing with pure glee.

'Your asters? Your sunflowers? Your marrows? Your cinerarias?'

'Scorched. Doomed. Had it.'

Complete strangers come up to me and shake me by the hand saying: 'Funniest thing I've ever heard of. You've really made my day. Thanks awfully old man, you've properly bucked me up.'[4]

If you prefer to opt for a 'relaxed' wilderness garden, heed the words of Beverley

Nichols, who cautions fellow gardeners about wild flowers such as valerian (*Centranthus ruber*), which seeds itself in the chinks of stone walls:

> Any beginner who has a walled garden will see his walls as canvases on which he can paint charming pictures ... he will grow ambitious and realise that these walls are potential 'hanging gardens', not necessarily of Babylonian proportions, but none the less delightful. On them ... he can suspend pleasing patches of pink and mauve and white ... then nature comes along in the shape of, let us say, a seed of that very pretty plant the red valerian, which may have been borne on the wind or – less poetically – ejected from the innocent posterior of a pigeon ... Valerian takes roots in the crevices, sends out its shrill green leaves, and eventually bursts into song in a series of rosy arias ... from the moment it takes root the wall is doomed. Unless you have actually seen the strength and persistence of this plant, thrusting deeper and deeper, displacing the mortar, lifting the bricks with a relentless pressure, you would not believe it could do so much damage ... the plant will go on seeding until one day, with a loud crash, the wall falls down.[5]

At this stage in our musings, weeds and weeding begin to take on the aspect of the nightmare described by English gardeners W.C. Sellar and R.J. Yeatman. They suffer somewhat exotic weeds in their garden, and have an enthusiastic predilection for the exclamation mark:

> In theory the most tedious occupation in the world, weeding in practice is a dangerous hysteria. It comes suddenly without warning ... You see a plantain here, a bindweed there ... you stoop down. A little groundsel in the rose bed ... you grab at it. A whorl of goose-grass among the asters ... you're off!
>
> *Ground ivy* among the sweet peas. Have at it! *Cat's whiskers* among the carrots, *Job's comforters* choking the phloxes, *Leechwort* bleeding the dahlias to death! Down on your knees, pulling, gouging, tearing, cursing! Not a moment to lose!
>
> An hour goes by, two hours, three hours, you haven't scratched the surface of it! *Creeping thistle* undermining the whole herbaceous border!
>
> *Charlock, chickweed, horse-tail, coltsfoot, pig-sporran!* Still pulling, still tearing, still swearing. Dinner time. Grab a cutlet as if it were a hemlock-and-two-vetch and hurl it into the fireplace. At it again, prising huge dandelions out of the lawn by light of the hurricane lantern.
>
> Bed at last. But what a sleep! Hands clutching, knees shaking, body writhing, brain reeling. '*Calf's-tail!*' you bellow as nightmare grips you, ripping the cord out of your pyjama waist. '*Crowsfoot!*' you mutter, poking yourself in the eye.
>
> '*Joshua's-beard!*' you jibber, lurching over in bed tearing at your partner's chin. 'Upsidaisy!' you prise the baby out of its cot and plunge it into the dirty clothes basket.

'*Deadly nightshade!*' With final shout of victory you wake up pouring with perspiration to find you have weeded the whole bedroom beyond repair.[6]

The only antidote for a nightmare of such gruesome proportions is to stagger to a hypnotherapist, who will put you straight back to sleep, having taught you to chant: 'There are few weeds in my garden. I have them absolutely under control. I shall grow old peacefully, feet up, dreaming the afternoons away while less diligent gardeners, bent double, struggle in deadly combat with the implacable enemy.' This has been known to work – sometimes.

Do not despair. We will end on a more positive note with lines penned by one gardener who has managed, despite a preoccupation with plants of dubious parentage, to retain a sense of humour:

Dandelions: you fight dandelions all weekend, and late Monday afternoon there they are, pert and in full gorgeous bloom, pretty as can be, thriving as only dandelions can in the face of adversity. —Hal Borland

Which might be said to sum things up pretty thoroughly, really, apart from a last word from Karel Capek:

Lord, give me the courage and tenacity of a weed.[7]

GARDENER'S LAMENT
The things I sow somehow don't grow
I'm sorely disenchanted;
But, oh, what luck I have with stuff
I never even planted.
—Anon

# 7

# LAYING DOWN THE LAWN

*Lawn: A number of sods that become one large sod later in life.*

We have diligently put in the mandatory 40 per cent time-span weeding the blessed plot, which moves us to the 35 per cent required by the lawns.

If, before creating your garden, you have studied your garden landscaping books diligently, you will have been persuaded of the desirability of the pleasant restfulness of an unbroken expanse of lawn to balance the carnival of flower colour. But before undertaking such a task, give serious thought to paved, patio, or concreted walking mediums. Ask yourself the following questions: are you young and strong or noticing an increasing tendency towards feeling old and feeble? Are you prepared to dig the whole plot over, break it down and rake it perfectly smooth for seeds? Risk hypertension watching the birds scoff the lot? Spend endless hours flogging up and down behind a noisy smelly mower when you could be lazing in a deck-chair on a paved garden entertaining area? If you balk at the very thought of such unceasing toil, or answer in the affirmative to even one of these questions, you lack the necessary enthusiasm to become the owner of the lawn of your dreams. Accept that the perfect lawn requires more cosseting and attention than a newborn baby.

> Have you heard the one about the American tourist who asked the head gardener at one of the Cambridge colleges how he managed to have such perfect lawns?
> 'Just cut 'em and roll 'em,' says the gardener.
> 'That all?' asks the incredulous visitor.
> 'Ah!' affirms the gardener.
> 'How long for?'
> 'About 400 years.'

So you set aside large areas on the master plan for sweeps of greensward. I did so too, and the brutal toil of creating my first lawn at Valley Homestead is inscribed indelibly on my heart.

The lawn I envisaged would have been revered in front of an English stately home. The reality, here on our farm in New Zealand, was a jungle of kikuyu grass with tentacles as thick as rope, which rampaged up and down a series of curious mounds, trying to strangle the giant tufts of paspalum grass and other noxious weeds in its path.

Fired with all the zeal of a pioneer given her first land grant, I hacked my way into the interior. The strange mounds, I decided, must be piles of rich topsoil dumped there during the excavations for re-siting the house. They weren't. At the end of day one I'd made acquaintance with the fact that they were heaps of rubbish dating back to the 1950s, roped together with giant kikuyu roots.

I dragged out old bicycle frames, endless metres of barbed and fencing wire, old pots, pans, buckets, shoes, clothes, bottles, heaps of unidentifiable bits from defunct farm machinery, cans, even an almost entire gas cooker complete with claw feet, a fridge, and more – much, much more. In the levelling of all those mounds, the only item I found that was of any use was a large quantity of old red bricks that must once have been an outdoor privy.

Suffice to say that by the time I had levelled that paddock, even the blisters on my callouses were blistered.

The great day finally came when I was able to take the mower into the interior. Even on its highest setting it choked and smoked, gasping piteously over the vicious web of kikuyu. After mowing on each of the six blade levels, even my faith was foundering that something remotely resembling a lawn would ever emerge. I had an area of unsurpassed ugliness, snarled with the bleached hair of the lowest levels of kikuyu, which hadn't seen the light of day in decades, and punctuated by dozens of bald spots where I had levelled the mounds.

Nothing daunted, the indestructible kikuyu put forth fresh growth, and multifarious weed seeds, liberated from the dark blanket in which they had been cocooned for years, germinated overnight in the warmth and sunlight.

Eventually I raised a lawn of kikuyu and cut-down weeds. The fine and expensive lawn seed I had sprinkled lavishly over the bald patches was choked by a weed crop of unparalleled magnificence. I decide to join the exponents of the CDW (cut-down weeds) lawns. I observed that 25 out of 50 suburban lawns were of this variety and comforted myself with the thought that although

---

*Our forefathers ran a farm with less machinery than we need to run a lawn.*
—Howard Scripps

it wasn't quite the billiard table top I'd had in mind, it was at least a tough and durable lawn.

After four years of relentless mowing, the all-kikyu and CDW lawn is quite presentable. It was hard-won. It is, I tell myself, fit for a garden party any day.

It was also my lot to attempt to create a new lawn on an area devoid of topsoil but rich in builders' rubble. When this infertile debris was cleared the soil beneath was not the sandy loam beloved of gardeners, but of impermeable yellow clay.

In summer it was as hard as a brick and resembled the Gobi desert – baked and cracked by the sun into ankle-wrenching fissures. In winter it was water-logged and incredibly sticky. I managed to break it into lumps with a fork. After it had remained thus over the winter months, I was sufficiently recovered physically to repeat the process in early spring. The result was an area that looked as though it had been ploughed up by a herd of bullocks. I despairingly cast grass seed all over it and, being by now older and wiser in the ways of gardendom, planted it with hundreds of tiny twigs wound about in black thread to snare sparrows, self, etc. I set slug traps, mouse traps, man traps and, having suffered the gastronomic depredations of wandering cattle beasts on an earlier new lawn, cattle traps of electrified tape.

In time, a sward of the CDW variety again emerged, which flourished until the subsequent winter. In my ignorance I had imagined that grass, like any other plant, would relish all the water it could get. I learned the Great Truth that grasses need good drainage too, and a badly drained lawn produces only moss, toadstools and sickly yellow grass.

Even at this stage I still had not learned. Refusing to be beaten and unutter-ably weary of mowing my rampant kikuyu and CDW jobs, I determined to spray one of the areas and replace it with a lawn of *Dichondra*, or Mercury Bay weed. I was assured by a helpful garden centre assistant that this little low-growing clover-like plant was my salvation; I need never mow this lawn, ever. When the kikuyu had died back (that which was visible above ground, that is) I spent many back-breaking hours lifting and turning the clods and raking their reverse to some kind of soft soil.

Reverently I measured out the expensive seed per metre, raked, covered against the birds, and watered. In what seemed like a gratifyingly short space of time a delicate green blush covered the ground. Embryonic carrot weed vied with rag-wort, thistle and plantains; infant dandelions fought with clover and daisies.

Here and there in ragged patches the faintest sprinkling of tiny kidney-shaped leaves struggled for their very lives.

Another week and the delicate *Dichondra* was invisible beneath this luxuriant blanket of weeds. Draconian measures were required. The same helpful assistant who had sold me the Mercury Bay seed sold me a bottle of selective lawn weedkiller. The instructions read 'Use only on mature lawns, or not until nine months after planting.' I vacillated uneasily and the weeds grew and grew. In desperation, I sprayed on the selective killer. The *Dichondra* turned a sickly yellow but so did the weeds. They keeled over in the most gratifying manner, and slowly the small spade-shaped leaves recovered and began to spread.

Their hold on life was brief. The weeds had subsided into but temporary oblivion, and it was at this stage that the tenacious roots of the kikuyu, which had been lurking in a vicious network *beneath the ground*, began to shoot to the surface.

No matter how large or small our plots, gardeners are all, to some degree, lawnatics. But as Karel Capek concludes, a lush and verdant greensward is a vision that lives only in the gardener's heart:

> June is the time for making hay; but as for us, owners of small gardeners in towns, please do not think that one dewy morning we shall whet the scythe, and then with open shirt, with powerful rustling sweeps, and singing popular songs, we shall cut the sparkling grass. Things are rather different with us. First of all we want to have an English lawn, green like a billiard cloth, and dense like a carpet, a perfect lawn, a grass-plot without blemish, turf like velvet, a meadow like a table. Well, then, in spring we find that this English lawn consists of bald patches, dandelions, clover, clay, and a few hard and yellow tufts of grass. First it must be weeded; we sit down on our heels and pull out all the mischievous weeds, leaving behind a waste land, trampled, and as bare as if bricklayers or a herd of zebra had been dancing on it. Then it is watered and left to crack in the sun, after which we decide that it really needs cutting.[1]

Yes, once the wretched lawn is established, then we must keep it mowed.

Mowing in the good old days was done by a stout pony wearing boots made of felt or leather; the soothing hum of the mowing roller blades that it pulled must have been one of the pleasures of summer. How preferable to the noisy, smelly petrol-driven monsters that roar with their two-stroke cacophony through suburbia today, announcing spring or the weekend.

The wits and wags have plenty to say on the subject of lawns:

Spring hasn't really reached the suburbs until you are awakened by the first lawnmower. —*Dan Kidney*

If the grass is greener in the other fellow's yard, let him worry about cutting it. —*Fred Allen*

The kind of grass I've got in the garden lies down under the mower and pops up again as soon as it's passed. —*Basil Boothroyd*

I love the sound of a lawnmower. It means something is being done and I'm not doing it. —*Helen Hayes*

And from British humourist Richard Briers:

Now that I have a motorised mower I can agree with a certain amount of complacency that a lawn like the surface of a billiard table should be the aspiration of every British gardener who has more space than a window-box. If I still relied on a handmower I should have given way to the temptation of astroturf long ago. I once received some rather ingenious advice on the subject of lawns. 'Add a little brandy to your watering can,' counselled a gardening friend. 'That way you can be sure your lawns will come up half cut.'

We might threaten, from time to time, to concrete the whole thing over but, like Rumer Godden's nine-year-old Lovejoy, who created a garden against all odds on a ruined London bomb site, which of us has the moral fibre to resist having a hand in the miracle of germination and growth? Let the last word on the labour of the lawn be Lovejoy's:

The packet had said the seeds would come up … when Lovejoy planted them she supposed she had believed it, but it had been more hope than belief. Now, on the patch of earth under the net, had come a film of green; when she bent down and looked closely, she could see that it was made of countless little stalks as fine as hairs, some so fine she could scarcely see their colour, others vividly showing their new green. They're blades, thought Lovejoy, blades of grass! In the borders were what she thought at first were tiny weeds, until she saw real weeds among them. The weeds were among the grass too; she could tell them because they were bigger, a different pattern, and when she looked again the borders were peopled with myriad heads, all alike, each head made of two flat leaves, no bigger than pinheads, on a stalk; they were so many and so all the same, that she knew they were meant; no weed seeded like that. They must come from a sowing … my sowing, thought Lovejoy suddenly, the seeds I planted.

She knelt down, carefully lifted the net away, and very gently with her palm, she brushed the hair blades; they seemed to move as though they were not quite rooted, but rooted they were; when she held one in her thumb and finger, it did not come away. 'It's like … earth's fur,' said Lovejoy.[2]

# 8

# A THORNY ISSUE – THE ROSARIAN

*And if you voz to see my rozis*
*Which is a boon to all men's noziz,*
*You'd fall upon your back and scream –*
*Oh lawk, oh crikey! It's a dream!*
　　　　　　　　　—Edward Lear

A rosarian may be defined as a gardener with problems. As though a passion for gardening were not liability enough, he or she suffers from a disease that manifests itself in a manic passion for, and obsession with, all things related to the *rose*.

So if it is to be a rose garden, do not choose those stunted, unnatural earth-loving strains, which have nothing of vigour and wildness in them, nor banish other flowers which may do homage to the beauty of the rose as courtiers to a queen. Let climbing roses drop in a veil from the terrace and smother with flower-spangled embroidery the garden wall, run riot over vaulted arcades, clamber up lofty obelisks of leaf-tangled trellis, twine themselves around the pillars of a rose-roofed temple, where little avalanches of sweetness shall rustle down at a touch and the dusty gold of the sunshine shall mingle with the summer snow of the flying petals. Let them leap in a great bow or fall in a creamy cataract to a foaming pool of flowers. In the midst of the garden set a state of Venus with a great bloom trained to her own hand, or of Flora, her cornucopia overflowing with white rosettes, or a tiny basin where leaden amorini seated upon the margin are fishing with trailing buds.[1]

Extravagant stuff! Delicious prose crystallising our enslavement by the rose. The Minoans painted it, the Romans spent fortunes on it (sometimes even suffocating their guests at banquets beneath its petals), the Greeks enshrined it as a deity in their mythology. Poets, writers and artists down the centuries have struggled to capture the essence of the flower on canvas and pin it down with words. It has been a political symbol and the emblem of a dynasty. Soldiers throughout history have followed, and died beneath, banners decorated with the rose. Homer tells us that the shield of Achilles was decorated with the flower, and England's medieval War of the Roses was fought by the House of Lancaster bearing the red rose, *Rosa gallica*, against the House of York bearing the white rose, *Rosa alba*.

We are suitably impressed to know that the rose is older than the human race, older than the hands that drew the first picture of it. The flower originated in Central Asia some 60 million years ago, and fossils found in Oregon and Colorado are said to be 30 million years old. Some 5000 years ago the Chinese, appreciating the beauty of the flower, began cultivating it widely. The species was christened 'Queen of the Flowers' by Sappho, a Roman poet, in 600BC. She wrote: 'O'er all the flowers shall reign a queen, the rose – that royal flower … she is of earth the gem, of flowers the diadem.'

Not satisfied with cramming our gardens with the flower, we surround ourselves with it in our homes too – not only in vases. We have it climbing up the curtains and soft furnishings and cavorting across the wallpaper. It seduces us from placemats, china, chocolate boxes, and calendars, and enslavement is complete when we wish not only to smell like a rose but to eat it too. We slosh on lashings of rose-perfumed toiletries and cosmetics, and drool over rose-flavoured crystallised candies, conserves, teas and vinegars. Last but not least, we have made it the subject of songs, poems and television series, and there are more books on rose species and culture than on any other single aspect of gardening.

We do not stop to ask ourselves whether peonies, camellias or azaleas are equally beautiful. We are superior and remark that these are paltry tribes (though they do have some admirers) compared with the aristocrat – the rose. We ignore the fact that like all prima donnas they make their devotees pay dearly for their admiration, by exacting a year-round intensive-care schedule of watering, spraying, pruning, deadheading, and fertilising. We forgive them in winter when they become weather-beaten, black spot-infested prickly monsters prevailing over the gardens like knights that have been thrashed in a jousting tournament. The fact that rose lovers down the ages have (with only a modicum of exasperation) obediently put up with all this, together with the fact that we are still doing so, merely emphasises the truth of the matter.

Countess Elizabeth von Arnhim, writing on the subject of a recalcitrant rose in her German garden last century, has this to say:

> I was disgusted with 'Dr Grill'. He had the best place in the garden – warm, sunny and sheltered – his holes were prepared with the tenderest care – he was given the most dainty mixture of compost, clay and manure – he was watered assiduously all through the drought when more willing flowers got nothing – and he refused to do anything but look black and shrivel. He did not die, but neither did he live – he just existed – and at the end of the

summer not one of him had a scrap more shoot or leaf than when he was first put in. It would have been better if he had died straight away, for then I should have known what to do – as it is, there he is still occupying the best place, wrapped up carefully for winter, excluding kinder roses and probably intending to repeat the same conduct next year.[2]

Rose fanciers today fall into two schools: those who sing the praises of the modern hybrid tea, and those who swoon over the old-fashioned shrub rose. Make no mistake, the horticultural élite judge one by the type of rose one grows. Old or 'heritage' roses are *de rigeur* in the gardens of the cogniscenti – it does not matter that they grow into monsters in months; that many of them have a three-week blooming period; that most of them are viciously barbed and will wreck your expensive Country Life/Lakeland knitwear.

Germaine Greer has never used her pseudonym of Rose Blight more aptly than in this recommendation:

> If your garden is all that stands between your domestic hearth and a tourist-junkie-drunk-and-football-fan-infested street, you need to cultivate plants which actually inflict pain upon the unwary interloper … *Rosa felipes* 'Kiftsgate' is able to strangle full-grown elms. The euphoric freak about whom she throws her hammerlock will indeed die in aromatic pain. If he struggles to break free of her iron caress he may well flay himself to the very bone. The very exist-ence of the 'Dunwich Rose' is justified by its astonishing ability to draw blood with its larger spines and to cause weeks of agony with its myriad tiny ones. *Rosa spinosissima* is so extravagantly prickly that it tears all its own leaves off in a high wind.
>
> Most of the really vicious roses only flower as an afterthought, so that passers-by are not actively lured to donate blood and curses. The way to do that is to plant the showier hybrid roses on the far side of a killer rose. Passers-by will willingly run the gamut as soon as the buds begin to blow, and will abuse you roundly when they hurt themselves, all of which is very amusing.[3]

If you do grow heritage roses, and the hybrid tea man questions the wisdom of devoting your entire garden to them, do not admit that they have swallowed up everything else, and reply to the effect that they have 'such incredible his-tory … old-world charm … unparalleled perfumes … delicate and refined flow-ers … beautifully shaped heps (not hips) … and need so little pruning and spraying'. Ignore his chortles when he points at the gentle grey mist of mildew engulfing the Bourbons and Gallicas, and pretend not to hear when he rudely suggests chainsaw pruning.

If his philistine lack of sensitivity enrages you and you must enter into a debate, you can try towing him round the garden eulogising over the delicacy and refinement of the blooms of 'Assemblage des Beautés', or 'Baron Girod de l'Ain'. Refuse to be intimidated when he dismisses them as 'wishy-washy heretodays and gone tomorrows', and when he visits next time bearing a bunch of modern hybrid teas, sneer politely and suggest that you can't help feeling they are just a *little* 'vulgar', 'blowsy', 'coarse in form', 'garish in colour' etc for your taste.

Similarly, the élitist rosarian will have no truck with miniature roses except in expensive containers on the terraces, and floribunda hybrids are just passable but a little flashy. The only modern hybrids that are absolutely *de rigeur* in his garden are those of the English hybridist David Austin.

Austin hit the jackpot by establishing a highly sought-after range of modern roses in the 1960s. Named for Shakespearian and other literary characters, they combine all the scent, form and colour of the old-fashioned rose with the re-peat blooming qualities and high health of the modern rose. In other words they look old but aren't, impress with intellectual names, and are generally quite stunning. Above all, they lack the coarseness and blowsiness of which the hy-brid tea varieties are accused.

> 'I want them every month,' he cried,
> 'I want them every hour,
> Perennial rose and none beside,
> Henceforth shall be my flower.'[4]

You can acquaint the hybrid tea person with the fact that there are famous gardeners and writers who have had the temerity to question the perfection of modern roses, and even to to express positive dislike of them.

Vita Sackville-West sums up the modern hybrid tea thus:

I have heard conventionally minded people remark that they like a rose to be a rose, by which they apparently mean an overblown pink, scarlet or yellow object, desirable enough in itself, but lacking the subtlety to be found in tra-ditional roses which might well be picked off a piece of medieval tapestry.[5]

Beverley Nichols, with his usual wit, wrote in 1969:

I have been drawn into many heated arguments through my deep-rooted aversion to hybrid tea roses ... for to whisper a word against roses in England or America is simply not 'done'. When one suggests one can have too many of them and that the role they play in the garden is limited, one's remarks are received with the same sort of horrified incredulity as if one had observed, *en passant*, that all dogs are not the noblest creatures in the animal kingdom nor all babies the most beautiful example of God's handiwork … an honest moment's reflection must reveal the fact that many dogs are not noble, and that most babies are of considerable hideousness, with bald pates and lunatic expressions.

We are besotted with roses. We can no longer see them straight because of a mist of sentimental tradition. 'My love is like a red, red rose rose,' sang Burns and for the 100,000 members of the Rose Society this fits in nicely with their personal predilections, evoking as it does a picture of a young woman waiting to be wooed – but one hopes not too painfully scratched – against a background of 'Dorothy Perkins'.[6]

Nichols demands:

Why should nature approve of a hybrid tea? Without its flowers, which means for the greater part of its life, it is gaunt, gawky and deliberately deformed by man, with its tortured, amputated limbs sticking out in all directions, demanding pity rather than praise … really look at them … what do you see? A long row of hospital cases.[7]

British writer and rose fancier George Orwell was no snob when it came to buying roses:

In the good old days when nothing in Woolworth's cost over sixpence, one of their best lines was their rose bushes. They were always very young plants but they came into bloom in their second year, and I don't think I ever had one die on me. Their chief interest was that they were never, or very seldom, what they claimed to be on their labels. One that I bought for a 'Dorothy Perkins' turned out to be a beautiful little white rose with a yellow heart, one of the finest ramblers I have ever seen. A polyantha rose labelled yellow turned out to be deep red. Another, bought for an 'Albertine', was like an 'Albertine' but more double, and gave astonishing masses of blossom. These roses had all the interest of a surprise packet, and there was always the chance that you might happen upon a new variety which you would have the right to name 'John Smithii' or something of that kind.

Last summer I passed the cottage where I used to live before the war. The little white rose, no bigger than a boy's catapult when I had put it in, had grown into a huge vigorous bush; the 'Albertine' or near 'Albertine' was smothering half the fence in a cloud of pink blossom. I had planted both these in 1936. And I thought 'All that for sixpence!' I do not know how long a rose bush lives; I suppose ten years might be an average life. And throughout that time a rambler will be in full bloom for a month or six weeks each year, while a bush rose will be blooming on and off for at least four months. All that for sixpence – the price before the war of ten Players, or a pint and a half of mild, or a week's subscription to the *Daily Mail*, or about twenty minutes of twice-breathed air in the movies![8]

Regardless of which school one belongs to, it is a dead cert that we have all planted far too many roses, yearn for those we can't fit in, and order new ones every year, keeping all our other plants determinedly mobile.

Enslavement? Absolutely. Utterly.

Many rosarians suffer from a complication of the disease, which manifests itself in an obsessive desire to 'Grow to Show'.

The Wars of the Roses are annual events staged by the Rosarians' Society. The condition is an addiction and there seems to be no cure. The discomfort may be alleviated temporarily by staging the biggest, brightest and most lucious blooms in any competitive show, and the subsequent acquisition of car boots crammed with vases, bowls and trophies (preferably made of precious metals).

For all the euphoria, such glory is not to be attained easily. First, the 'Grow to Show' type of rosarian must go to inordinate lengths to cheat the shattering rain that threatens to reduce prized blooms to sodden mildewed heaps just days before 'The Show'.

His neighbour will stagger back clutching his heart when, on pulling back the drapes in the morning, he sees that every single bloom has disappeared from the rose-mad garden next door. 'This time they really have taken leave of their senses, flipped their lids,' he tells his wife. 'They've gone and planted rows and rows of multi-coloured golf umbrellas!'

It takes the poor fellow a few moments' rational thinking to deduce that the roses are still there, dry-headed and blushing coyly beneath a kaleidoscope of parasols. But that is not all.

The rosarian's car is out in the rain because the garage is heaped high with mountains of insulated polystyrene boxes, buckets full of water, piles of old newspaper, bubble wrap, tissue paper, wads of cotton wool, boxes of cotton tips and hand sprayers full of water.

There is worse to come. As the bemused neighbours close their drapes at bedtime they see the rosarians creep into the garden, sneak beneath the umbrellas and perform the astonishing act of felling the most excellent of their roses in their prime. Peeping through the drapes into the garage, they see the long-stemmed beauties plunged up to their necks in the buckets and further stems hacked off underwater. The heads of the blooms are then padded out with moistened tissues, petals reshaped with cotton wool buds and foliage with the slightest blemish firmly snipped off and discarded.

The moonlight rituals continue. The stems of roses are tenderly folded into bubble wrap and packed into the polystyrene boxes. When the lids are sealed the bewildered neighbour concludes that the rosarians have now come to their senses and are going to hit the sack – get some shuteye. Not a bit of it; the cool boxes and all the attendant paraphernalia are lobbed into the back of the car. The rose fanciers leap in the front and the car speeds off into the night to the airport, or towards some far-flung town.

There are banners and placards in these areas proclaiming National or even World Rose Show or Convention, Rose Breeders' Conference etc. These advertisements cause the rosarian to hyperventilate and thrust his or her foot down on the accelerator. Flasks of black coffee are tossed around the car.

On arrival at the exhibition hall at dawn, the bleary-eyed rosarians jump out, unpack their blooms, examine them anxiously, then wrestle with trestle tables, vases, staging cards and documentation. Their adrenalin leaps when, titivating their blooms, they see that those of their rivals on either side obviously did *not* spend their days under golf umbrellas and have not been protected from anything that blew, flew, crept or crawled.

I do not suffer from the 'Grow to Show' complication. The lust within my matronly bosom is for the rampant beauties of yesteryear. My problems are more of a 'hunt the house, garage, farm' variety, as my lusty beauties of ancient lineage threaten to engulf them forever.

I must admit that should Prince Charming pass this way, he'd have a devil of a job rescuing the building from the thorny thickets, leave alone Sleeping Beauty. But oh, those many-quartered blooms of ancient lineage – damasks and velvets, mosses and musks, jewelled colours, velvet red-blacks, sultry purples, languishing lavender lilacs, their rich sensuous perfumes.

It appears that those of us in the terminal stages of the rosarians' disease have no desire for redemption. We are happy to remain irretrievably addicted, unsaved, unconverted, and would wilt, mildew, rust or break out in a rash of black spot at the mere thought of being rehabilitated or, perish the thought, *cured*.

Our passion and *enslavement* by the rose shall continue unabated, encouraged by the words of the Reverend Samuel Reynolds Hole, Dean of Rochester, in 1869:

> There should be beds of roses, banks of roses, bowers of roses, hedges of roses, edgings of roses, baskets of roses, vistas and alleys of roses.[9]

# ROSE QUIZ

1. When **pruning** roses you should always:

   a) Make an advance deposit at the blood bank.
   b) Hire a neighbourhood kid you don't like.
   c) Wear spouse's gorse-clipping gloves and body armour.

2. **Grafting** is defined as:

   a) What politicians do when they run short of cash.
   b) Cultural payoffs known as Arts and Grafts.

3. **Hybrid** is:

   a) The opposite of lobrid.
   b) How birds greet each other.
   c) The plant that results from crossing two distinctly different species.

4. **Humus** is defined as:

   a) Something amusing or funny.
   b) When the air is moist and muggy and you wake up covered in mildew.

5. A **deadhead**:

   a) Perfectly describes your last date.
   b) Perfectly describes the competitor who beat you in the last floribunda show.

6. When **staking** you should always:

   a) Wear a black cape.
   b) Light the barbecue.
   c) Make sure someone else holds the stick while you hold the hammer.

7. A **picket** is:

   a) An unhappy jobbing gardener carrying a sign and refusing to work.
   b) What you long to do to another rosarian's prize bloom.
   c) A lethal type of decorative fencing useful for supporting rampant roses.[10]

Temptation looms large in a gardener's life. There are two ways of contemplating the danger: William Shakespeare's view …

'Tis one thing to be tempted but another to fall.

or (much nearer the gardener's heart) Oscar Wilde's theory:

The way to get rid of temptation is to yield to it.

It's called greed. That vice that assails every gardener as soon as he or she sets foot in a garden centre or nursery. There are plants you will kill for; plants that are bigger, brighter, better, rarer. Plants you cannot live without; plants that promise panoplies of prodigious colour and performance. The fact that you cannot afford them and will have to give half a dozen other plants a long ride in the wheelbarrow to find room for even one new acquisition is entirely beside the point. The latest acquisitions will have to serve a lengthy initiation period of standing in their planter bags for several weeks, while you wander round desperately trying to find a gap into which they might just squeeze.

Jonathan Cox brings this thorny issue to a close in this soliloquy, exposing us rosarians for the acquisitive creatures we are:


## MY LAST ROSE
*A brief drama for one player and two voices.*

**Scene:** A large garden centre in suburban Auckland.

JC: Look – wonderfully healthy plants of 'Graham Thomas' just coming into bud. I've always wanted to grow that rose.

JC: It is a fabulous rose. You should get it.

JC: Out of the question. Don't you remember? I bought my last rose last month.

JC: Don't be ridiculous. No one ever says 'This is my last rose' and means it. It's like saying 'This is my last potato chip'. Everyone knows you'll go right on and scoff the rest of the packet.

JC: 'Maigold' was absolutely my last rose.

JC: You're always saying 'This is my last something'. 'This is my last gardening book,' you'll say. Next minute you're signing up for all four volumes of the new *RHS Dictionary of Gardening*. 'That was my last ride on the beach,' you said after Barnaby threw you off into the tide and you had to ride home covered in sand with your riding boots full of seawater. Next week you were back on galloping faster than ever.

JC: It's not the same thing. There's not a spot of room left in the garden any more. It's like gardening in a huge bouquet. I keep expecting to hit one of these steel brush things that florists poke flowers into, with the spade. The whole thing has got entirely out of hand. One minute you're standing admiring the day lilies, you take a step backwards and you're up to your waist in *Rosa omeiensis* 'Pteracantha'. My entire lower torso resembles a cat's scratching post.

JC: You said you wanted a wild, blowsy look.

JC: I've changed my mind. Now I want absolute formality. Rows and rows of box hedging and clipped yews everywhere. Symmetry and garden rooms and more perspective than a town planner's sketch.

JC: This isn't getting us anywhere. If you just curbed 'Wedding Day' a bit, 'Graham Thomas' could share the back fence with her.

JC: Curb 'Wedding Day'? Curbing 'Wedding Day' is like trying to fight a forest fire with a damp handkerchief. Besides, that fellow next door is dedicated to curbing 'Wedding Day'. He likes everything just so. I've seen him out there with a square set measuring the angle of his tulip stems. 'Wedding Day' has only to poke up two centimetres above the fence and the minute my back's turned he's up that ladder with his loppers hacking her back.

He thinks I don't notice. I peeped through and saw two huge canes poking out from behind their tool shed where he'd stashed them. The other day I came home unexpectedly and caught him up the ladder with his loppers poised. He got such a fright to see me that he nearly fell right over the fence. He quickly cut two branches off their apple tree just to make it look as though he wasn't really up to something.

JC: Why not move 'Wedding Day' onto the carport? Then 'Graham Thomas' could have the run of the back fence. He's not so vigorous, so Harry the Hacker would be happy.

JC: Are you mad? That carport's on its last legs. One day a fat sparrow will land on the roof and the whole lot will be history. I'll have to try to pass the heap of rubble off as some kind of artistic statement. We could probably grow 'Wedding Day' over it then and call it 'Back to Nature' or something.

JC: Well, why not strengthen the carport with some more supports and trellised sides, and coax her up those and onto the roof? She'd look fabulous from the upstairs window.

JC: Actually, that's not such a bad idea. She would look fabulous from upstairs and she could amuse herself by billowing down over the front and trying to snag the car as we drive in and out. But, more importantly, I could have 'Graham Thomas' after all.

JC: You look happier now.

JC: You're a genius. You always know what I really want.

JC: I know you so well.

JC: I've got 'Graham Thomas'. Now, quick! For heaven's sake, let's get out of here before I see anything else!

JC: Wait! Look! What's that lovely blue thing? Clematis 'H.F. Young'. Just think how that would look rambling through 'Graham Thomas'! And you could do a yellow and blue planting at their feet – *Ageratum houstonianum*, yellow day lilies ...

JC: Don't say another word! The blue and yellow planting is out! Out! Do you hear? But I may just take 'H.F. Young'. It will look superb with 'Graham Thomas' and it won't really be any more trouble than just having the rose by itself.

JC: You won't regret it.

JC: This is absolutely my last clematis.[11]

Let's end with a spot of beheading as (opposed to deadheading) from New Zealand rose breeder Sam McGredy:

### HENRY VIII

> If Henry's roses grew
> black spot,
> They'd quickly pay the price,
> And with his pruners
> trusty he'd
> Behead them in a trice!

... and a word of warning:

### FRIENDS IN NEED

> Beware of your friends in springtime
> Who speak of the roses they've got;
> They'll ask your advice on the pruning,
> And you'll end up by doing the lot!

# 9

## GARDENING ON THE ROCKS

*The rock garden: a place where hardier plants
may be set advanced survival exercises.*

The wags of gardendom have a good deal to say about rock gardens. It appears that a rock garden is an ideal project for beginners. Rocks are very easy to grow and require very little attention. In general the gardener should aim to grow as wide a variety of rocks as possible, especially big ones, since they cover a lot of space and suppress weeds.

Horticultural manuals instruct that this is a nice easy style of garden for the beginner, and as we are usually only too keen to do something desperately creative with the piles of boulders lying round the place, we obey. Crushed digits, ruined backs and a knowledge born of bitter experience are our reward.

Reginald Arkell puts the whole thing neatly into context for us:

> Rock gardens are really ridiculous things,
> Like peaches with pepper and donkeys with wings.
>
> You make out a list of the plants you must buy,
> You stick them in pockets and most of them die.
>
> And if you are foolish enough to suppose
> You can keep them alive with a hose –
>
> What dire disillusionment awaits you next day:
> The water is certain to wash them away.[1]

English gardener Reginald Farrer had definite views on the design of the gardens constructed with stones:

> The ideal rock garden must have a plan ... there are three plans, none of which are good. The first is what I may call the Almond Pudding Scheme ... you take a round bed; you pile it up with soil; you then choose the spikiest

pinnacles of limestone you can find, and insert them thickly with their points in the air, until the effect is that of a tipsy cake stuck with almonds.

The second style is that of the Dog's Grave, which is affected by growers of alpines ... the pudding shape remains more or less the same, but the stones are laid flat in the Dog's Grave ideal.

The third style is that of the Devil's Lapful ... the plan is simplicity itself. You take a hundred or thousand cartloads of bald square-faced boulders, you drop them all absolutely anyhow, and you plant things amongst them. The chaotic hideousness of the result is something to be remembered with shudders ever after.[2]

The irrepressible duo of Sellar and Yeatman also offer somewhat tongue-in-cheek advice about landscaping the rock garden:

The rock garden ... on the face of it appears to be an attempt to pile up rocks and then hide them with invisible plants or to pile up invisible plants and then hide them with rocks. The true purpose of rock gardening, however, is to triumph over nature as well as the neighbours by first making gardening as difficult as possible, and then succeed in growing minute flowers – tiny saxifrages, teeny febrifuges and weeny-weeny sweet sarcophaguses – in the face of all the difficulties or even on the faces of all the rocks.[3]

Beverley Nichols, writing in 1932, gives less frivolous advice in this essay:

## HOW NOT TO MAKE A ROCK GARDEN

When I first came to the cottage, I decided that there would not be a rock garden, partly because there seemed no place for such a garden, but principally because in my ignorance I did not care for rock gardens ... visualised them as gaunt damp rubbish heaps on southern promenades over which there brooded a few diseased palms, while in front of them passed a procession of nurse-maids, wheeling perambulators in which revolting infants glowered and spat. Rock gardens seemed to be the monopoly of garden gossip writers, who were always telling one to tidy up the saxifrages, and throw the snails over the left shoulder. I had, in short, the gloomiest views about rock gardens, and it was only by accident I ever possessed one.

It happened like this. The first summer at the cottage was phenomenally dry ... sinister cracks appeared in the herbaceous borders. The roses drooped flushed, exhausted heads. Even the pansies protruded purple tongues over the crumbling earth, demanding mercy. For several anxious weeks I scrambled about the neighbourhood in search of water. There was a pond in a distant field which was often raided, at dusk when its owner was safely in the pub ... Accompanied by a friend we would make guilty excursions ... sweat pouring off our foreheads, scurrying silently over the fields, cursing as the pail made an indiscreet clatter, thinking always of the dry, dying roots we were soon to succour.

After a few nights we were bored with scurrying and decided it was really far more agreeable to sit at home and play bridge, and drink brandy ... it was therefore decided that the water problem must be solved by the creation of a pond ... which led to the creation of the rock garden. The pond was dug by a young man from a neighbouring village ... before it had reached any appreciable depth I had to return to London, and it was more than a month before I was able to return. Judge, therefore, of my surprise when I discovered that I had created not only a pond, but a mountain which towered over the pond in a most menacing manner.

At all moments of crisis my interfering gardening neighbour Mrs M has a habit of popping up, and I had hardly seen the mountain and was still wondering where to put it when I heard her footsteps.

'Ah, good evening. Going for a climb up Mont Blanc? He! He! Ho! Ho! You'll have a job getting all this earth away.'

'Getting it away?'

'Well, you're surely not going to leave it here – like this?'

'Not like this, no.' My mind was working with desperate speed to try to get some valid reason for keeping the earth. Then suddenly I had an inspiration. 'This,' I blurted out, 'is the beginning of my rock garden.' And it was.

Mrs M stared at me with undisguised suspicion. 'Rock garden?' she cried. 'What do you mean rock garden?'

'By a rock garden,' I replied, 'I mean a garden containing a quantity of rocks.'

'But you haven't got any rocks.'

'Not yet, no.'

'Where are you going to get them?'

I had not the slightest idea where I was going to get them, so I said in a sepulchral voice 'They Are Coming,' rather as though the skies might open at any moment and deluge us with a cascade of boulders.

'Yes, but where from?'

'Yorkshire.' This was partly guesswork and partly memory, because I had remembered reading in some book of a man who had a quarry of stone in Yorkshire which he used to export.

Mrs M snorted again. 'That'll cost you a pretty penny,' she said. I could hear signs of fierce envy in her voice. She glared at my mountain and then she said:

'But you're surely not going to stuff a lot of rocks on all that mud?'

'Stuff them? No. I shan't stuff them.'

'Well, throw them, then. You've got to have some sort of design.'

'I have.'

'What is it?'

'It is being Done For Me,' I said.

'By whom?'

I could think of nobody but Sir Edward Lutyens, who designed Delhi. So I said 'You will catch cold, Mrs M, if you stand on that wet grass.'

I am glad to be able record that she did.

I was therefore committed to a rock garden. I spent a restless night cursing myself ... On the following morning, when I visited the mountain, the prospect did not look so black. The site was promising. A fair slope led down to the pond. Two green arms of a hedge encircled it ... the mountain only had to be slightly sat on, and carven into shape, and decorated with roses, cunningly disposed, to be transformed into a rock garden.

So I fondly imagined.

I ordered the rocks. I was told that it was cheaper to order a truckful, which would contain about eight tons. It seemed a great deal, especially since they had to come all the way from Yorkshire. I was assured that if less were ordered 'it would come out dearer in the end'. There constantly rose before me the sneering face of Mrs M, who did not believe the rocks were coming at all. She believed it well enough a few days later, when she had to drive four miles out of her way because the road in front of my cottage was completely blocked by the collapse of an enormous vanful of best-quality, fully weathered Yorkshire rocks.

She believed it still more when she discovered she would be deprived of the services of her odd-job man, who had secretly deserted her in order to earn double pay in transporting my rocks across the field ...

At last the thing was done. All the rocks were safely ensconced in the mountain ... the big ones at the bottom, the small ones at the top. Looking back at this adventure, it seems almost incredible that I could have been such a fatuous and ignorant optimist as to imagine that this was the way to make a rock garden, without any plan, without even an adequate preparation of the soil. Yet, I did imagine it – until I saw it in being.

The thing was horrible. It was utterly out of keeping with the rest of the garden. I tried looking at it from this way and from that, half closing my eyes and putting my head on one side. I regarded it before and after cocktail time. It looked much worse after, which is proof that alcohol stimulates the aesthetic sense. No amount of self-hypnotism could persuade me that I liked it.

It reminded me of those puddings made of sponge-cake and custard, which are studded with almonds until they look like some dreadful beast thrown up by the sea. It had no sort of design. It was so steep that the earth was already showing signs of falling away in the slightest rain. The best I could say about it was that it made a very good shelter from the wind.

Had it not been for Mrs M I should have destroyed it overnight. False pride made me keep it there for several days. But there are stronger emotions than false pride. One morning, a few days later, I went out, saw the hideous thing and decided that it could remain no longer. Urgently we summoned the same men who had put it together. By the following afternoon, the earth had been taken away and deposited in a neighbouring field. There remained only a quantity of rocks, scattered about the grass.[4]

Life is too short to weed a rockery.

# 10

# A DEADLY PURSUIT

*Only folk with permanently soiled hands and almost permanent cricks in their backs during the growing season are aware of the manifold delights and dismays in the outwardly mild vocation of gardening for fun. Actually, it is a furious and nerve-straining exercise/pastime. A sixteenth of an acre can furnish space for the violent exercise of virtually all the human emotions.*— Frederick Van Der Walter

Bungy jumping? Free-fall parachuting? Rock climbing? The theory is that the time-honoured gentle pursuit of gardening is for both sexes more dangerous than all three put together. I have been informed (at length) by a member of the medical profession that horticulture is fraught with hazard and should be banned. So stern was his lecture, so comprehensive his list of garden-related injuries that my mutterings of 'therapeutic', 'keeps us fit' and 'healthy hobby' tailed feebly away, because I have to admit to inflicting a good deal of grievous bodily harm upon myself in the cause of decking the earth with flowers and cornucopias of fruit. Gardening friends admit the same.

At the end of a good gardening day I am invariably bruised, battered, blistered or bleeding somewhere. My daughter, white-faced, scolded severely when apprehending me in a bloody bathroom using six band-aids to 'mend' a secateur wound to a vein. It is probably accidents such as this that cause the physician to growl that an unacceptably high proportion of the patients in his waiting room are there as a result of garden-related injuries.

'Gardeners,' he accuses, 'push forks, spades and hoes through their toes, inflict gaping gashes with pruning saws and half of them have never had a tetanus injection in their lives.' If you are among this number, I should make an appointment to have one pretty damned smartly. The deadly tetanus bacteria, present in manure and soil, can enter the body through open wounds and lead to a most unpeaceful and uncomfortable demise.

---

*One of the most pleasing sounds of springtime to be heard all over the country is the contented cooing of osteopaths as Man picks up his garden spade.*— Oliver Pritchett

He launches into a gory and highly graphic account of accidents with lawnmowers, weedeaters, hedge and edge trimmers. 'Old Mr So-and-so,' he says, 'ran over his foot with his Flymo and mowed off three toes. Mrs G clipped off the top of her left index finger with the secateurs and had to have it stitched back on.' I have a revolting mental vision of a garden strewn with gardeners' hacked-off digits. I must have paled, because he stops fairly early on in his fountains-of-blood description of what gardeners do to themselves with chainsaws. I am grateful.

If you can manage to hang on to all your digits in the course of cultivating your plot, then beware of broken bones. The doctor's next target is those gardeners who are careless enough to require medical attention for fractured femurs and broken ankles, arms and wrists incurred by tripping over tools left lying carelessly lying around, or by falling on slippery garden paths or sloping sections.

'These gardeners,' he snarls, 'are usually of more mature years and therefore old enough to know better.'

Being of less ancient vintage won't get you out of trouble either. He rants and raves for quite five minutes about the young gardeners who consult him complaining of blinding headaches, nausea, skin irritation and inexplicable fatigue while admitting to having used toxic chemical sprays wearing only bikinis, singlets, shorts and sandals.

And 'gardeners all have bad backs,' he thunders. 'Use their backs like cranes when lifting and wonder why they can't move for days.'

A real third degree follows and I am asked to answer the following questions. 'Have you, in this last gardening week, wrenched your back trying to right a too heavily and unevenly laden barrow as it catapulted over sideways? (Yes.) Hauled boulders for landscaping? (Guilty.) Used your back as a lever to lift large sacks of compost/potting mix into the barrow? (Correct.) Spent hours doubled up weeding, planting and digging so that you groan horribly when you try to straighten up? (Affirmative.) Crawled in diabolical pain to your GP? I am evasive and less than truthful in my replies, wondering if he has heard the adage 'What a man needs in the garden is a cast-iron back with a hinge on it'.

I mutter about having spent the week doing less strenuous chores since it has been so hot and sunny. 'Ah, the sun,' he smiles, before hurling the dart, 'rewards gardeners with melanoma …' To have told the inquisitor that I never sally forth for a 'head down, bottom up' *therapeutic* gardening session without first locating my sunblock and wide-brimmed hat would have been a barefaced lie.

Did I know, he demands, that over-exertion in the garden and sudden unaccustomed violent physical exercise is a primary cause of coronaries in the over-40s?

My attention begins to wander and I mentally paraphrase Dorothy Frances Gurney's 'Garden Thoughts':

> The kiss of the sun for pardon
> The song of the birds for mirth
> One is nearer God's heart in a garden
> Than anywhere else on earth.

> ... Kiss of the sun – melanoma – no pardon
> The throb as your arteries harden
> As you dig to reduce your girth
> One is nearer death's door in a garden
> Than anywhere else on earth.

Did I know, the good doctor continues, how many gardeners suffer severe allergic reaction to wasp and bee stings which brings them, literally, to death's door?

I am fortunate enough not to suffer such adverse reaction, which is just as well since last summer, thrusting my hand into a clump of dense plantings to pull up a weed, I closed it firmly around a wasps' nest. I did not lapse into instant unconciousness and stop breathing but the pain was excruciating. I suffered an enforced rest as I sat eating anti-histamine tablets, with that sausage-jointed and inflamed hand in bowls of iced water for the rest of the day.

Less dramatic related reactions can include hayfever or allergic response to some plants. The gardener who is allergic to pollens is stricken by swelling of the mucous membranes that line the eyes and nose. He or she gropes blindly around the garden clutching jumbo-sized boxes of tissues as the membranes become irritated and stream with fluid.

Other gardeners suffer severe skin rashes or blisters from some everyday plants which, although innocuous-looking, are, in fact, quite toxic. Even notorious *Clematis vitalba*, pretty *Clematis recta*, the humble buttercup and ranunculae can cause painful and spectacular eruptions of the skin.

We may think that the gentle gardeners among us who are rose fanciers can come to little harm among their blooms. Not so. I am informed that the rosarian is a frequent visitor to the surgery.

He or she often exhibits the symptoms of advanced anaemia from the pints of blood lost at peak pruning time. His or her flesh is permanently scarred by railway-line networks of infected scratches and tears; or the rose person requires minor surgery for the removal of thorns that ungrateful pampered

---

*Gardening is mostly a matter of taking pains – in the small of the back.*

darlings have embedded in the hands that feed them. Septic fingers, it seems, are the rosarian's lot. In the wars of the roses, the roses always win.

Then, continues the medical man remorselessly, there is the unfortunate consequence of pricking a part of the hand near a joint. This results in painful swollen knuckles or a condition he refers to as 'digital bursitis'. I admit to suffering from this incapacitating syndrome quite frequently.

Eye injuries are under discussion next. 'On an average,' he declares darkly, 'I have two or three gardeners a week in the surgery suffering sight-threatening injuries from impalement by twigs and branches, stones thrown up from mowers or from foreign bodies lodged in their eyes.'

If it were not for the fact that I have had cortisone injections in my right elbow for Repetition Strain Injury (too much digging, pruning, lifting heavy rocks etc) I would not have believed it possible for the doctor to think of any more dangers present in our tranquil plots.

'Worn-out wrists, elbows, shoulders, knees – gardeners have them all,' he growls. (I hope he has forgotten my Victorian and vapourish inclination to faint when the astonishingly long needle of his syringe is inserted and manoeuvred around my elbow joint.)

'Even the minor ailments,' he continues, 'coughs, colds, chills, aching joints – all are to be had by working in the garden in rain and remaining in damp clothes and footwear.'

If, like me, you are thinking at this stage of slinking off for a nice, quiet potter in the potting shed – bad move. If tetanus, melanoma, heart attack or allergic reaction to an insect sting haven't yet carried you off, that innocuous sack of potting mix or compost could. For in its wholesome depths lurks a fate for gardeners more sinister than all these others – legionnaire's disease, a deadly form of pneumonia that can be contracted by inhalation.

You may open your polythene sack and breathe deeply of the earthy smell that issues from the compost. But if soil infected with the fatal bacteria *Legionella pneumophila* has been incorporated into the mix and bred in the warm, moist, organic material, your exit from the ranks of gardeners will be swift and certain.

So: do we throw down our spades and enrol in a nice safe course of white-water rafting, ladies' rugby, pot-holing? Only the most brazen amongst us would now deny that gardening is anything but fraught with peril. Melanoma amidst the marigolds, anaphylaxis among the annuals, discarded digits in the delphiniums, coronaries in the cabbage patch, RSI in the rose beds and tetanus in the topiary!

And my friend the physician – what does he do for kicks? He has one of the best gardens in town.

# 11

# THE STRESS OF IT ALL

*The garden always makes sure one has something to worry about.*
—Pam Brown

One simply cannot ignore the tricky subject of the stress of gardening. The greatest single cause of this stress is the gardener's frantic race to try to exert some control over the garden. We have abused our bodies all day taming one area only to realise that the rest looks just like a stage set for *Sleeping Beauty*.

This is why I love autumn. I adore autumn. Not only because it is the season of mellow mists and fruitfulness and all that, but because with winter at its heels, it brings me a glimmer of hope that summer's rampant growth is almost at an end.

'Almost' is the operative word here at Valley Homestead in the subtropical belt of the northern North Island of New Zealand. I am prepared to admit that in our gardening we are all sometimes less than satisfied with the horticultural conditions dictated by individual geographic and climatic conditions. I can be magnanimous and agree that as gardeners we spend a goodly number of our gardening hours trying to cheat both. Be that as it may, I want you to understand exactly what I mean when I refer to rampant growth.

I speak of trees and shrubs that become forest giants in a matter of months; of climbers that become dense tangled thickets strangling and suffocating all in their path; I tell of thug-like perennials slugging it out in the parterres; of lawns that cause the mower to smoke if not hammered into submission every three or four days. As though this fearful fecundity were not enough, I tell of giant weeds that flourish prodigiously all year round; of grotesque insect bugs that breed prodigiously all year round; and of disgusting diseases that thrive all year round.

My frost-free winters may be the envy of rugged snow-bound gardeners in colder climes, but they dictate that there is almost never a rest in the demon gardens of subtropical zones such as ours. Okay, we can grow subtropicals you would die for, but consider their appalling growth-gone-mad habits in balmy climates. They must be constantly hacked back to prevent them assuming the proportions of an Ecuadorian rainforest. Labour-intensive isn't the word – only slashing with a machete will keep them from pushing over one's neighbours' fences. Consider the capital outlay invested in the maintenance and replacement of secateurs, loppers, pruning saws, chainsaws and mowers – worn out (or lost) in weeks. Imagine the tortured wrist, elbow, shoulder, hip and knee joints, and abused backs. In this advanced jungle control and survival exercise body parts wear out faster than the tools they wield.

It's enough to make the gardenperson declare a new RSI (Repetitive Strain Injury) syndrome called RSBI (Repetitive Saw Blade Injury). Enough to make them offer themselves dead or alive to horticultural scientists researching CGFS (Chronic Gardener Fatigue Syndrome).

In the southern hemisphere CGFS is most clearly observed during the months of January, February and March, and probably in September and October in the northern hemisphere. All plant material that was the glory of spring and summer needs massacre and mutilation. In Northland at this time our mean temperatures are around 28-34°C (in the shade) and the humidity count comes in at around 99 per cent. The blinding sweat oozing through a pancake layer of factor 45 sunblock and pouring into my eyes from beneath sensible wide-brimmed hat has been known to cause slightly less than accurate application of loppers and pruning saw.

Does the pathetic lopsided stump expire decently, leaving all that lovely space for the smothered underplantings beneath to burgeon forth? Does it tentatively put out a little polite restrained growth after a decently observed period of rest and recuperation? No. A couple of good old steamy Northland downpours and Godammit, the thing has merely been encouraged and has shot to three times its original height.

Can you even begin to imagine what a 'favoured subtropical climate' does for fungal diseases? It presents them with a spore-solarium. They sail (multiplying) through the soggy air, smothering precious plant material in spots, dots, blotches and mildews such as gardeners in less temperate zones have never dreamed of. Many of the old roses seem to float in some kind of creeping grey mist, while the more modern hybrids have foliage interestingly dappled in fetching shades of black, rust and purple. It does not seem too black a lie to tell visitors from further south that these are variegated hybrids indigenous to the Far North.

On the subject of species *Rosa*, I dare say that in autumn those who enjoy colder climates are still flaunting unblemished dark green glossy foliage and sporting blooms of clear colour. Their owners will snarl and say that our roses are in bloom months before theirs and deserve to be clapped out by January/February. I am prepared to concede that point. They are. Those cultivars that have tried for a second blooming have had their flowers scorched and bleached by the brassy northern sun. They are long, leggy and menopausal, producing miniature blooms and inclined towards defoliation. At least the frenzied perennials falling into each other's arms like unruly children hide their desperately unattractive thorny legs. When I summon up the courage to decapitate the frenzied perennials I am going to have desperately unattractive slashed wrists.

Species *Rosa* are goners for this year. 'But did you mulch well?' I hear you ask earnestly. The answer is utterly. So utterly that a logging truck would not go amiss among the vengeful thickets presently formed by the shrub and climbing varieties. With vision granted only to inspired gardeners I planted *Wisteria sinensis* and *Rosa* 'Souvenir de Mme Leonie Viennot' along the side of the garage. In early October, garden visitors indulge reels of film capturing the ephemeral beauty of the lilac-lazuli mist of the wisteria racemes dripping down through Leonie's beautifully blowsy blooms of coppery apricot-pink.

The visitors of early January retreat nervously as the garage sways dangerously beneath the weight of their combined enthusiasm. Their trunks have assumed the proportions of a Sumo wrestler's thighs; dangerous octopoid tentacles and barbed canes whip out towards the roof of the house and savage the unwary. The Non-Gardening Husband is disbelieving when I tell him that the rope-like trunk advancing across his garage workbench through a broken window pane is a mere wisteria 'tendril'. I am despairing at having to hack this lot back. Pruning in Northland is not a process for the faint of heart.

Weeds are discussed elsewhere in this volume, but in a subtropical climate they come into the despair category too. They choke your rows of seedlings, smother the early lettuce, and by the time you've finished hoeing between the rows they've already started to grow again at the other end. A shower of nice warm subtropical rain and those you felled are rooted and away again.

Have I told you about the prodigious quantities of 'wandering jew' (*Tradescantia*

---

*Gardening: eleven months of hard work followed by one month of disappointment.* —Lord Heathcote-Amory

spp) I inherited when we acquired this property? (In the northern hemisphere this thug of thugs is potted up and cossetted as a houseplant in centrally heated rooms.) Given a water-retentive clay soil and moist atmospheric conditions, its bolting fingers root down faster than one can blink. It actually builds up three-dimensional layers then scrambles up into shrubs and trees, letting fall terrifying canopies of jointed tentacles. A small shoot accidentally dropped onto the too-hot-to-walk-on asphalt driveway lies fresh and perky for days attempting to root down even there. Similarly, my Elizabethan parterres of old roses provide a sanctuary for underplantings of oxalis and other unmentionables, all growing tumultuously in the humid warmth. I have tried every method known to man to halt their growth – except of course prolonged searing frost and cold.

My potato vine (*Solanum jasminoides* 'Alba'), planted to do a quick cosmetic cover-up on an aesthetically displeasing water tank in the vege garden, is not fit to live. It has strangled the scarecrow and most of the veges. No matter how many times I try to murder it by felling it to the ground it resurrects itself, fighting back with spindly stalks bearing right at their tops a profusion of white flowers destined not for the ugly sides of the tank but for the tops of trees in an adjacent paddock.

'Well, you must put up with all that,' you say. 'With your climate look at all those marvellous things you can grow (and grow). We'd give our eye teeth to be able to grow some of those flashy subtropicals – plants that we nurture as tender treasures are almost naturalised weeds on roundabouts up your way.' Fair enough, but by the same token, I'd give my eye teeth to be able to grow some luscious winter-loving peonies, blue Himalayan poppies or, on a more prosaic note, even some good old-fashioned Brussels sprouts.

I've had repeated attempts at those in subtropical Northland and the results are truly phenomenal – Jack and the Beanstalk trunks bearing tiers of giant frilly leaves and not a tight little frost-kissed green head in sight. I can't grow cold-climate plants, but many of mine may be enjoyed in cooler locations with the protection of a little frostcloth, or by growing them in relocatable containers for when the shivery days of winter advance.

'So how would you like four months of freezing cold, ice, snow and frost?' snow-bound gardeners demand. I'd adore it. I'd welcome the searing cold that would deal death to insect pests and their eggs, and freeze the spores of creeping grey and black mildews off the face of the temperate north. This same cleansing cold would retard whopping weed growth, and chill deciduous trees into blessing our lush green subtropical landscape with the foil of autumn colour. *Liquidambar styracifolia* the American sweet gum, *Quercus palustris* the pin-oak and some of the maples do their best to sing crimsons, golds and tawny russets, but it is sometimes a little half-hearted in the long hot Indian summer which is our autumn. All those picture postcards, photographs on calendar pages, and glossy pics in gardening books of glorious autumn colour in the South Island of New Zealand, in England, Europe, Canada etc are positively upsetting.

While gardeners in less temperate climes are pulling on Swanndris and lambs-wool sweaters and piling logs on the fire, I am still faced with a huge garden in which every bloom needs brutalising, deadheads rule, and every shrub, without exception, is screaming for a mighty whack back.

'How would you like to be snowed in, imprisoned indoors for weeks on end?' I am asked. I'd absolutely relish cocooning blankets of snow changing the contours of the loved and familiar garden into a mysterious landscape of illuminated ice-green light. I'd adore just a couple of months when fierce frost, heavy snow, and sub-zero temperatures would prevent my even setting foot in the garden. With the thaw and rising temperatures I could come back to it as a whole new adventure, or as to a beloved after an absence.

At the first frost, gardeners suffering severe winters hurl their gardening gear and lawnmowers into the shed, throw away the key and hibernate for the duration beneath mountains of glossy catalogues. This is my cue to tell them about lawns in Northland. In rural gardens they are all, almost without exception, ex-paddock jobs comprising of every rank pasture grass that is a foe to the farmer – especially paspalum and kikuyu. Paspalum leaps upwards again as soon as the mower has passed over it, and kikuyu sends out claw-like tentacles that make edging the lawns a life sentence – carrot weed and prickly Onehunga weed, plantain, dock and daisy – you name it, we have it. Lawns do not stop growing in the 'winterless north'. They have to be mowed, rolled, aerated, patted, edged and the resulting mountains of clippings disposed of year round. They do slow down a bit in winter, but mostly the two-stroke symphony is a year-round serenade.

The only thing that remains untouched by snow in gardens of both the northern and southern hemispheres is the water in ornamental pools. Water lilies and aquatic plants have long gone dormant, leaving the water a calm quiet surface. But what is happening in the winterless north? 'Goodness, how lush the plantings around your water gardens are – how things have grown,' say visitors from further south, nervously eyeing the prickly man-eating foliage of *Gunnera manicata* from the rainforests of Brazil. 'Simply splendid,' they say of the giant green-white chalices of Arum lily 'Green Goddess' as they beat a pathway through the jungle of drooping ponga fronds and exuberant palms. I wholly agree that the greater part of the surface of a pond should be free of planting to ensure a tranquil reflective quality. At this moment in late autumn, I am sure there still is tranquil reflective water beneath the dramatic half-metre silver platelets of the oriental lotus, and between the prolific glossy green leaves of the tropical waterlilies. It's just that between them they have rendered it invisible.

Have you ever 'weeded' or 'pruned' the surface of your pond? In Northland you do so with monotonous regularity, cutting out and carting away more barrow-loads than you can dream of. If this is not done you are in danger of garden visitors constantly asking you where the water gardens are or demanding a refund. Creating compost from all that exotic foliage also renders you a complete philistine, of course. On the plus side, standing immersed to the waist hacking out foliage is a way of cooling down on sauna-steamy heat filled afternoons – but it's still such very hard work. Similarly, this activity does not negate the fact that it would be infinitely preferable to keep one's cool lolling in a hammock strung from the great willow with a drink and book to hand.

This shameless tirade of gardener discontent will reveal to the alert cooler-climate horticulturist that late summer in the garden is absolutely not my favourite time. I am hotter than the handles of my secateurs, loppers and saws. The garden has become a forest of densest foliage, a wanton regrowth of vine and fern, a glossy green wave of luxuriant vegetation which, if I pause from my labours, will overtake me with terrible speed.

As gardeners we learn that the acid test of any plot is how it looks in midwinter bereft of the colour, flowers and foliage of summer. We know that winter is a time of evaluation, of learning, when one looks to see what has pleased or displeased during the year, a time for rectifying mistakes, for planning and planting, for making changes and for laying the foundations of new gardens with optimism.

It is the time when the gardeners of cooler climates trip off to nurseries, to pile trolleys with luscious shrubs and trees and rush home to plant them in the still warm, damp soil of autumn. Optimum planting time, when the plants will utilise the winter months to build up and establish strong root systems before spring comes thundering into the garden.

*The garden: a thing of beauty and a job forever ...* —Anon

In the winterless north? I shall still be out there, hacking, pruning, cutting, killing, weeding, spraying, hoeing and mowing, subtracting rather than adding. But there is hope – the coming of late autumn and winter even in these temperate latitudes promises some release, halting furious growth and allowing the gardener to exert some control over the demon garden, if only for a little while. Just visible on the edges of all those subtropical specimens with 'luxuriant foliage' is the tattiest tinge of brown and surely they are displaying the slightest loss of vigour?

In the meantime, 'pruning' for today involves three specimens of *Lavatera* 'Barnsley' which, having become small trees, are fighting it out with the architecturally splendid but frenzied foliage of the globe artichokes. Dahlias with dishmop heads so splendid they have resisted all my attempts at staking are also fighting to the death chrysanthemums with heads of equally vulgar proportions.

The coming of winter does wonders for my disposition.

A short aside from American gardeners Henry Beard and Roy McKie:

Scab: Disorder in plants caused by fungi.

Scald: Disorder in plants caused by excessive sunlight.

Scorch: Disorder in plants caused by drought.

Screaming Meemies: Disorder in gardeners caused by observing the effects of scab, scald and scorch.[1]

So, you think, the answer to stress in the garden is simply to take a holiday? Think again. British writer and gardener Anne Scott-James recounts how she and her husband once rented an old house in Greece for the summer month of August. The owner left them with a lengthy list of instructions for watering the garden in his absence, commenting that they would find the zinnias particularly rewarding. Ms. Scott-James recalls that on going round the garden they were delighted to find that all the flowers were already quite dead, especially as all the water had to be hauled up by bucket from a well. They were more fortunate than the persecuted friend of Czech gardener Karel Capek.

## THE GARDENER'S HOLIDAY

August is usually the time when the amateur gardener forsakes his garden of wonder and goes on leave. The whole year he vehemently swore that this year he would not go anywhere, that a garden is worth more than all the summer resorts; nevertheless when summer sets in he departs with a heavy heart, full of fears and care for his garden; and he will not go until he has found a friend or relation to whom he entrusts his garden for that time.

'Look here,' he says, 'there is nothing to be done now in the garden in any case; if you come and look once in three days that will be quite enough, and if something here and there is not in order, you must write me a card, and I will come. So, I am relying on you then? As I said, five minutes, five minutes will be enough, just a glance round.'

Then he leaves, having laid his garden upon the heart of an obliging fellow creature. Next day the fellow creature receives a letter: 'I forgot to tell you that the garden must be watered every day, the best time for doing it is five in the morning, and towards seven in the evening. It is practically nothing, you only fasten the hose to the hydrant and water for a few moments. Will you please water the conifers all over as they stand, and thoroughly, and the lawn as well? If you see any weeds, pull them out. That's all.'

A day after: 'It is frightfully dry, will you give the rhododendron about two buckets of tepid water, and each conifer about five buckets, and other trees about four buckets? The perennials which are now in flower ought to have a good deal of water – write by return post what is in flower. Withered stalks must be cut off! It would be a good thing if you loosened all the beds with a hoe; the soil breathes much better then. If there are plant lice on the roses, buy tobacco extract, and syringe them with it while the dew is still on, or after a rain. Nothing else need be done at present.'

The third day: 'I forgot to tell you that the lawn must be cut; you can do it easily with the mower, and what the mower does not take, you cut with clippers. After mowing the grass must be well raked, and then swept with a sweeper! Otherwise the lawn gets bald patches! And water, plenty of water!'

The fourth day: 'If a storm comes, will you please run and look at my garden? A heavy rain sometimes causes damage, and it is good to be on the spot. If mildew appears on the roses, sprinkle them early in the morning while the dew is still on them with flowers of sulphur. Tie high perennials to sticks so that the wind does not break them. It is glorious here, mushrooms are growing and the swimming is beautiful. Don't forget to water every day the amelopsis near the house, it is too dry for it there. Keep for me in a packet the seeds of *Papaver nudicaule*. I hope that you have already mown the lawns. You needn't do anything else, but destroy the earwigs.'

The fifth day: 'I am sending you a box of plants which I dug up here in a wood. There are various orchids, wild lilies, Pasque flowers, pirolas, bugworts, anemones, and others. Immediately you have got the box, open it, and damp the seedlings, and plant then somewhere in a shady place! Add peat and leafmould! Plant immediately and water three times a day! Please cut the side branches off the roses.'

The sixth day: 'I am sending you by express post a box of plants from the country ... They must go into the ground at once ... At night you ought to go into the garden with a lamp and destroy the snails. It would be good to weed the paths. I hope that looking after my garden doesn't take up much of your time, and that you are enjoying it.'

In the meantime the obliging fellow creature, conscious of his responsibilities, waters, mows, tills, weeds, and wanders round with a box of seedlings wondering where the devil he can plant them; he sweats, and is muddied all over; he notices with horror that there is some damned plant fading, and that there are some stalks broken, and that the lawn has become rusty, and that the whole garden is somehow looking blasted, and he curses the moment when he took upon himself this burden, and he prays to heaven for autumn to come.

And in the meantime the owner of the garden thinks with uneasiness of his flowers and lawns, sleeps badly, curses because the obliging fellow creature is not sending him reports every day on the state of the garden, and he counts the days to his return ...

Finally he returns; still with baggage in hand he rushes into the garden and looks round with damp eyes:

'That laggard, that dolt, that pig,' he thinks bitterly, 'he has made a mess of my garden!'

'Thank you,' he says dryly to his fellow creature, and like a living reproach he snatches the hose to water the neglected garden. (That idiot, he thinks in the bottom of his heart, to trust him with anything! Never in my life will I be such a fool as to go away on holiday again!)[2]

As a little light relief from The Stress of it All Jonathan Cox invites us to take time out with an extract from his new thriller.

## MAYHEM AMONG THE MIMULUS

I've always been jealous of Jackie Collins. I can imagine her dictating the closing chapters of her latest steamy bestseller, cool drink in immaculately manicured hand at a poolside in Miami, before flying off by private jet for a season's skiing at Aspen ... Jackie seems to me to hold the key. 'After all, how hard can it be to write a sultry Hollywood pot-boiler?' I ask myself, visions of lazy afternoons spent sipping mint juleps on a verandah dancing in my brain.

And then, one day as I was struggling with an enormous dock intent on suffocating my best daylily, it came to me – a new literary genre: the Horticultural Horror Murder, mystery and mayhem among the mimulus, dark goings-on in the glasshouse, poltergeists in the potting shed – all that sort of thing. Horror and horticulture! Not exactly cloak and dagger, more like cloak and trowel. Just the kind of thing reading gardeners can get their teeth into between bouts of dead-heading and tying-up.

(Years later when I'm rich and famous I'll coyly admit to an interviewer that I got the germ of the idea from a chapter entitled *Gardening with a Knife* in Margery Fish's *We made a Garden*, even though Margery had more innocent pursuits in mind.)

Without giving too much away (no endings may be revealed, for example), I can let you in on the outlines for the first three Horticultural Horrors, each one guaranteed to be more terrifying than a bad attack of black spot. All totally original of course, and as the saying goes, in the best possible taste.

The first Horticultural Horror to be unleashed on the unsuspecting public is entitled *Lady Chatterley's Cleaver*. It tells the story of Bonstance Chatterley who is torn between two men and two different styles of gardening, with horrific consequences.

Having long tired of her insufferable husband Stifford, Bonstance has engaged in a passionate affair with the local coal-man, Sellers, a fervent 'greenie'. Stifford's suspicions have been aroused by the constant traces of coal dust upon Bonnie's person, which she has so far managed to explain away as faulty mascara refills.

The hard feelings between the three have come to a head over Stifford's plans for the grounds in front of Wragby Hall, ancestral home of the Chatterleys. Stifford's scheme involves a series of formal beds, to be planted out in *Salvia* 'Bonfire' and bedding begonias, which will spell out 'Welcome to Wragby' when viewed from the air.

Bonnie and Sellars want the grounds left to revert to a wildflower meadow garden, but their pleas to Stifford have fallen on deaf ears. Even though he has started dibbling the first begonias into their beds, Bonstance attempts to appeal to Stifford one last time. He is adamant that, as long as he is Lord of the Hall, there will be no meadow garden at Wragby.

After a passionate encounter in Wragby Wood, Bonnie and Sellars return to the Hall and burn down Stifford's potting shed as a symbol of all that distasteful Victorian bedding schemes represent. Stifford is furious, mainly because he is in the potting shed at the time. Escaping with his dibber badly singed, he threatens Bonstance with divorce and public humiliation and, as a measure of his wrath, has an acre of woodland bulldozed in front of her horrified eyes.

That night a terrible thunderstorm rages above Wragby Hall. Stifford is up late, working on his horticultural masterpiece, a manuscript entitled *Eighty Awful Arrangements with Auriculas*. Alone in their bedroom, Bonnie tosses and turns as lightning flashes and thunder rolls. Vowing to end matters once and for all, she leaves her bed and creeps downstairs in her coaldust-smeared nightie.

Tiptoeing into the kitchen she picks up a large meat cleaver and climbs back up the stairs to Stifford's study. A blinding flash of lightning illuminates the whole house, as Bonstance throws open Stifford's door and stands there with her cleaver raised...

While the critics search for superlatives and gardeners everywhere clamour for more, *Slaughter at Sissyherbs* will hit the bookstands. This devilishly clever follow-up goes something like this.

Suffering from a bad case of paeonies envy, after her own blooms are relegated to second place in favour of those belonging to a rival gardener, Vita Bagville-East vows to eliminate the competition. Acting out of a combination of murky Freudian motivation and a dastardly plan for vengeance, she has a high tower built at Sissyherbs, her garden deep in the countryside. Once her tower is completed she invites her unsuspecting rival to come and admire the panorama from its height.

Sensing next years paeony prize within her grasp, Vita is in good humour as they wend their way up the steep stairs. In the tiny room at the top she has been nurturing a plant of ornamental rhubarb, *Rheum palmatum,* on the sunny window-sill.

'Look,' says playful Vita, 'A *rheum* with a view!'

Laughing uproariously at her own joke, she swiftly administers a vicious left hook to her victim's jaw. (Her left arm has become immensely strong through years of doing battle with the intractable bindweed in Sissyherb's borders.) She then despatches the body to certain death on the cobbles below.

'And rhubarb to you,' Vita mutters, bending out of the window to view the lifeless corpse below. So callous is she that the spilled blood on the cobblestones below immediately suggests a dramatic colour scheme to her and she later plants a cottage border in blood red, yellow and orange tones.

That evening, in the long twilight, Vita buries a suspiciously large bundle halfway down her Beached Lime Alley, so called because she obtained the lime trees very cheaply after a foolhardy French gardener attempted to ferry a boatload of them across the channel. A terrible storm sank the boat and the limes were later washed ashore on the English coastline.

Life at Sissyherbs continues apace. Sure enough, Vita wins the next paeony prize and taking up an offer from a prestigious newspaper she begins a weekly gardening column – 'Wry Vita: Witticisms and Wisdom from the Weald'.

However, after seeing a huge barn owl swoop down on its prey, Vita is overcome with guilt and remorse. Vowing to atone for her guilty past, she plans a huge white garden as a testimony to her new purity of spirit. Hardly has this plan come to fruition than a grisly find shatters the peace at Sissyherbs. One of Vita's gardeners, weeding among the hundreds of spring bulbs that line the Beached Lime Alley, discovers the remains of a human foot, prompting the headline 'Toe Tip Through the Tulips' in the local rag…

The third Horticultural Horror rejoices in the catchy title of *Miss Jekyll and Mistress Hyde,*

Driven to distraction by her neighbour's incredibly gauche sense of colour in their garden (puce dahlias with orange daylilies), Gertie Jekyll schemes to do away with them, purchase their property and extend her own tasteful herbaceous borders even further.

She lures her victims deep into Funstead Wool on the pretext of viewing her enormous *Cardiocrinums*. While they stand awe struck before the huge milky blooms Gertie slips into her secret laboratory cum potting shed. Downing a secret formula she turns into her terrifying alter-ego, Mistress Hyde.

Fleeing Funstead Wood with Mistress Hyde in hot pursuit, her intended victims manage to make it to the village bookshop. Cowering before the magazine racks while Mistress Hyde bears down on them through the paperback section, they are suddenly seized by a brainstorm. Each grabbing a copy of the periodical *Garish Gardening* they stop Mistress Hyde in her tracks as page after page of shocking tonal indiscretions are flashed before her.

The tables are turned – Gertie becomes the hunted!

Hot-footing it back to Funstead Wood and the laboratory, with the magazine-wielding pair close behind, Gertie's progress is impeded when her cape snags on the spikes of a large *Yucca filamentosa* which she had foolishly placed as a focal point right at the edge of a border. Her hated neighbours gain the potting shed before her and gleefully paper its sticky creosoted outer walls with retina-wrenching magazine photos. Unable to enter her sanctuary and change back, Gertie is forever trapped as the vampirish Mistress Hyde …

# PARASITE'S PARADISE

The garden holds the high, still peace of summer.
All creatures hush; no bird song, beetle yell.
My deck-chair hushes; I could not be dumber.
Emerald peace! And, underneath it – hell!

This sun-spread scene of woodland, lawn and orchard,
This green Jerusalem, this Mon Repos –
The whole half acre's being slowly tortured.
(A rhyme designed to stimulate real woe.)

Look at the lily, dreaming on her lover,
Drooping towards his wild embrace or hug!
Look. Very closely. What do you discover?
The drooping's caused by some revolting bug.

The nodding rose, the pendulous carnation,
Wilt in the greenfly's nauseating grip.
Massed aphids of every coloration
Are giving the herbaceous border gyp.

No noise! No rumour! But the broad-bean narrows,
The drowsing pea is riddled by the worm,
Uncounted molars masticate the marrows
And make the sleeping spinach squirm.

Unheard, ten million mandibles are smacking,
Five million silent mouths are bulged with shrubs;
The whole pleasaunce is getting a shellacking –
Eden is being eaten by the grubs.

Justin Richardson[1]

# 12

# A PLETHORA OF PESTS

*On every stem, on every leaf ... and at the root of everything that grows, is a professional specialist in the shape of grub, caterpillar, aphis, or other expert, whose business it is to devour that particular plant.* —Oliver Wendell-Holmes

No book about gardens will fail to have lengthy chapters devoted to insectiferous garden pests. Poets and artists wax lyrical about flowers, but gardeners wax even more articulate and eloquent about the winged plagues of biblical proportions that destroy them.

> CABBAGE WHITE
> Butterflies – dainty things,
> Drifting round on delicate wings,
> Turn pacifists into compulsive killers,
> Thinking of myriad caterpillars!
> — Elizabeth Pack[2]

Garden pests are, ever have been, and ever will be. Invent a new pest deterrent and the pests will produce a new pest.

Modern British writer Douglas Sutherland offers the following thoughts on growing fruit:

> ... the gentle gardener would do well to think before he acts in the matter of cultivating fruit. Thinking is a perfectly reasonable occupation and one which may be carried out in comfort. Thinking in the case of fruit growing (and much else) should be directed towards assessing the value of future rewards as set against present effort. Obviously a lifetime spent defending anything you might produce against predators does not represent a reasonable investment of initial effort.[3]

Quite so.

---

*Insect: any creature that conflicts with the gardener's own idea of a balanced ecosystem. Insecticide: spray used to destroy that part of the environment on which insect pests do not live.*

Insectiferous pests do not discriminate between rural and city gardens. They torment either with the disgusting degree of voracity described by Germaine Greer:

> If left to its own devices the city garden will become repellent in a day or two. The famed air of the 'greenhouse effect' is much more conducive to insect reproduction than it is to any vegetative activity. Every variety of plant-louse, greenfly, blackfly, blight and termite breeds exponentially.
>
> All are regenerated from their artificially heated winter quarters long before the swallow or ladybird dares to come. Legions of bugs hover on the winds of March, waiting to overwhelm the new shoots in a seething mass, like commuters boarding a train. The ratio of vegetation to predators remains pathetically small. Plants which elsewhere would be immune to sucking insects are, in London, attacked by them *faute de mieux*.
>
> Demented earwigs chew the growing tips out of clematis, while woodlice wantonly gnaw through their stems at ground level. Any leaf which manages to mature is gradually overwhelmed by leaf-miners. Airborne filth settling on aphis honey-dew asphyxiates all those plants which survive the sucking, biting, chewing, riddling activities of insects. [4]

Aphids exist only to break gardeners' hearts. They are the vampires of the insect world, decimating vegetable and cereal crops, roses, and just about any other ornamental species you care to grow. Giving birth to living young, their rate of increase is prodigious. When they have saturated one plant, their smart little offspring sprout wings and whizz off to infest another.

But this sport is not enough; the little ghouls produce honeydew, a sticky substance from their digestive tracts. This provides the food for a disfiguring fungus called sooty mould, so that plants that were hitherto a delicate shade of green turn midnight black. The midnight mould interferes with the plant's foliar food-making and respiration and is invariably fatal. To dispense with the bad news as quickly as possible, there are some 80 species of sap-sucking aphids.

Racial discrimination notwithstanding, we have a colour choice between them: there is the greenfly, the whitefly and the blackfly. Their absolute favourite abode is a warm sunny greenhouse; if you can provide this, they will reward you by breeding in their millions.

Extermination of these beasts can be most satisfying. If the greenhouse should contain a treasured plant that is heaving with the beasts, take it indoors and try the 'up the spout' method on it. Place the plant on the floor, taking care not to disturb the aphids. Get out the vacuum cleaner, remove the nozzle from the end of the hose, and hold it over the plant. Tilt the plant and the flies will swarm into the air; watching the little pests being sucked into oblivion is most rewarding. More advanced students may like to try this with an extension lead in the flowerbeds surrounding the house.

Another innovative approach to pest extermination is advocated by an earnest gardener writing to a horticultural magazine. He or she suggests that belligerent teenagers should be weaned from spray cans of graffiti paint by being provided with aerosols containing non-toxic insecticides. The theory behind this methodology is that while still allowing them full expression of destructive tendencies, it may turn vicious shaven-headed little thugs into long-haired greenie Friends of the Earth types.

Aphid infestations have so upset gardeners in the past that some have been moved to verse. British gardener A.P. Herbert, writing in the 1920s, manages to retain a sense of humour in the face of pests devastating his flowers and chewing his roses. He pens his anguish in true lament:

Greenfly, it's difficult to see, why God who made the rose, made thee.[5]

There are, of course, other pests in the garden that are such a pain (literally) that they must be dealt with in a category of their own – such as wasps. It is probably true that wasps do not set out each morning with the intention of leaving their barbed rear end embedded in people. But they will readily do so if swatted at, trapped in clothing or hair or, worst of all, downed with a swig of beer.

When the bee stings, we grin and bear it, since we all accept the bee is the gardener's friend, providing honey etc. We will take considerable pains ('in' word in this section) to protect their lives. But wasps are different. One useful purpose they serve is to prey on greenfly, but in autumn they negate this helpful policy by ravaging one's fruit crops.

They are also a thorough nuisance during any picnic meal in the garden. Their antennae can detect softdrinks, sugared goodies etc from miles away, and they nose-dive in without further ado. At the first threatening buzz, set a saucer of jam or, in a real emergency, a large rum and coke on another table. With any luck all the wasps in the vicinity will zoom in and look no further.

If you suspect the presence of a wasps' nest in the garden, find it by observing their flight homeward in the evening. Then destroy them at dead of night

*We hope that, when insects take over the world, they will remember with gratitude how we took them along on our picnics.* —Bill Vaughan

when they are all at home and snoozing. This may be done by discharging a generous blast of insecticide from an aerosol can, or by pouring petrol or paraffin into the nest and sealing up the exit. The fumes will kill them, so try to resist the temptation to use a match to set the nest alight. Your exit from this mortal coil could be speedier than theirs.

As jam is to the wasp, al fresco dinners or drinks in the garden are to the mosquito. Guests' legs fidget nervously under the table in accompaniment to the high-pitched whine of mozzy music. They peer miserably at the long-legged corpses in their drinks, start upright and slap the back of their necks violently, and hiss 'That's got the little bugger.'

Female guests scrabble surreptitiously into evening bags and pass round little rolltop containers of astringently malodorous repellent. These taint the delicate flavour of the meal their hostess has spent all day slaving to produce. Mozzies are bad news.

It is a common fallacy that sandflies of the tiny vampire jaws reside only at the beach. Not so. In many parts of the world they choose to reside in any light sandy soils so that they may attack the gardener most viciously. Weeding on hands and knees gives unlimited access to tender flesh, as does laying paving stones or any other low-down garden activity. Sandflies and mosquitoes are worse pests than wasps because whereas the pain from a wasp sting subsides reasonably rapidly, sandfly and mozzy bites erupt into painful itching swellings that last for days. But all of these insects require gardeners to include in their toolboxes an armoury of stinking repellent lotions, potions, sting soothers and 'death-from-the-air' aerosols.

Next to aphids, slugs and snails must surely be top of every gardener's hit list. Slugs range in size from big black monsters 15cm long to sluglings of only 12mm. It appears that slugs are species of snails that lost their shells somewhere along the evolutionary line. Perhaps this is why they have few friends – the snail does at least look presentable with its convolute attractively marked shell. Even so, Vita Sackville-West leaves us in no doubt that this does not excuse their deadly intent:

The snail, the exquisite, the brindled snail
Creeping with horny threat towards the foison,
Leaving a glistening, an opal trail,
A smear of evil, a signature of poison.[6]

Slugs have fat slimy bodies and are ... so repulsively sluglike. Of all the pests, writes Celia Thaxter in 1894:

> ... worst is the loathsome slug, a creature that is beyond description repulsive, a mass of sooty shapeless slime and he devours everything that is fair and exquisite in the garden.[7]

Every one of us can pontificate (at length) about the depredations of slugs and snails upon our plots, each trying to outdo the other in tales of their sheer awfulness. The slug is regrettably a gastropod with whom I have been forced into intimate contact on several occasions.

The first of these remains etched in my memory. Just before half term I stayed with young gardening friends. Their small daughter arrived home from school breathless, announcing that she had been chosen for a great honour. She had been made a prefect? Been elected captain of the netball team? Was to present a bouquet to some visiting dignitary? Nothing so mundane. She was to be in sole charge of some of her class 'mini-pets' for the holidays.

Susie had got the snails, Michael had got the slaters, but she – Emma – *she* had got the slugs – a mother and a father one who were big and brown, and eight little black baby ones who were darlings! *We* were to host the invertebrate family for the week.

Her father made one thing quite clear – he would have nothing to do with them. After all, he had fed, cleaned out and generally looked after 'her' pets for six years, even delivering moving eulogies at the funerals of mice, rats, hamsters, guinea pigs, rabbits and cats in the back garden.

Emma had a full set of instructions. These included what the slugs were to eat. Not, her father was relieved to hear, the young lettuce in the *potager* nor the new tips of his clematis shoots. The slugs would apparently thrive on a diet of apple and potato. Whereas most invertebrates seem to survive outside, these were to stay inside at night, as Emma was worried 'something would get them' – touching concern marred only by her mother's hysterical giggling in the background.

Her father's sarcastic responses were met with disdainful looks. After all, he was asked, why did they have to kill slugs; couldn't they be thrown into next door's garden? Her parents do have a wildlife area and pond in the garden well stocked with frogs but their numbers would have to grow to biblical plague proportions if they were to protect the flora of the garden from attack.

The week's holiday proceeded uneventfully, adults ignoring the icecream container with its pampered former inhabitants of the school playing field – until late on Sunday evening.

Disaster! Emma said the slugs were supposed to have been cleared out and given new bedding in order to return to school next day. This had not been done. She would not accept that this could easily be done tomorrow, the slugs have an extended holiday and go back to school on Tuesday. Early morning was no good as she had to arrive at school at some unearthly hour to collect incoming books as she was the library monitor.

A tearful confrontation loomed. 'We might need them for some experiments,' sobbed the surrogate mother. Her father replied that he did not think Mrs Jameson would have spent her half-term devising a series of biological tests to kill slugs. He also voiced the thought that Mrs Jameson could probably manage very well without them. That was it. Feet thundered up to bed, accompanied by howls of hatred.

'I think you got it wrong!' his wife pointed out quietly. Guiltily and very carefully, her father opened the container. The two big brown slugs, engorged on apple and potato,were certainly there, but a desperate search failed to reveal even one of the black baby darlings. Where had they gone? Had they made a slimy dash for freedom or had they just shrivelled up?

The wails at the top of the stairs increased in crescendo – 'I've *got* to take back *eight*!' she howled. 'To bed!' shrieked her mother.

Gloved and booted, torches in hand, we all trekked down the garden in search of infant invertebrates. It was drizzling. Where to look? Where had the most recent damage been done? The delphiniums were being stripped nightly so that seemed to be a good place to start. Not a gastropod in sight. Exasperated, we combed the vegetable plot, crawled wet and frozen in the flowerbeds, turned up pots and uninviting piles of garden debris.

'I must be mad,' snarled Emma's paternal parent.

Muddied and stiff with cold, we eventually found, tucked away at the base of one of the compost bins, a whole sluggy family awaiting adoption. Carefully, they were placed in the container.

Whether their whole sluggy lives passed before their eyes I do not know but doubtless they were surprised to find themselves suddenly dining on a diet of lettuce and cucumber rather than being squashed underfoot.

Next day they went to begin their primary school education as part of the 'mini-pets' project. At the end of the week they were to be released at the edge of the school field, where some homing instinct would undoubtedly operate to bring them straight back to Emma's parents' garden.

As a result of this intimate observation of gastropods I began some in-depth reading on how the gluttonous ones shred, chop and decimate our gardens.

I discovered that what slugs and snails have in common is that they are eating machines. Underneath those tentacles that go in and out at the end of the soft foot there is a mouth hole equipped with a thin, ribbon-like tongue called the radula. This has up to 15,000 teeth on it, which means these voracious heaps of slime are supremely well equipped for mass destruction. Besides all those teeth, they lay eggs – hundreds and hundreds of them, producing an infinite, eradicable army of tiny babies with file-like teeth, rasping away all night long while Mum potters off and lays a couple of hundred more eggs between meals.

I was further depressed to learn that, even if snails are trapped somewhere without any food at all, they have supernatural powers of survival. The British Museum records the case of a snail that was mounted as an exhibit on a tablet for a number of years. When removed and put in tepid water it emerged from its shell and started rasping away on a cabbage leaf!

Hand-picking gastropods is effective but slow. It is better, armed with a flashlight, to don a pair of 'crunching' boots after dark.

Another alternative is one I was taught when very small; I was encouraged to go on slug hunts armed with a tin of Cerebos salt. The brand did not really matter, but Cerebos came in a tin with a handy little pouring nozzle in the top. This method is extremely satisfying as the pest literally turns to water before one's eyes. Rather a dirty trick, but marginally better than pulling the legs off flies. Allow one tin of Cerebos to approximately 40 brace of slugs.

If you are a gardener of kinder disposition or more humanitarian turn of mind you can treat your slugs to an alcoholic demise. Put out easily scaled dishes of beer – they love it and will topple in happily and rapidly drink themselves to death. A good way to go by any standards.

The advance of medical science has brought us toxic slug pellets. These are scattered around the battle fields and gastropods will obligingly slither over them and commit suicide by frothing and foaming all over. The disadvantage of this method is that domestic pets, birds and hedgehogs may be despatched also.

Perhaps it is a case of 'if you can't beat 'em, join 'em', by finding a reason for their existence. Organic gardeners may care to try farming snails and selling them to upmarket restaurants, where they could appear in new guise drenched with garlic butter and dressed with parsley. But resist the temptation to rush out into the vege patch (should you be so lucky as to have any left) and scoop up buckets of snails. Gastropods for culinary purposes must be lovingly reared on bran meal like thox- of a Roman nobleman called Fulvius Hirpinus. This august gentleman was so impressed with snails as dietary delicacies that he kept a snail farm, a 'cochlearia', at Tarquinium in about 50BC. He fed his prey on wine and various types of meal and the good Fulvius's snails were renowned throughout Rome for their size, juiciness and 'nobility'.

To invent a *raison d'être* for slugs, however, poses more of a problem. Subscribing to research by scientists interested in homoeopathic medicine may be our only course. We may refer to Pliny the Elder, who, back in AD50, was advocating slugs raw, beaten, boiled or roasted for ailments as diverse as swelling of the joints, corns, asthma, pleurisy, colds and coughs, and 'obstructions'.

English herbal journals from medieval times instruct that a plaster of decapitated slugs may prove most beneficial if one has a bad headache coming on. As late as early this century in Europe, decoctions of slugs, snails and earthworms were swallowed daily as a precautionary medicine against tuberculosis. One cannot be too careful. For gardeners interested in natural remedies the recipe reads thus:

> For consumption take thirty snails, thirty slugs and thirty earthworms of middling size. Bruise the snails, wash them and the worms in clear water. Cut the worms into pieces. Boil these in a quart of spring water and reduce to a pint. Pour it boiling on to two ounces of candied Eringoe root sliced thin. When cool, strain through a fine flannel bag. Take quarter of a pint of it warm with an equal quantity of cow's milk at twilight. Continue until well.[8]

Or exceedingly *unwell* ...

When all else fails you can try praying, as did the holy martyr Trypho of Lamascus (11th century AD), whom we suspect was a keen gardener:

> O ye caterpillars, snails, slugs ... I charge you by the many eyed Cherubim ... the six winged Seraphim ... by all the holy Angels, the Supreme powers ... (etc, etc,) hurt not the vines nor the land, nor the fruit of the trees, nor the vegetables of the servant of the Lord, but depart into the wild mountains, into the unfruitful woods, in which God hath given you your daily food.

Some chance. I have read enough. I find myself on the side of unmitigated violence. Where did I leave my crunching boots?

The gardener fights back according to his or her personal philosophy. There are few subjects more emotive among horticulturists than that of chemical versus organic sprays. The subject causes a great divide: some of us drench pest-ridden plants with cocktails of poisonous chemicals; others opt for witches' cauldrons in which to boil and bubble stinking organic decoctions.

When I began as a novice gardener making my gardens I would drench my plants with any prettily packaged poison the helpful garden centre staff would sell me. Night after night as I read my 'How to' gardening books, lurid and highly graphic pictures would leap from the page of pests and diseases grotesque enough to strike terror into any amateur's heart. Their very names smacked of foul decay – rot, corky scab, wilt, blight, fungus, leaf curl, black spot, rust, botrytis and mildews. It seemed as though only the Black Plague was excluded.

As though this weren't enough, there followed lists of disgusting pests whose destructive capacities were apparently legendary. I used to go to bed envisioning whole armies of arthropod vampires invading my new gardens. I bought a backpack and enough toxic chemicals to annihilate plant life from several acres and dispensed death vengefully whenever I saw a few aphids.

One day a friend much older and wiser in the ways of gardening than I, seeing me striding around goggled, hooded, booted and suited like a demented astronaut, commanded that I stop and think what I was doing. I vacillated uneasily between the use of diabolical chemicals and the dread of plant decimation by gruesome plants and diseases, watched a queen bee staggering round wheezing pitifully after my ministrations (the guilt was terrible) – and defected to the ranks of the Cauldron Club.

The aphids, mites and caterpillars incumbent in my beds now quail beneath cocktails of garlic and pyrethrum – and sport extremely bad breath.

Stinky beetles, those bronze and green sap-sucking bugs that smell so foul when you crush them, can be given a dose of their own medicine – literally. The recipe, which was pressed upon me by an enthusiastic old gentleman, involves hand-picking a jarful of the beasts from your roses or vegetables. Drop them into a bowl of soapy water to kill them, then hurl the awful mixture into a kitchen blender. (Male gardeners ask wife first.)

The evil-smelling green goo that results must stand, then be strained and diluted and sprayed around the affected plants. Readers may rest assured that the diabolical method truly works – whole plagues of stinky beetles have departed my plot for someone else's, or flipped over and waved their legs in the air.

If you suffer from an outbreak of flea beetle (which gets its name because it jumps when disturbed) a more satisfying method of extermination than a puff of Derris Dust is to get a flat piece of board and grease it generously. Pass it over the beetle-infested plants and the infuriated creatures will leap into the air and superglue themselves to your plank.

If you are a smoker, there is another gruesome insect demise for scales, woolly aphis and mealy bugs – the white furry ones that are ingesting the life blood from your best ornamentals. Remove the filter tips from 30 butts and infuse the butts in about four litres of water for five days. Strain before spraying and, as with the garlic brews, remember not to drench your roses etc with gallons of the stuff just before a coach-load of visitors is due.

W.C. Sellar and R.J. Yeatman retained their sense of humour in the face of depradation by insect pests, suggesting some inventive remedies:

> *Aphid.* Send it to the laundry. When it comes back send it to the wash again. After two or three goes it will shrink so tight on to itself that it will suffocate.
> *Weevils.* Ignore them – remember the old warning: 'Hear no weevil, see no weevil, speak no weevil', and cut them dead.
> *Basic Slug.* Innumerable weighty pamphlets on slug control are available. Obtain a ten pound one. Read it aloud to the slug. If the slug doesn't play the game, slug it with the pamphlet.
> *Greenfly.* Likes roses. A splendid subject for finger and thumb work, enabling you to acquire green fingers in a few seconds without all the bother of having to inherit them.[9]

By employing alternative methods such as these, horticultural destruction may be halted, but not, alas, stopped. Dismal tomes instruct that this is a very crowded planet – there are over a million species of insect pests. Despite chemical warfare they remain ahead, for not one of them has been eliminated.

If temporary respite for your plants is not enough and you think all this organic stuff is a load of bunkum, Professor John Carey has a message for you:

> In this situation the only adequate response is to thank God for chemical pesticides, and use them liberally. Unfortunately the strongest and most effective ones keep being withdrawn from the market on the grounds that they have been found to damage the environment. So when you hit on a really lethal source it's a good plan to buy it in large supply, which will enable you to go on using it after it has been outlawed.
> I did this for several seasons with a splendid product, now alas unobtainable, which wiped out everything from snails to flea beetles. It had no adverse effect upon the bird population as far as I could see, though the neighbourhood cats did start to look a bit seedy. That, of course was an advantage from my point of view, for cats are filthy insanitary beasts, and a fearful nuisance to the gardener. One of the anomalies of English law is that whereas it would,

as I understand it, be an offence to clamber over your neighbour's fence and defecate among his vegetables, you can send a feline accomplice on precisely the same errand with total impunity. It has always amazed me that manufacturers of slug bait, and other such garden aids, should proudly pronounce on the label that their product is 'harmless to pets'. A pesticide that could guarantee to cause irreparable damage would, I'd have thought, sell like hot cakes.[10]

✤

Gardeners fall not only victim to every life form that creeps, crawls, flies, sucks and stings, but to pests of their own kind. Germaine Greer, is terse and delightfully acerbic about the thieves, passers-by, and builders with whom she must reluctantly and inevitably share her city garden:

> Ever since the Christmas garland disappeared off the front door an hour after it had been put up, we at Blight's Folly have tried to take precautions against thieves. Unfortunately, grappling the replacement wreaths to the door with hoops of steel rather spoiled the effect. It used to be thought that gardeners were honourable folk, but since my *Thymus* 'Aureus' was lifted out of its bed like a tooth from a gum, I've had to alter my opinion.
>
> Blackouts are the garden thief's delight. He stands admiring your carefully tended *Ruta graveolens* 'Jackman's Blue', by daylight and then, when the street light goes out that evening, whammy – he's away down the street under a spout of green leaves which you will not recognise, even if you do see it in a street-market next day ... The garden burglar is a different species, who knows to the last penny how much value has accrued to your shrubs for each six inches they have put on.[11]

Passers-by present equal hazard:

> As the spring sunshine gains in confidence, the gardener creeps forth and is promptly assailed by passers-by. It is a curious fact that nearly all the fair-rented tenants of run-down London were once gardeners ... now, without the least temptation to grab a spade, they are extremely anxious that my gardening live up to their standards. A passing crone fingers *Rosa* 'Fruhlingsgold', who has actually survived youths lashing her with sticks, soccer balls crashing into her midriff, a sodden root run and the omnibus tortrix moth, and tells me reproachfully that she has greenfly. The old beast will not move off until with her own eyes she has seen me spray the rose, and off she goes, uttering her boundless contempt of me to anyone who will listen.
>
> Crone Number Two insists that the quince tree needs a drink. Actually, the poor old *Cydonia vulgaris* needs to move as far from the city as she can get. To get rid of this one I have to go inside and watch through the kitchen blinds until she has gone. No sooner have I returned than Crone Number

107

Three appears, regards me sombrely and tears off a whole branch of *Rosa* 'Maigold', thorns and all, and bears it off ... While I'm cutting off the damaged wood, an off-duty bus conductor stops sucking his can of Carlsburg Special to give me a pruning lesson, in the course of which he actually attempts to take my secateurs and attack my roses. I pretend I can hear the phone ringing and flee.

When I sneak out again, the old man from next door but one is wanting to know if I intend to grow 'them awful nasturtiums' again this year ... They bring, he opines, the greenfly ... is equally certain that my wonderful [dahlia] 'Bishop of Landaff' brings the eary-wigs.[12]

Any gardener who has suffered the destructive proclivities of builders on, in, or even near the garden, must agree with Ms Greer that on the scale of human pests they are the kiss of death – they are in a class of their own:

Call no London gardener happy until she is dead. Everything was going as well as could be expected ... The neighbour's children only hacked down one rose-bush this year, and broke off the main stem of *Clematis orientalis*. 'Sheriffi' because it impeded the free exercise of their favourite summer sport, petty theft. In the front garden the tree peony bloomed for the first time and *Abutilon megapotamicum* decided that the back wall was hers to climb up to the stars. I reckoned without builders.

Builders are the sworn enemies of all green and growing things. Into the house they came, swarmed up to the top storey and threw the roof off through the boughs of the lime trees. The roof was followed, amid a storm of mangled foliage, by sofas, armchairs, linoleum, carpeting, several tons of lath and plaster, a few hundred bricks, and several gross of pop cans and cigarette packets.

When the back garden was quite full of this detritus, in faithful pursuance of their scorched earth policy, they set fire to the lot. A mad cretin fed the blaze: if the flames sank below the level of the second storey he would appear at a window with a seething mattress or plastic-coated kitchen cupboard ... Over all lay the most abominable stink ...

Peace returned. The kipper smell gradually faded out of my carpets and curtains. Lime blossom scented the air ...

Alas, alas, they have returned, to the house next door this time. Their inscrutable ends may be served only by erecting scaffolding all over the front garden. I am no match for a gang of stalwart fellows armed with pickaxes and club hammers. They may break the law with impunity, for complaining about illegal bonfires, and the hurling of rubbish down five storeys simply means more or less accidental damage is supplemented by deliberate sabotage ... What plants they do not succeed in slashing and trampling, they will slowly engulf in a poisonous rain of lime and mortar.

I dare not protest.[13]

# 13

# ANIMALS IN THE GARDEN

*The garden: one of a vast number of free outdoor restaurants operated by charity-minded amateurs in an effort to provide healthful, balanced meals for birds, animals and insects.* —Beard & McKie

Like insect pests, animal pests have tormented gardeners since ages past; many are common to gardens world wide, but others, such as possums, are peculiar to one particular part of the world.

Many gardeners in New Zealand are locked in mortal combat with a pest that operates well above ground level.

Rage, horror, disbelief. Revenge. This creature, clothed in fur, turns gentle gardeners into vengeful hunters armed with guns, flashlights, bait, traps and cages. It makes serial killers of us and drags us from our beds uttering foul oaths or incantations that smack of witchcraft.

Night after night rural gardeners try to remain unconscious, trying not to hear the rising crescendo of the dogs' hysterical warning that the enemy is in the garden, leaping about full of *joie de vivre*, holding feasts of Bacchanalian proportions amongst (scream) the rose bushes and tender shrubs.

Burying our heads beneath the pillows, our vain hope is that perhaps they'll go away, (dogs and predators both). This hope evaporates as fitful sleep is permeated by nightmarish visions of the horticultural devastation the creature is wreaking in its gastronomic orgy.

Groaning and cursing, we drag ourselves out of bed, fling waterproofs over pyjamas and nighties (a sight that should frighten anything), unlock the gun cupboard and plod bleary-eyed into the cold wet night. The rain fuels our outrage as we creep through the shrubbery and orchard towards the rose gardens. The low cunning in our stealth and the black murder in our hearts would do justice to the most brutal and licentious of soldiers on a mission to kill.

Our quarry? The brush-tailed opossum, *Trichosurus vulpeca*, the appealing little furry marsupial that was introduced into New Zealand from Australia in 1837, to support a fur industry. When the fur trade collapsed in the 1890s the animals were released into the wild, where the subtropical climate and balmy moonlit nights of the North Island in particular were greatly conducive to nocturnal marsupial romance and the possum population exploded. In between reproductive preoccupations, these despoilers with appetites that would turn a piranha green with envy gobble away indiscriminately at anything that is growing.

These are sobering facts to be included in a book of garden humour, but it is necessary for the (gentle) reader to understand the gourmets' devour-a-garden-overnight policy and the subsequent determination of rural folk to perpetuate foul murder, toting gun and flashlight through the night. So often we are just in time to see the dogs chase a pair of possums across the lawn into the bush, where they are just out of range of our weaponry. They sit in the trees laughing their throaty laughs as we return indoors in a fury of ill-humour. Teeth chattering, I fling two glasses of milk to warm in the microwave. The husband sloshes an impressive amount of amber liquid into his.

I remember the night eight years ago when, new to New Zealand, we settled down to sleep in our new country home. We were shocked awake by noises that sounded like old men with laryngitis, but a walk around the garden armed with a stout stick (we were not into firearms at this stage) did not reveal any itinerant superannuitants suffering from respiratory tract infections.

The disturbance the following night sounded as though a mob of catarrhal tigers was on the prowl. A trifle uneasily, thinking we were either very brave or very foolish, out we went again, and there they were, all bright-eyed and bushy-tailed, partying in the fruit trees – our very first possums.

I thought they were cute and was puzzled when our new Kiwi neighbours let forth a stream of invective at my naiveté.

Then I started making a garden and planting roses. As I dug beds and planted, I learned in double quick time the nature of the herbivorous adversary and its voracious appetite. I threw grand tantrums, frustrated beyond belief at the sight of young bushes stripped of every last leaf overnight.

I resorted to all sorts of recommended folk methods and remedies, such as mothballs, which did not deter the possies in the least but were capable of exterminating one's child or pets. I embezzled from the housekeeping for expensive 'keep off' toxic chemical sprays with such impressive names as Despatch, and Pushoff Possies (they did not). I tried spraying tender new treasures with abominably odiferous liquid fish manure. The foe was perhaps slightly repelled but my new garden, to put it mildly, stank of well-rotted silage or something not only dead but in an advanced state of putrefaction.

I abandoned fish manure concentrate after one hardier rose bush (escaping the enemies' fangs for a few nights) actually sneaked forth several blooms. It gave

110

forth an unmistakable whiff of putrefying fish, effectively repelling gardener and visitor.

My next deterrent, black nylon mesh draped everywhere, wrecked mowers and snared birds. The pests still got their suppers by bypassing the net at the base of the trees and swinging Tarzan-like from branch to branch with their prehensile tails.

I resorted to bandaging precious saplings with rags dunked in creosote which looked and smelled terrible; I scarred my hands for life tangling barbed wire along the top of the rose trellis. The beasts strolled across the spikes snacking with contemptuous ease.

The more precious the plant the faster they ate it. I sought advice from my new rural neighbours. They encouraged me to bribe their teenage sons into joining my husband's nocturnal shooting parties. These purges kept the pests at bay for a while, but stripped plants would herald their return only too soon.

The next suggestion was to ring my new beds with electric wires just above ground level. Turning the beds into mini-stalags was one of the first gardening chores the Non Gardening Husband kindly did for me. The hot wires certainly were effective in that new growth burgeoned forth on the poor skeletal bushes, but it disappeared with the speed of light if I forgot to turn the power back on before leaving the garden in the evening.

This was the flaw in the system: the power had to be turned off during the day. Hot wires at ground level cause dogs to race for cover beneath the house, tails between their legs, yelping piteously, from where they peer out with bewildered brown eyes, whimpering 'How could you do this to me?'

Hot wires around island beds on the lawn cause children to scream for hours and refuse to go into the garden again. Ever. They electrify lawnmowers, barrows, feet and ankles, not to mention inflicting undignified shocks on the rear as one crawls around weeding. They act as stinging trip-wires to the unwary and seriously disturb sleep when one remembers from the depths of a snug warm bed that one forgot to turn the power back on at dusk.

They are aesthetically displeasing and definitely gardener-unfriendly. The possums, cheated of their snacks at ground level, retaliate by devouring everything above the height of the wires.

Hot wires are also self-limiting in that, as the naked ambition in the gardener's heart causes her to dig more and more beds, the long-suffering husband runs out of the time and the patience required to erect more. 'You'll have to get some cages,' he said. 'You'll have to learn to use a gun,' he declared.

The struggle between the gardener and the gourmet continued unabated for some time because it took courage and a number of lessons before I was confident enough to handle a firearm safely. When my Annie Get Your Gun meta-morphosis image was complete we bought the cages and I indulged in impassioned oratory with the neighbours on the efficacy of various baits. These included flour mixed with cinnamon or linseed oil, apples and apple-scented shampoo, citrus fruits and cinnamon toast. One neighbour actually made little cinnamon dumplings for her cages, and swore they were infallible.

I found the possums needed little culinary enticement to 'come into my cage' and when the husband was away I would stride womanfully towards the traps, .22 beneath my arm, dreading that they would be tenanted. They always were, and only by reciting to myself 'One dead possum, one live tree' could I bring myself to shoot the poor creatures cowering in the light of day.

I continued to dispense death until the morning I found a female in one of the cages with a youngster on her shoulder and another in her pouch. I raised the gun and two pairs of sad, frightened eyes looked into mine. I lowered the gun and considered the cowardly alternative of leaving them terrified in the cage all day until Brian returned from a business trip.

I shot them because I had to, but the guilt was awful. I tried to justify the murder I had perpetrated by reminding myself that the poor creatures had reached epidemic proportions and that it was the responsibility of all individuals to help cull and control them. I began to believe stories I'd heard of old ladies putting the caged captives into the boot of the car and driving away to release them 'somewhere nice and safe'.

There had to be another way involving less trauma for both assassin and victim, and inasmuch as any tale of 'pesticide' can have if not a happy, then a more satisfactory ending, this one did. During the time that had elapsed while I struggled with my folklore, wires, cages and guns, a solution to possum control for the home gardener had arrived in the shape of a cheerful yellow plastic box called a Timms trap. The boxes contain a highly efficient guillotine system, which is entirely humane since it causes instant death. The bait is put on the tip of a steel spike, and the trap is sprung by means of a pull cord. When the peckish possie puts its head into the small hole at the front of the box, a powerful spring-loaded bar drops, breaking its neck instantaneously.

As a back-up to our traps we live in hope of training the two resident lady labradors to deal with any snacking marsupial at ground level, without any of the baying and howling of werewolves, which makes it impossible for us to stay in bed. The only problem with this method is that the younger dog is enormously possessive of her catch and tends to secrete possie corpses away until such time as she deems them fit to exhume for dropping as a noble (and desperately odiferous) present at the feet of garden guests.

I have to admit that possies make excellent manure and that they are buried nose to tail in the gardens at Valley Homestead (position is important).

Each evening, however, when the time comes for setting my traps, I still experience this horrendous guilt, and pity the poor possum, because the herbivorous midnight marauders are with us in such devastating numbers through little fault of their own. Nothing for it but to maintain (wry) good humour and remind oneself that when all is said and done, it *can* only be a case of 'One dead possum, one live tree' – and *vive le jardin*!

October 8, 1763: Hares or some vermin have gnawed all the fine pheasant-eyed pinks, and the newly planted cabbages.[1]

Rabbits, with their sharp incisors and twitching whiskers, are universal pests, driving gardeners world wide to despair. Is there a gardener among us who has not foamed at the mouth on discovering trees ring-barked, tender greens nibbled to their roots, flower-heads scissored off, lawns scratched up into bald patches and bulbs exhumed?

Germaine Greer, battling to create a garden at Stump Cross in Cambridgeshire in the British Isles in 1992, sums up succinctly every gardener's battles with this most populous of burrowing mammals:

We have a thousand or so rabbits and about the same number of rats on my three acres because there is nowhere else for them to go. The population that should be spread over the 100-acre field lives with me because I neither plough nor poison my ground with fungicides, herbicides, insecticides and fertilisers. Because of the environmental stress none of the critters who lives under my hedgerows and my poultry houses is quite sane or quite well. The rabbit population is full of myxomatosis. Because none of the predators will take a sick rabbit, the myxy ones are compelled to live out a normal life-span, and to reproduce. When the ferreters come they get no hassle from me. Strange to relate they get no hassle from the anti-blood sports people either. Funny that, when you think about it. Foxes live by hunting and could expect to die the same way, but rabbits? What harm did rabbits ever do?

Well, I'll tell you. Rabbits are bloody bastards. Absolute bloody bastards. They don't kill other animals. They kill plants. Foxes, unlike dogs, and mink, kill for food for themselves and their young. Rabbits don't kill trees for food. I don't know why they kill trees. They will do just enough damage to a young tree to ensure that it dies, and then they will move on to the next one. They will nose their way through spiral guards and gnaw out a neat half-inch strip all the way round the tree; that's all it takes to kill even a mighty tree. They will climb on each other's shoulders to attack the tree above the guard – I reckon, because otherwise I don't know how the hell they do it. Build a cage for a young tree, and they will burrow under it. If they can't get at any other part of the tree, they will dig under it and eat the roots – I have planted more than seven hundred trees since I lived in this house and they have destroyed four hundred of them, some when they were already twenty centimetres in girth. They have eaten whole yews and lived to tell the tale. They even managed to strip a monkey puzzle of its scales.

I do not protest when rabbits eat bulbs or gnaw their way into the cage to eat my salad. But I cannot bear it when for the sake of a slightly different taste, some sort of oral novelty, they kill one of my trees. Do something for our struggling tree population. Kill a rabbit today.[2]

An anonymous author writing in 1706 is stern in his or her admonishment that:

> Dogs and cats ought not to be suffer'd in a Flower Garden. Your dogs do, by their continual leaping, leave ugly Marks or Impressions upon the Surface of the Ground and the Cats scattering their Ordure all about, and then scraping the Earth to cover it, do grub up many Plants.[3]

Rock-solid advice.

In theory, keeping a dog will scare off stray cats, but in practice the cat will sit smugly on top of the wall or fence jeering at the dog. The furious canine crashing through the flowerbeds in pursuit will cause more damage than 20 cats. He may even dig frantically under your fences to get at the cat next door. Taking him for long, exhausting walks will help to burn up his energy a little, but yours will burn up faster. If you try tying dogs up on a long chain, out of reach of visiting moggies and your more precious plants, they will howl heartrendingly until the SPCA arrives. Frivolous friends (mostly of the non-gardening variety) will proffer advice like 'Take him for a long walk down the motorway', 'Put him in kennels and move to another town', or 'Swap him for a chihuahua'. Animals and gardens, contrary to what fervent animal-lovers claim, are not made for each other. They co-exist, but in a state of uneasy disharmony.

When the children join in cat-dog warfare as well, all hell is let loose and the boundary dispute extends to the neighbours', who demand to know 'What the *# *#! is going on?' When things get to this stage, drag your slathering canine

---

*Dog: form of automatic digger suitable for turning over any garden.*

away as fast as you can and never admit that its rabid fangs were drawn with the intention of dining on their cat.

Cats are probably the lesser enemy in the wreck-a-garden stakes, and would be quite acceptable residents if only their natural digging abilities could be channelled. Would that they could be trained to cultivate the garden and keep it free from weeds in an orderly fashion instead of the horribly haphazard methods they employ to scratch up beds of seeds and seedlings. Felines are extremely fastidious about where they choose to deposit their droppings. You can bet your last dollar that the choicest position is the very one you selected as worthy of the newly planted hybrid raised from seed. The neighbours' moggies show true appreciation of the soft, finely sifted loam bed (prepared just for them) and after they have scratched it to blazes the tender new hybrid will lie in a mangled heap, roots pointing skywards.

It is necessary to arm yourself with a weapon that will give them enough of a shock to keep them out of your garden without actually harming them, which is not allowed. You might get funny looks from the neighbours (especially if it's their little Whiskers you're stalking) but your weapon is a water pistol. Conceal yourself in a vegetative bivouac and give the moggie a belt on the nose. The more powerful the squirt the longer it will be deterred.

If you don't think you can get away with this method you could try mothballs. Cats hate the smell of these so they're quite effective, though not half as much fun as the water pistol. There are of course, expensive commercially prepared forms of cat repellent, which cost more than the seedlings you are trying to protect. Most of these come in powder form and wash away as soon as it rains or you water the garden. A friend of mine recommends sprinkling curry powder on small plants. Go easy in the vege garden, however, unless you want to cultivate ready-made vindaloo.

If armed warfare is frowned upon, perhaps a little lateral thinking is the answer. An alternative way of keeping cats away from a seedbed is to be kind to them – plant its edges with extravagant clumps of catmint (*Nepeta faassenii*). Cats adore its smell and will roll in it ecstatically and loll, glazed of eye, transported on a catmint trip. A kilo of catnip has an 'alley value' of five to 10 mice since its narcotic effect on moggies is similar to that of cannabis on humans. You must learn to like the prostrate habit of the plant since it will never attain its upright form.

Unlike dogs, cats can also be a nuisance above *terra firma*. Any ornamental structure such as a pergola, trellis or archway provides a speedy escape route and vantage viewing point over the whole garden. If chased by the dog or kids, cats will scramble up a rose pole in seconds, and freeze their pursuer with malevolent feline eyes from their safe vantage point. Constant cat-claw traffic can be the kiss of death to the delicate climbers with which you have adorned elevated structures. Lateral thought again: think twice before you tip that damned cat off your favourite lounger. While it is snoozing without as much as a twitch of a whisker on a cushion in the sun, it is not vandalising seedlings or clawing climbers to death.

For fear of sacks of hate-mail arriving Fast Post from outraged cat-owners I will here acknowledge that many gardeners are inordinately fond of their cat companions. Famous gardeners and writers such as Gertrude Jekyll, Beverley Nichols and Marion Cran devoted whole chapters in their erudite gardening tomes to the exploits of their feline friends. In 1968 Nichols dedicated his book *Garden Open Tomorrow* thus:

> To the Memory
> of
> Certain Feline Companions
> who
> While this Work was being Completed
> were
> Constantly by the Author's Side
> Not only in the Garden
> but
> At his Desk
> Giving to his Words
> The Approval of their muted Purrs
> and
> The Authority of their muddy Paws.

Ursula Bethell, gardening and writing in New Zealand in the early 1920s, kept a much-beloved tom called Michael, her 'Garden Lion':

> O Michael, you are at once the enemy
> And the chief ornament of our garden,
> Scrambling up rose posts, nibbling at Nepeta
> Making your lair where tender plants should flourish,
> Or proudly couchant on a sun-warmed stone.[4]

Even the stern and revered Miss Gertrude Jekyll's learned garden prose softened when she spoke of her feline companions:

> My garden would not be half the pleasure it is to me without the pussies …
> They are perfect garden companions. When I am out at work there is sure to

be one or other of them close by, lying on my jacket or on the bench if there is one. When it is Tabby, if there is an empty basket anywhere handy he is certain to get into it … Like most cats he is devoted to the pretty catmint. It is in several places in the garden. He knows where every plant is and never passes one when we are out walking together without stooping to nuzzle and nibble at it … when he has had his first taste he will push himself right down into the middle of the plant and sometimes roll down and roll in it to get all he can of the sweet smell.[5]

Try as one might to adopt a 'live and let live' philosophy in the face of feline vandalism, things get really tricky when the family demand a dog for a pet.

Dog ownership is fun – ask any gardener. Dogs add a whole new dimension to life in the garden. They have a unique relationship with plants – whereas newly sown annuals do have a chance of resurrection after a feline has lain atop them sunbathing, species that are sat/leaned upon by 40kg canines never recover. Ever. Then there is the 'raised leg' syndrome, which withers tender vegetation at a blast. There is also something very peculiar about bitches' urine. It will finish forever any pretensions you had of aspiring to velvet greensward. The reality is an expanse of lawn liberally blotched with brown, bald and horribly scorched patches.

This sets a teaser for the gardener whose gardens are open to the public, and full marks must go to the British gardener who came up with the following solution. Every morning when his dogs were let out they would race across the terraces to 'water' the lawns. He debated how to keep them off and came up with the idea of a 'watering post' on a discreet corner of the terrace. The male dogs, following atavistic instincts, obediently 'cocked a leg' at the required spot, and the bitches followed suit in their own fashion. The post proved a great success, but was hardly an object of great beauty. To imbue it with dignity he invented an erudite-sounding Latin name, which he had engraved on a hand-some brass plate. It read *Apis Spole Canis*.

His satisfaction was complete when a particularly overbearing garden visitor asked what it was. 'A rare specimen recently discovered in the Himalayas,' he answered solemnly. 'Oh,' came the reply, 'I do hope you will let me have a cutting if it takes.'

'It will be a pleasure, madam,' smiled the ingenious one.

If you have overlooked provision for pets' lavatory requirements in your initial garden landscaping plan, you must now incorporate a sprint-round-the-lawn-bucket-and-shovel routine before anyone can be allowed in, or polluted footwear and offended sensibilities result.

Dog-owning gardeners must learn to accept the half tree trunks, punctured balls, old shoes and bones that litter the lawns because they are pets' playthings. Robbed of occupational therapy, dogs can become bored and may inflict impressive damage around and about the plot. You must learn also to suppress shudders when offspring or visitors hurl the half tree trunks the length of the lawns. This is absolutely the best garden sport. A duet executed to perfection by a couple of dogs is the slamming-on of claw brakes at the final moment of retrieval. This results in spectacular skid marks that can reach two metres long. On the other hand, emergency stops by heavyweight canines also rake up an astonishing amount of moss.

If the arm that hurls the missile is not too accurate, plant treasures raised from seed or purchased from expensive catalogues are lost forever. Fragile garden statuary adorned with cherubs and garlands topples as the beasts lunge after their tree trunks.

Kind mums visiting the garden with small children often provide them with balls to play with. They do not know about dogs. Many are the occasions when I have had to break off an impressive garden lecture to placate a screaming child by prising a spitty ball from slathering fangs.

If you have chosen to share your garden with bitches you must also share it with the endless procession of mangy male dog suitors who beat a well-trodden path across the irresistibly pungent blotches on the lawn. In our present garden situation we are the owners of a pair of labrador bitches of youth and beauty. They are not renowned for their morals, and the lascivious lovers are welcomed warmly, to say the least. Even with the most elaborate of precautions, miles of aesthetically displeasing fencing, putting the animals under house/garden-shed arrest – we find ourselves with monotonous regularity inviting them into the car and heading for the vet for a 'morning after' injection. The dubious parentage of their suitors and the horrendous vet's bills have caused us to abandon any ambition of breeding thoroughbred gun dogs from ladies whose pedigrees are impeccable but whose morals are disgracefully permissive.

Bones, burial of – a distressing subject. Rabbits have nothing on labradors when it comes to sniffing out a patch of newly turned earth. This patch instantly becomes number one bone and plant cemetery. Flowers wilt and shrubs keel over as their root systems are exposed to the elements. Bone interment involves frenzied digging, which sends black showers all over the drive or pathways.

Dogs will tell you that the best time for the exhumation of old bones is just before a carload of guests is due to arrive. This ensures that the newly mown

118

lawn is littered with malodorous skeletal relics. The cool shady verandahs on which the guests might like to rest are also improved by being strewn with rotting bones in advanced stages of decay. The front door mat is a good place too.

Every gardener knows that dogs, like plants, require frequent watering. During the summer months a great battle ensues between me and our bitches over ownership of the lotus and lily pond. It is a bone of great contention (excuse the pun). Spectacular canine leaps are executed through the delicate foliage of the irises and hostas edging the pool. Then they plough like battleships straight through the lily and lotus blossoms with epic splashes and crashes. I tell myself that the flower heads skidding across the turbulent waters look most attractive. Wet dog showers all over garden guests in pretty frocks are also a feature of this time of year.

Take it from one who knows. Trying to garden-train dogs and cats is injurious to the health, and a 'Free to Good Home' ad in the local rag costs little.

Leaving the fur-coated pests to their depredations we move on to those of the feathered varieties. With regard to fruit on trees, the main enemy is the birds of the air, except for apples, pears or plums, where the enemy is boys from neighbouring properties. In both cases it is essential to accept that you cannot win. If you fight it, coronaries, strokes, high blood pressure and red spots before the eyes will negate the advantage of what fruits are left to you.

The best ploy with the itinerant scrumpers is to invite them into the orchard. They find nothing more discouraging than being invited to help themselves. They will half-heartedly pull a few apples from the low-growing branches and beat a hasty retreat to a garden where the thrill of looting is greater.

Birds cannot be expected to appreciate the psychology underlying this 'what's mine is yours' attitude. Nor does one wish to waste money and labour erecting Alcatraz-type high-security fruit cages – desperately expensive and usually the prerogative of filthy rich gardeners. This leaves you wrestling with tangled miles of cheap netting as a barrier. But when your cunningly erected network collapses in a heap around your head and those of the birds that have inevitably got in, you will experience difficulty in feeling enthusiastic about this method.

Australian gardener Barbara Wenzel shares this experience:

> I enjoyed the notion of harvesting something from my own garden, so I planted a fruiting grape to grow over a pergola at the back of the house. This was a mistake. Far from being the haven of green and dappled shade I had envis-

aged, the back terrace in summer resembled an overcrowded wildlife enclosure. Birds and possums nightly held Bacchanalian revels of such epic proportions that the end results, so to speak, were disastrous. Anyone rashly venturing out in the morning found himself knee-deep in guano. In desperation I bought some bird nets of fine black mesh and with some difficulty draped them over the whole vine.

The birds simply flew in and ate their fill from underneath. The nets did seem to discourage the possums, though, so they remained in place. Then I arrived home one day to find my daughter, tears streaming down her face, precariously balanced on a ladder trying to free an enmeshed bird with a pair of nail scissors. A confused scene ensued. The bird's role consisted of spirited attempts to blind us both as we swayed about on the ladder. My daughter, a passionate animal-lover, alternately made soothing noises at the wretched thing and hurled imprecations at me as a murderer and assassin.

The bird was finally cut free from the net and hurtled to the ground where it began a demented dashing about, obviously unable to fly. A mad pursuit followed to the accompaniment of mounting hysteria from at least two of the cast. Cornered at last, the bird was freed of the remaining strands of netting at no greater cost than a couple of Samaritan fingers slashed to the bone. Although the bird had escaped apparently uninjured, the point was made quite forcefully to me that the nets had to go.[6]

The foremost of avian pests is undoubtedly the sparrow. It does not destroy orchards as comprehensively as blackbirds and thrushes, and might be said to be gardener-friendly in that it feeds its young on caterpillars, white butterflies and beetles. It is, however, primarily a seed eater, and that thick-billed, seed-crunching beak is one of the reasons the gardener's wrath descends regularly upon its pert little head.

The sheer persistence with which the sparrow will hunt and devour seeds is astonishing. I have personally tried every method known to man to keep grass seed down when reseeding lawns. I have concealed it beneath layers of fine soil or grass clippings; abused my back and knees crawling round tangling crazy spiders' webs of cotton between twigs thrust into the soil; and swathed the seeded patches beneath layers of shade cloth or netting. As soon as my back is turned the mini-vultures descend in gleeful anticipatory hordes.

They stomp all over the area with sturdy little legs and feet, pushing those tough beaks through whatever form of deterrent material I have used, until they have devoured virtually all the seed.

---

*The good gardener always plants three seeds: one for the grubs, one for the birds, and one for himself.* —C. Collins

This hardy little villain may be found in almost any geographical location and climatic extreme in the world – anywhere, in fact, where there is human habitation. Gardeners the world over must endure its torments. Even Vita Sackville-West implored her readers for advice regarding the destructive habits of the sparrow:

> How does one protect the choicer sorts of primroses from the attack of sparrows? Has any reader a sovereign remedy against this naughty, wanton, wild destruction? Short of putting automatic cartridges among my primroses, I have done everything I can think of. I have made a sort of cat's-cradle of strong black thread, pegged down in the hope that the birds would catch their nasty little claws in it as they alighted and thus be frightened and discouraged. It doesn't work. The sparrows don't seem to mind. I can only suppose that they crawl underneath the threads and nip the flowers off, scattering the buds and heads all over the ground at dawn before I have got up in the morning.[7]

Celia Thaxter, gardening in the 1890s on the Isle of Appledore off the coast of New Hampshire in America, also laments:

> Another enemy to my flowers and a truly formidable one is my little friend the sparrow. Literally he gives the plot no peace if I venture to put seeds in it … I am obliged to lay newspapers or some protection over the seeded beds, and over these again, sheets of wire netting, to keep off the sparrows until the seeds are safely sprouted. Last year I put a border of mignonette seeds around every flower bed. When I came again to the garden in the afternoon, it was alive with flirting tails and saucy beaks and bright eyes and stout little legs and claws scratching like mad … Hardly a seed had those merry little marauders left in the ground. Around the edge of each bed a groove ran, nicely hollowed out by their feet, and as empty as my hopes.[8]

The petite adversary is indeed formidable; frustrated observation will show that even if a few seeds should germinate and raise delicate green spears through the protective materials, the sparrow will murder them by yanking and twisting their stems in the vain hope of uprooting the remains of the seed.

In the vege garden this thuggery must be thwarted by covering the lettuce, beet and other seedlings with bottomless jackets made from two-litre plastic softdrink bottles.

I have harboured thoughts of sparrow pie when faced with industrious mobs of incorrigible little thieves yanking up my newly transplanted sweet pea seedlings or persecuting the wisteria, flowering cherry and fruit trees, making dietary delicacy of the buds – the flowers to be! I have also watched the villains tearing the fragile petals of precious early primroses and crocuses.

Sparrow thuggery, when it comes to foodstuffs, is extended to birds whose size is vastly in excess of their own. As far as grain is concerned they are never more audacious than when I feed the doves and fantail pigeons with whom we share the gardens at Valley Homestead.

With unerring sense of timing they decorate the fences and trees waiting for my call, and unless I stand, a stern human sentinel, the tiny muggers swoop down, virtually elbowing aside the gentle fantails, stealing grain from under their very beaks. The same happens at the hen house when I call the chickens and turkeys to feed – the sparrows' audacity knows no bounds. I will the impudent thieves to get trodden on by the turkey's large feet but it never seems to happen.

If they have any virtue at all, I suppose it is that the little pests treat us to so cheerful a song that we have no need of an alarm clock. We have the lusty old rose 'Alberic Barbier' scrambling above one of our bedroom windows, and the flamboyant bougainvillea 'Scarlett O'Hara' over the other. The sparrows regard both these climbers as the most desirable of nesting sites and cram them with huge, untidy, trailing nests in what seems like minutes, their construction taking place with the maximum amount of raucous territorial squabbling.

At dusk there is more hullabaloo as a thousand sparrows quarrel over roosting branches. Then peace reigns, until the moon fades to a pale crescent, and first light, the colour of a dove's wing, feathers the sky. All hell breaks loose as the first tentative chirps and cheeps burst into a double-note 'Chissick, chissick!' and anthems of joy from a thousand small throats welcome the new day, rousing those who lie abed.

Other avian pests include blackbirds and thrushes. These play havoc with fruit and have other trying habits that make for a love-hate relationship between gardener and bird. In spring, with nests of hungry fledglings to feed, they follow the gardener's footsteps, uprooting seedlings and newly planted annuals in a keen-eyed search for worms and bugs. The hunt involves scooting soil and mulching materials with monotonous regularity all over drives and pathways.

With spring come the starlings. In New Zealand and many other countries they are welcome since they dine on vast quantities of grass grubs. But their innovative and eccentric choice of nesting places sometimes causes problems. On one occasion we were preparing to light a large brick barbecue for a charity luncheon in the garden. My husband had just put a taper to the charcoal when an indignant starling mum erupted out of the top of the chimney, leaving a nest full of piteously squawking fledglings.

Pa starling scolded us noisily from an adjacent fence, and as 80 hungry guests arrived, festivities had to be halted while a rescue operation was mounted by volunteer visitor force. It was an extremely delicate procedure, my husband (having moved the smouldering charcoal) twisting himself up into the base of the chimney and pushing the nest, intact with its precious cargo, further towards the top so that others could pull it out.

We put the nest in a plastic plant pot, covered it with dark cloth and hung it from the side of the barbecue. Ma starling ruffled her feathers crossly, hopped back in, and settled down to rear her young in the new abode without further ado.

We suffered few grass-gobbling grubs in the lawns that season.

For gardeners possessed of a rural garden, the ravages of itinerant poultry can be pretty discouraging. Their powerful scratching claws can strip the surface of an entire flower bed of its tender plant materials in minutes. Sharp beaks can shred a bed of tender spring greens faster than a multitude of sparrows or slugs and snails.

It was our misfortune to be obliged to share one garden with an ancient hen who was a constant illegal immigrant. She added insult to injury by invariably bringing along her latest brood of chicks. A hen of intelligence, she had sussed out the fact that the best place for infant scratching lessons was in the fine soil of my newly worked flowerbeds. Time and again I would do my mad-woman-with-a-broomstick act, shooing them out, until the day she scratched up an entire bed of newly planted annuals. Enough was enough. I lurked in the undergrowth until she brought her little family into the garden again, determined to teach her a lesson by catching her and confining the whole family to the poultry run as punishment.

When she was deeply engrossed beneath taller perennials I crept up behind to grab her. I lunged, she erupted into the air squawking blue murder, and my little finger hit a stone, doubled back and snapped. While I leapt about mouthing foul epithets in howling agony, she gathered her infants about her with immense dignity and, fixing me with evil stare from beady malevolent eye, ambled haughtily out of the garden.

Our gardens at Valley Homestead are in an area where wild turkeys roam, and the ravages they can inflict on small plants with huge horny feet and sharp beaks is impressive. Fortunately they are shy in nature and are more easily intimidated than the hens. The wild-woman-with-a-broomstick act usually keeps them away for some time, but they are eventually attracted back again by our peacocks. When the turkey mob see them strolling imperiously around the lawns, they see no reason why they should not do so too.

The leaders of the peacock tribe are Old Blue and (latterly) his hen Plain Jane, but the tale is sad. An elderly stag turkey took a fancy to Plain Jane who duly became utterly besotted with him. Old Blue was desperately jealous and wore himself to nervous exhaustion, unfurling his tail in a great arc of quivering greens, electric blues and burnished gold, but the faithless hussy trailed round with blind adoration after her unhandsome lover. His technicolour blue and scarlet head looked just like something from a sci-fi movie, and as he was of mature years he was always in moult, looking like something the cat had dragged in.

However, he and Plain Jane eloped one day and were never seen again, proving perchance that love is blind and that mixed marriages do work. We hoped they would bring their offspring *(perkies?)* back to the garden for a visit, but they never did.

Fury. Panic. Disbelief. Anguish. Among the immutable laws of gardening it is ordained that at one time or another rural gardeners all over the world will have their hearts and herbaceous broken by the devastating syndrome called 'wandering stock'.

From time immemorial gardeners have described the depredations of beasts that have evaded field and fence to feast on domestic gardens. In 1794 Fanny Burney described such gastronomic pillage thus in a letter to her father:

> My husband, Mr d'Arblay, had worked most laboriously in his garden, but his misfortunes there might melt a heart of stone. The cattle of our neighbouring farmer broke through our hedges, and have made a kind of bog of our garden, by scampering in it during the wet; the sheep followed, who have eaten all our greens, every sprout and lettuce destined for winter, while the horses dug up our turnips and carrots, and the swine, pursuing such examples, have trodden down the young plants, besides devouring whatever the others left of the vegetables.[9]

In 1896 Elizabeth von Arnhim recorded sadly:

> My eldest baby born in April is five years old. While I was stooping over a group of hollyhocks she, who had been sitting close by, got up suddenly, and began to run aimlessly about shrieking and wringing her hands with every appearance of terror. I stared and saw that a whole army of cows were grazing perilously near my tea roses and most precious plants. The nurse and I began

to chase them, but not before they had trampled down a border of pinks and lilies in the cruellest way, and made a great hole in a bed of China roses.[10]

Heartbreak or *what*?

City gardeners, it is true, have their gardening trials in the form of unwelcome invasion by neighbours' bugs, plant diseases, children, balls, cats and dogs, leaf fall and creeping roots of over-sized trees, but never in their wildest dreams could they believe the amount of damage a herd of vagrant cattle can do to a garden. Short of uprooting mature trees I do not believe a herd of elephants could do more. Cows' wicked cloven hooves will most cruelly mangle and crush all that is underfoot; their great jaws tear branches from trees, uproot shrubs and savage all plant material without discrimination until nothing remains but a shattered skeletal framework.

When they are fatigued with laying waste to all that is around them the beasts will crash down, inevitably upon something fragile such as one's dwarf maples, and sit complacently chewing the cud, a variegated green vegetative mix that minutes ago (scream) was the delicate lace-like foliage of Acers *Dissectum viridis* and *Atropurpureum*. As a final bonus they will blast lawns, paths and beds liberally with jets of khaki-green liquid manure.

I have a modern-day tale to relate of a gardening friend who experienced the ultimate horror at the hands (feet?) of wandering stock:

> One day while I was weeding the phone rang and I ran indoors to answer. It was for my husband. I don't know how it happened but Bonny, our house cow, who had been grazing in the paddock next to the garden, walked through the open ranchsliders right into the house past my husband (who swears to this day that he didn't see her). She strolled through the kitchen and up the two steps leading into the lounge and onto the pale cream carpet. As she raised her tail, I stood frozen in stricken horror.
>
> She rewarded me with several arcing sprays of olive-green liquid dung. My screams, turning into howls of purest rage, eventually caused my husband to terminate his telephone conversation. He drove her out, but not before she had trampled through the great pools of dung, patterning the rest of the carpet, knocking over furniture and smashing ornaments. She ambled out contentedly, dropping several more heaps of dung in the kitchen, and in between hefty whacks across her offending rump from my husband, snacked her way across the flower gardens until he finally got her back into her paddock. The offspring who left the gate open after retrieving a ball was disinherited.

Beside this tale, the odd gastronomic orgies perpetrated by bovine tribes upon the gardens at Valley Homestead seem to pale into insignificance, but I find it difficult to forget the day when Daisy, our nursing cow, got out (as only nursing cows can) with her two calves. We had recently had a truckful of topsoil delivered and laid a large new lawn. Weather conditions had been favourable and the seed had germinated quickly, spreading an even carpet of small green blades.

Daisy the Beast went walkabout, sinking her huge hoofs some 15cm deep all over the new lawn, making great craters that filled with water when the self-timed sprinklers went on shortly afterwards. Her calves executed a wild west rodeo by way of a freedom celebration and were eventually apprehended, all long-lashed innocence, sleeping (bellies distended with precious plant material) in the herbaceous borders. As for the new lawn, what little tender new growth the three hadn't eaten they'd tugged up by fragile roots, or crushed underfoot. A sort of dung-coated, mouldy green, terrible lunar landscape remained. I threw a tantrum on a scale that impressed the husband even after 26 years of marriage. We spent a dipsomaniac evening, and next day went out to rotovate, lay and seed that lawn all over again.

A rural gardener will, shortly and succinctly, declare that there is no such thing as a *stockproof* fence. Under, over or through, stock *will* find their way into the domestic gardens because electrified fences have a fatal flaw. The beasts lingering longingly behind the wires sense the electrical impulses travelling through them, and every electric fence must be turned off sometimes. The very second the current is turned off they detect the lack of vibration and barge merrily through.

Similarly, one has to be a rural gardener to believe just how hard cows can *lean* on a fence to reach a precious shrub some several metres over the other side; or how long cows' or horses' tongues actually are – curling out octopus-like to pull into their vast cavernous jaws vegetation that is a seemingly impossible distance away. I can personally, on my life, swear that a cow can squeeze its great head, horns and all, through an eight-strand wire fence to devour an entire herbaceous border beyond (sob). Horses are one up on cows in the 'reach and stretch' stakes since their tongues are carried in bigger heads borne on longer necks.

There is not a great deal of difference between equines and bovines in terms of the damage inflicted by hooves upon sweeps of velvet greensward and flowerbeds. Having escaped into the gardens from the stalag of a perfectly good spacious paddock of green pasture, both will communicate victory and j*oie de vivre*, with much thundering about and unseemly kicking up of legs in the air. Great clods of turf, entire plants, branches of shrubs, garden statuary adorned with smirking cherubs, rustic furniture and mortgage repayment pots all sail merrily through the air beneath thudding hooves as they execute the *danse de despoliation.*

Should you have the gross misfortune to inadvertently allow a herd of young bulls or steers access to the garden, the lawn on which you have expended the labour of years becomes a bullring in which the heavyweight vandals play 'headsies'. They growl and roar, practising male dominance with much fearsome pawing of the turf into huge bald craters. But there is *worse.*

When bored with laying the lawns to waste and devouring trees, the playful young things will 'toy' with ornamental garden structures. When this palls – usually because the picket fences, trellis archways, pergolas and gazebo have splintered like matchsticks and collapsed beneath their combined assault, they will play at lifting gates off their hinges and trampling them.

My neighbour's bull, in the enthusiasm of uplifting a heavy four-metre metal barred gate from between his paddock and the garden, got it inextricably tangled upon his horns. In his efforts to remove it he careered across a the large courtyard in front of the house, crashing the gate up and down on the paving stones, chipping them and flattening patio furniture and flower-filled containers en route. Fortunately his owners were nearby in the vege garden and, hearing the racket, raced to the scene.

They tell me that driving him (and the gate) back into the paddock and thence to the confinement of a pen was a memorable experience – and this wasn't the end of the tale. Their fraught-with-danger attempts to divorce maddened beast from metal head-dress proving quite futile, they had to pay the vet to come and surgically excise each from the other. They are still reticent about the details of his bill and the cost of replacing paving stones, ornamental containers and gate.

Finding their way onto the domestic scene, even peaceful heifers and matronly cows have been known to score the sides of buildings with their horns or, as in the case of one couple I know – the sides of the new family car as they idly 'scratch' their heads and shoulders.

Escapee goats demonstrate much the same enthusiasm as far as treasured plant material is concerned, and will ring-bark shrubs and trees in minutes, but their dung is easier to clear up. They are obdurate, stubborn and cantankerous when you make known your wish that they should vacate the herbaceous area, and evade capture by leaping onto narrow ledges and by kicking viciously. If they are getting on a bit and are especially cantankerous, expect to be head-butted also.

Sheep are marginally less destructive on the mangling and crushing front, but nibble everything right off until only bare soil remains. Sheep and goats are equally hard to catch and re-route into legalised grazing territory.

In this depressingly comprehensive list of wandering stock the porcine tribe may not be excepted. The ravages inflicted upon the precious plot by pigs are not as astonishing as that by cattle and horses, but pigs *dig*. Having devoured the tops of the perennials they will 'root' for the roots, thereby effecting the extinction of entire plant species from the garden.

This vegetative consumption frees the soil for swines to plough it up in search of their absolute favourite food – the earthworms that were lurking in the hitherto concealing roots of the perennials. The landscape of the moon has nothing on that of a lawn on which a sow and her litter of piglets have gone to work.

Wandering stock, regardless of variety, ensure that any flowers and perennials that escape being eaten, are mangled, dug up, crushed underfoot, sat upon or simply scorched to death by a blast of urine or a cloak of dung. Fresh cow manure is a river of khaki death, sheep and goat droppings present a lesser problem, but pig manure is something else again. It is revolting in the extreme, uniquely odiferous, and there is not a plant that can survive its caustic embrace. Any gardener knows that well-rotted animal manure is worth its weight in gold to any garden, but fresh and undiluted it is the kiss of death.

(Did I latch that gate securely or not?)

After all this carping about animals that are pests, it is time for some unstinted praise – there are small animals which are friend to all gardeners. An advertisement in a prestigious British newspaper in 1890 read:

> One is amused in walking through the great Covent Garden Market, London, to find toads among the commodities offered for sale. In such favour do these familiar reptiles stand with English market gardeners that they readily command a shilling apiece ... The toad has indeed no superior as a destroyer of noxious insects, and as he possesses no bad habits and is entirely inoffensive himself, every owner of a garden should treat him with the utmost hospitality. It is quite worth the while not only to offer any simple inducements which suggest themselves for rendering the property attractive to him, but should he show a tendency to wander away from them, to go as far as to exercise a gentle force in bringing him back to the regions where his services may be of the greatest utility.

Around the same time Celia Thaxter, gardening on the island of Appledore on the coast of New Hampshire in America, was plagued by legions of slugs despite her every effort to annihilate them. One day a friend remarked to her:

'Everything living has its enemy and the enemy of the slug is the toad. Why don't you import some toads?'

Ms Thaxter tells of sending of an order to Europe and of the toads' arrival:

In June a boat brought a box to me from a far-off express office. A piece of wire netting was nailed across the top, and upon the earth with which it was half filled, reposing among some dry and dusty leaves, sat three dry and dusty frogs, wearily gazing at nothing. Is this all, I thought, only three! Hardly worth sending so far. Poor creatures, they looked so arid and wilted. I took up the hose and turned on them a gentle shower of fresh cool water. I was not prepared for the result! The dry, baked earth heaved tumultuously; up came dusky heads and shoulders and bright eyes by the dozen. A sudden concert of liquid sweet notes was poured out on the air from the whole rejoicing company ...

I surveyed them with eager interest as they sat singing and blinking together. 'You are not handsome,' I said, as I wrenched off the wire cover, 'but you will be lovely in my sight if you will help me to destroy mine enemy.' I tipped the box on its side and out they skipped into a perfect paradise of food and shade. All summer I came upon them in different parts of the garden, waxing fatter and fatter till they were round as apples. In autumn baby toads no larger than my thumb nail were found hopping merrily over the whole island.[11]

Ms Thaxter learned that toads will not only bolt down legions of slugs but, like whales sieving plankton, will intake oceans of caterpillars, beetles, ants and worms as well. Under no circumstances will they ever attack a plant even if hungry and thirsty. Toads, with admirable self-restraint, make love (in the bath) just once after this springtime awakening, and then settle down to a year of serious eating. The only enemies of this highly desirable gardener's friend are cats, dogs, lawnmowers and curious children.

If you do not fancy toads but are fortunate enough to have hedgehogs around the garden, they will do an equally efficient job of despatching slimy pests. When you put the cat out before bed, take a nocturnal stroll around the garden with a torch and see who's having a wild night out:

A TONGUE OF QUICKSILVER,
HIS EYE BRILLIANT BLACK

Under the moon and stars without number
I noticed a hedgehog starting to lumber
over the lawn, spines glinting with dew,
trundling along as though still in slumber[12]

129

With any luck *Erinaceus europus*, the common hedgehog, will be present, beginning a delectable supper of succulent slugs and crunchy creepy crawlies. A rustling and shuffling of leaves and a snuffling, grunting sound is the prelude to this feast, but to pretend sorrow for their uncomfortable demise would be extraordinarily hypocritical.

The soft grunting sound the small creature makes as it searches for supper explains the origin of its common name, the hedge-pig or hedgehog. In times past the inoffensive creatures were persecuted in rural areas because farmers alleged they robbed hen's nests. This is unlikely, since it would take the largest and most persistent of hedgehogs to break a hen's egg. Another serious charge made against them was that they milked cows! This resulted in accusations of witchcraft and further persecution. In our more scientific and enlightened days it has been recorded that hedgehogs have been drawn to the milk smell on wet udders, when a cow has been lying in a prone position. Tiny teeth marks have been found, but the small inoffensive creature is no sharemilker!

If Mama hedgehog takes up residence in one's garden she will bear a litter of up to five young once a year. Doubtless she thinks them quite stunning, but the skin of the young is bright sugar-pink and covered with white pimples. Within an hour or two the skin dries ands shrinks, allowing the first coat of spines to appear. Two more coats follow in the next 10 days and after about 14 days the small creatures are protected enough to go out with Ma, and make the acquaintance of sumptuous slimy suppers around and about the garden.

Researchers tracking the night-time wanderings of hedgehogs estimate that one individual will travel more than 2.5 kilometres in search of supper. In the course of one night, one's gardens may be visited by as many as 10 hedgehogs – pretty bad news for the slug population. Primarily a nocturnal creature, a hapless hedgehog may bumble out onto the lawns during the day, to the delight of children and the bewilderment of dogs.

If a hedgehog is at peace with the world its spines lie flat and smooth upon its back. If the animal is frightened or threatened, the spines become erect, a sharp deterrent or mouthful for the would-be attacker. Our dogs have learned to their cost that hedgehogs jump if touched!

Hedgehogs have some surprising habits for such gentle creatures. Although they suffer poor eyesight, they are equipped with a keen sense of smell. If a food source is detected up a tree or on top of a wall, they have an excellent head for heights and have been known to climb to six or seven metres. When they have finished feeding they simply launch themselves into thin air, dropping to the ground like a ball, their spines acting like a soft blanket to cushion the fall.

English gardeners regard this small creature as such an ecological treasure that tunnels are built under motorways for them, and there is even a hedgehog hospital called St Tiggywinkles!

Admirable little fellows though they might be, hedgehogs are not recommended as children's pets. It is their misfortune to carry some rather unsavoury diseases and a fair number of fleas, so it is best to encourage junior to put down a saucer of milk and leave it at that – to feed but not to fondle.

Like the toad, Ma and Pa hedgehog will look for a snug place to hibernate in areas suffering severe winters, although they remain on duty year round in temperate climes. A favourite place for their comatose winter sleep is under a pile of leaves or brushwood, so it is wise to move any such pile about gently before lighting a bonfire. There would not be a gardener among us who would wish inadvertently to consign this valued predator of garden pests to such a painful end.

They will waken ravenously hungry with the rising tempeatures of spring and despatch the plague of slugs that would otherwise devastate your garden.

> So it's out with the saucers and –
> Wait under the hawthorns and stars without number
> For your pincushion friend to wake from his slumber![13]

# 14

# CHILDREN IN THE GARDEN

*Nothing grows in our garden, only washing. And babies.*
— Dylan Thomas[1]

Germaine Greer sets the ball rolling on the subject of children in the garden by leaving us in no doubt of her feelings regarding the youthful visitors who torment her London garden:

God, how I do perfectly hate all children! There was a time, before I became a gardener, when I quite liked children. That time is past. A child, admittedly a bloated, grey-faced, pimply thug of a child, has cut my best rose bush in half. The reason for this highly unreasonable act is that I asked her not to use my garden as a goal mouth in a form of play resembling soccer in that there was a ball – but more like a wall game in effect, the wall in question being my rose-bedecked railings. Broken bottles and revolving spikes set on top of walls are, I believe, illegal – if you don't live in Buckingham Palace, that is. Round the Revolting Back-garden runs a six-foot brick wall, which children use as a thoroughfare.

The wall being only nine inches wide, there are frequent collisions, which result in thrashing tangles of children falling into and onto the Revolting Garden. When a child finds itself in a garden, it feels that it must at once seize a stick and start thrashing the plants. This pastime is evidently very gratifying for it is accompanied by ear-splitting screams of delight. The mirth becomes more jubilant the more minced leaves fly through the air. Picking flowers is, perhaps a comprehensible activity, especially if you have not had the fag of actually growing them, but children these days have no time for daisy chains or garlands.

They apparently see the flowers as weapons, for they tear them up by the roots, and brandish them or start hitting each other with them. If you turn the hose on them you have their appalling parents to deal with. Not a child in my street but is menaced by some dire pulmonary ailment, it seems ...

To think that I once contemplated paying a child to help take care of the garden! Nowadays the mere sound of a childish voice brings out the cold sweat-drops on my skin.[2]

Mature gardeners may sigh for the 'good old days' when children existed to be seen and not heard, or handed back to nanny after a shortish interval of exposure to parents and adults. In those days and on those terms it was possible to keep quite a decent garden, and the presence of children was tolerable.

Such infants are described by Elizabeth von Arnhim, writing about her German Garden in 1897. In 1890 Elizabeth had married a German count who was desperate for a son; she bore him, in as many years, three daughters to whom she refers with rueful affection as 'the April, May and June babies'. They make frequent entertaining appearances in the garden:

The April baby came panting up, the others hurrying along behind, and with flaming cheeks displayed for my admiration three brand new kittens that she was carrying in her pinafore. 'Look,' she cried breathlessly, 'such a much!'[3]

She describes the joy of her return to the garden and the babies after a trip abroad:

I got out into the brightest, purest snow atmosphere, the air so still the whole world seemed to be listening, the sky cloudless, the crisp snow sparkling underfoot and on the trees, and a happy row of three beaming babies awaited me, each with a kitten in one hand and an elegant bouquet of pine needles and grass in the other, and what with the presentations of the bouquets, the struggles of the kittens, the hugging and kissing was much interfered with.[4]

Gentle 19th-century infants. Idyllic days in tranquil gardens.

The role of the modern child in the garden is much more active and demanding, the emphasis being upon the 'demanding' bit. Whole tracts of deliciously fertile land are swallowed up on garden landscaping plans as 'play areas'. If one is to be considered a good parent one not only admits defeat without snarling, but takes the advice of skilled landscapers to ensure that the garden is as welcoming a place as possible for the progeny.

The first lesson to be learned by the Parent-Gardener is that despite this being the age of push-button entertainment indoors, a couple of children setting foot outside must be equipped with an astonishing amount of apparatus in order for the garden to entertain them satisfactorily. Outdoor areas under the windows of mature or childless gardeners' houses exhibit elegant herbaceous borders, fragile antique statuary, charming containers, tranquil ornamental pools and rose-bedecked parterres with miniature hedges of box.

The other sort of gardener's plot sports such essentials as a sandpit, paddling/ swimming pool, trampoline, climbing frame, wendy house and tenting area.

In order to meet safety standards, all these amusements must be sited on flat stable surfaces so juveniles will not skin their infantile elbows and knees or break their scrawny little necks. These structures therefore engulf areas originally designated as lawn and adult entertainment spaces for sun loungers, wine-drinking and barbecue pads.

If the garden is also for older children, the last remaining metres of lawn should be rollered and concreted to provide another flat stable surface where they can perform wheelies on mountain bikes, rollerblades and skateboards. If the garden started out as a large one and a remnant of lawn still remains, it should be marked out for games such as cricket, rounders, basketball, football, etc. When the childless couple with the monumental sweeps of greensward next door shake their heads pityingly over its bald, scuffed and hammered face, it must be explained that such games help the young develop gross motor skills and hand-eye co-ordination. You must help them understand that yours is a 'relaxed' garden, an easy-care garden, and try to ignore their knowing smiles.

If there are a few last desperate tufts of green cowering on the 'lawn's' face, the infant enemy will spy them and demand that hutches be erected for a menagerie of rabbits or guinea pigs. Having a cat and a dog is not enough. It is important to the child's social development that he is able to be responsible for the welfare of creatures smaller than himself. The experience will be educational and therapeutic for you too, since once the novelty of feeding and cleaning up their mess wears off (after two days), the pets' welfare will be entirely your responsibility. The good thing is that you will have plenty of time for the chore since you now have absolutely no lawns left to mow. The lawnmower may be sold and the proceeds put into a parental entertainment fund, which is only fair, because the diversions described will keep the juveniles off the streets.

If the garden is surrounded by walls or fences they should be left unplanted in order that both toddlers and teenagers can indulge inhibitions and tantrums by hurling balls, frisbees, projectile missiles and younger siblings against them. It would be little less than parental selfishness to harbour a desire to plant old-fashioned roses or fragile-stemmed clematis against them.

It is quite easy to make economical play equipment for older children; a trip to the tip will yield all sorts of filthy splintery timber that will make the project economical. A section of log and planks will make see-saws, while a series of half tree trunks sunk in the ground at varying heights will encourage children to leap recklessly from one to another.

If you do not have access to the city tip, timber may be acquired by felling the trees in the garden, but let one mature specimen remain. Its trunk will be disguised by a hanging ladder, which will give young access to the tree house in its branches. Ideally, this should be sited in the highest point of the tree. Providing the house with some kind of roof so that the des. res. is attractive in all weathers will sometimes give you enough time to yourself to indulge in a snooze with the newspapers in a deckchair.

The children will prefer the design to incorporate a rope ladder they can pull up after ascending so that no adults can get at them. The disadvantage of this system is that they readily can come down and get at you. Opt instead for a home-made rickety ladder which you can pull away as soon as they've ascended.

If you are really good Parent-Gardeners you will create an imaginative and challenging adventure trail *en route*. Level pathways are boring in the extreme.

You can devise a really dangerous assault course featuring high hurdles with deep water on the other side, narrow catwalks, child-eating climbing nets, fraying rope trapezes with strangle power and tunnels with inbuilt bottomless pits etc. A stack of old car tyres here and there will enable them to bounce back on course while acquiring more painful knocks and bruises.

The shrubbery (a grand misnomer for the pathetic clump of ball-battered shrubs in the farther corners of the plot) exists only so that the little beasts can play such infantile games as hide and seek, secret dens etc. The fact that the original blueprint of the garden layout sited the rubbish bins and a pungently rotting compost heap here (well screened by the shrubs) will only heighten their enjoyment. Shrubberies are extremely important to the child's developing maturity; it is here that they learn to smoke cigarettes lifted from Parent-Gardeners.

If, at this stage, you have any earth left at all, as good PGs you will naturally reserve this for the children, so that they may have their own gardens. At best it might be the start of a lifetime's passion, and the delinquent will be so inspired he or she will branch out and little by little until you find the original garden being reclaimed and returned to you. At worst, the precious plot will become a knee-high jungled wilderness of nourishing salad greens in the form of dandelions and chickweed.

When the unreasonable couple next door complain about weed seeds winging their way over the fence, explain that your children are learning by doing, and that contact with good clean soil is vital to the child's emotional and psychological development.

If you absolutely must keep a patch of soil for yourself, say for a vegetable garden, then the best line of defence is to give the child the meanest corner of the plot for his horticulture. Early successes are important for children; too many failures will probably put them off for life. For this same reason, when they demand seeds, don't give them easy-grow packets of nasturtiums, nigella, sunflowers, lettuce and radish etc. Choose species that take months to germinate – or preferably ones that do not germinate at all.

Play with sand gives the child tactile experiences that are vital in the early stages of sensory development. Careful thought must be given to the pit's construction; you can knock one up on the cheap with the old timber left over from constructing the assault course.

The sandtray is best sunk deeply into the ground, so that climbing out will challenge your child's ingenuity. It is recommended that the tray be filled with silver sand or fine washed builder's sand, but this is expensive. You can make do with ordinary builder's sand which will stain junior's designer play suits dark yellow, but *c'est la vie*. It is also recommended that a cover be made for the tray when not in use, to keep out falling leaves, cats, dogs and the inevitable consequences of their visits.

Although you have tried to be wise parents and have limited your family to a couple of offspring, what you have really achieved is to ensure that every last metre of space in *your* garden can be shared with every other kid in the neighbourhood.

Female children are easier on the garden than male. They are normally satisfied with a domestic corner containing an expensive shop-bought wendy house, perhaps a dolls' hospital and, for when both entertainments pall, a shop.

The corner must contain infant-sized tables and chairs so that elaborate tea parties for doll families may take place. A toy cooker is a nice addition, so that pint-sized parents can 'bake' mud pies etc. It follows that in order to encourage such vital creative play, you must ensure the small girls have a container of fresh soil and a water supply at hand.

As the play shop often becomes a flower shop, the caring PG sites the domestic corner near choice flowerbeds, so that the infant retailers may pick them in abundance. Little girls like to pick all the buds off the roses and perennials because their small hands can handle them better. There must be plenty of space in the corner for the wheeling about of dolly buggies and perambulators.

Young females can be persuaded into such quietly destructive garden pursuits as pressing the heads of hydrangeas, peonies, and interesting leaves. They may be encouraged to mount birds' eggs, twigs and slugs into nature albums, or tear off countless flower petals to make horridly cloying pot-pourris.

If you are PGs who have had the good judgment to ensure that your progeny are both girls, and have sacrificed the soil for play activities, comparative peace will reign in the plot until visiting nephews and male cousins see the delightful domestic scenario as the ultimate challenge.

They will launch vicious raids upon the female children, take them hostage, destroy their mud pies and floral arrangements and, with whoops of derision, tip dolls out of buggies and use them instead to whizz their mates around the garden. As the host PG you will know when this character-forming play is taking place: the small girls will be sobbing hysterically, the boys whooping with malevolent delight, and the neighbours complaining about the noise.

If you have male children only, your problems are of a more severe nature – viz, they attract hordes of other male children. (My sister-in-law, placed for some years in this predicament, has greyed prematurely and is now referred to as *Senecio greyii*.) The most interesting feature in the *modus operandii* of small boys is their pack instinct. They will never be found alone in a garden for more than five minutes before three or four like-minded male children will magically appear over the fence. They will be armed with bats, balls and pads of all types.

After half an hour of feverish garden demolition work and constant argument they all fall about exhausted and in desperate need of sustenance. Minutes later the garden is strewn with softdrink mugs, chocolate biscuit wrappers, lolly sticks and discarded jumpers.

The boy child may be classified as a non-floriferous, parasitic species that has great affinity for any garden situation. It does well in any soil type but thrives particularly well in damp, waterlogged areas that offer constant access to mud, and the opportunity of making lawn-scoring slides.

Boys do not ever venture into a garden without an assortment of cricket bats, balls and stumps, baseball and bats, rugby balls, basket balls, footballs, croquet balls, golf balls, tennis balls and boules. The balls will be hurled to all corners of the garden, rugby balls and basketballs proving to be particularly effective for flattening fuchsias and snapping new shoots off azaleas. At the end of play, balls are left where they land and absolutely never retrieved since small boys have an inexhaustible replacement supply.

When all other amusements fail, and when heavy rain threatens, there are always tents and camping. These are erected with much enthusiasm and filled to overflowing with creature comforts, and are then abandoned and left to start the work of indelibly blanching and subsequently killing the velvet turf beneath the groundsheets. It is the responsibility of the PG to dismantle and dry out the sodden tent.

Boys are hardy garden specimens; even the vilest of weather does not guarantee the garden any reprieve. They are blight- and damp-resistant and any attempt to restrain such exuberant garden activities will severely inhibit their emotional wellbeing.

This delightful cautionary tale comes from a rose grower in Christchurch, New Zealand:

An avid rose grower, I had been collecting rose cuttings all year. I potted each one and placed them lovingly on top of the backyard incinerator to acclimatise them to the elements, but I noticed that something was constantly taking the tops off them.

Determined to rid my precious cuttings of their attackers, I set out loads of slug pellets but the tops still disappeared.

It was only when I was sitting on the verandah one day, watching my bored son aiming his slug-gun at a bottle perched on the incinerator, that I realised I had been treating the wrong kind of slug.

I vow I will lace my son's food with the pellets if he ever tries that trick again.[5]

While your children are at home and in their formative years, it is better to settle for hobbies other than gardening, or to devise a Parent-Gardener's guide to survival.

From the moment they rise up from all fours and take their first footsteps, toddlers must be taught the phrase '*Off the garden!*'.

When they have sufficient language to be communicated with seriously, young children should be exploited as a form of slave labour. Parent-Gardeners have rights, and a bit of cheap help in the garden is not asking overmuch by way of return for feeding, clothing and educating the little beasts for years and years.

The degree of subtlety required for one's strategy depends on the age of the victim. For four- to six-year-olds who have not yet lost their innocence, the approach needs little in the way of parental guile. 'Whoever brings me a bucketful of dandelions by tea time will get a prize' will not provoke the enquiry of a more worldly-wise age group as to the exact nature of the prize. If you are vindictive enough to have organised a single jellybean as reward, the naive victim in the triumph of victory is unlikely to bear you a lasting grudge. Little children have trusting natures, so it is better not to corrupt them with monetary rewards.

If you have to target the 7-10 age range, more devious stratagems are required. If the school holidays (groan) are imminent it might occur to you that an outing to a funfair would be a pleasing *divertissement*. To state the possibility openly is to let the enemy breach your defences. You should only raise the possibility in order to point out how nice it would be, but how completely impossible.

'Oh, Mum/Dad, please! Please!' the enemy begs, to which you reply with a harassed sigh, 'It depends on how much work I can get done.' There is an avalanche of business correspondence, domestic rituals that simply must be dealt with, and then of course the garden is in a terrible state and will have to attended to. All this will take up most of the day – several days.

This stratagem places you in a fine bargaining position. Yes, yes, you know how much they would like to go ... You will bash your brains out writing your letters and wear your fingers to the bone cooking, cleaning and ironing by lunch-time ... If only someone would just mow the lawns, weed the borders, prune the roses and water the veges it might just be possible to get away by 2pm.

'Oh, thank you, thank you!' the grateful slaves cry, rushing out of doors to carry out their part of the bargain. If you are the male PG you retire to your study with the coffee-pot and a crossword, and if female, to the couch with a good book.

To cultivate a garden
Takes too much time and labour.
I'd rather live next door to one
And cultivate my neighbour.
—Stephen Way

# 15

# THE EDUCATION OF A GARDENER

*(With apologies to Russell Page)*

Not so very many years ago, if the weather was sunny and one was in the mood, one might have thrown on some terrible old gear and ambled forth to do a few hours' gardening.

One would mow the lawns, pull the worst of the weeds and, vastly impressed with the results of such diligence, one would leap into the car to a garden centre. After a happy hour spent browsing, a trolley (according to the state of the bank balance) would be piled with pots and punnets of instant (vulgar) colour and impulse buys of any pretty little thing that caught the eye.

Still caught in the fit of gardening enthusiasm, one spends all next day firing the plants in happily and haphazardly. The only soil preparation indulged in is the digging of the hole to receive the bursting-with-good-health plant in its planter bag. (The holes have to be dug first, so the money can be poured in ...) One remains serenely untroubled about the possibility that one is digging plant graves.

Friendly and helpful garden centre staff have declared them 'easy grow', so one naturally assumes this applies to any soil type, geographical location or climatic extreme. No problem.

Standing back, hugely impressed with one's creativity and the carnival of instant colour, one thinks: 'That's the garden finished for this season' and, emanating gross virtue, heads indoors to forget all about it.

What happens next? You sit back in your armchair and open the newspaper, and it contains a supplement full of seductive pictures from local nurseries showing their irresistible 'specials' for the coming weekend. You like the sound of

---

*I would like to differentiate between real style and the eclectic use of a borrowed style from another period or place. This will be a reflected mannerism deliberately imposed ... Such borrowings are fashions rather than styles and like all fashions sooner or later become dated and unfashionable.* —Russell Page

what they offer and feel you can't afford to miss out on such 'bargains'. A selection of these beauties would just put the finishing touches to your rehabilitated beds.

Instead of having a serenely slothful Saturday or Sunday lie-in, you join the hordes of other keen gardeners toting trolley-loads to the checkout. You get your loot home, realise you have spent far too much money, then wander round wondering where on earth you are going to find room for it all. You are prepared to admit that you have perhaps gone overboard a bit and reassure yourself that this is truly it – you are not going to set foot in the garden again, except for the odd mow and weed pull – for the rest of the year. (You suspect your back might not let you anyway, after the unaccustomed frenzy of digging and planting.)

You see your neighbours in their garden and give them a wave as you turn to go indoors. A nice quiet unassuming couple, you think, quite keen on their garden – then, what's this? A charabanc of tourists draws up outside their front gate. They've lost their way, got a puncture and, being a good sort, you sally forth to offer assistance. You are nearly flattened in the rush as 46 envious gardeners stride purposefully into your neighbour's plot to inspect every blade of grass, tree and shrub therein. Reeling from shock at the Jekyll and Hyde truth about the people next door, you totter inside, reach for the bottle, sit down and turn on the TV.

It is peak viewing time and a group of people dressed in trendy gardening gear are taking you on a guided tour of an over-manicured, over-cultivated, overlarge and completely unattainable garden. They leave the garden, return to a glitzy studio decorated with potted plants, and hold a gardeners' advice forum. They do not include information on how the grand park-like garden you've just seen on the screen might come your way. They answer questions from 'Les in London', 'Sal in Sydney' and 'Annie in Auckland' concerning unspeakable diseases that are knocking off their dahlias and roses.

You begin to perceive a Great Truth: the whole face of gardening as you know it is changing dramatically. Your days of pottering in the back yard are almost through. You begin to perceive that gardens have become big business and remember reading in a recent national survey that gardening was rated as one of the world's top 'leisure' activities. The Department of Statistics said that gardening had become a multimillion-dollar industry, with spending in the private sector assuming astronomical proportions.

The fact that your neighbours have opened their modest plot to the public says it all. Only a few years ago gardens inviting paying guests onto their immaculate lawns were large and impressive, famous nationally. Now it seems that the concept of welcoming visitors into private gardens for hard cash (or for fundraising activities if you are of a charitable turn of mind) is par for the course.

Turning to the 'What's On' section in the newspaper you find it full of reports of forthcoming garden safaris, parties, festivals and tours. You wander to the window and view your humble quarter acre with bemused but calculating eyes. You begin to feel left out – deprived almost – and decide that it is surely a case of if you can't beat 'em, join 'em.

You begin by tripping round other people's gardens conning ideas and picking up horticultural phrases that will make you feel one of the gang. You find yourself casually enquiring from your neighbours which day their garden club meets. You join, and find it to your benefit: you can get your hands on loads of luscious cuttings, buy heaps of inexpensive donated plants, go on outings to view and criticise yet more gardens. Someone lends you a copy of *Gardens Open to The Public* and every weekend is devoted to traipsing up and down the country viewing, reviewing, poaching ideas and amassing an acceptable plant collection. An overseas holiday becomes a pilgrimage to the shrines of the gardening élite of England and Europe.

While visiting the more prestigious gardens overseas, keep a keen eye out for their owners, whom you may be able to detain in conversation about their more obscure hybrids. This will be enormously useful later for name-dropping conversations back at the club. You will almost have gained élite status if you can mutter nonchalantly 'I was saying to Gordon at Titoke Point/Christopher at Great Dixter how much I agreed with his philosophy on plants with bold foliage and texture for maximum visual impact', or 'Sir Miles's formal gardens at Ohinetahi are equal to those of Sissinghurst any day' etc.

If you can pin down a well-known gardening or TV personality at one of the annual horticultural shows just long enough to say 'Gidday Maggie' or 'Afternoon David' that is quite enough for you to claim when you are among your colleagues back at the club to have had a conversation with them.

Your club may invite top horticultural speakers to educate you further in your new-found passion (as long as you stay awake). A burning ambition to be accepted by the nation's gardening élite has been born in your breast.

You spend every moment of your 'spare' time trying to improve your plot (or lot). Your garden is transformed: you are now in possession of a quarter acre of nervous land with a house in the middle. It is surrounded by a lawn that is no longer ankle deep in kids' toys, dogs' bones, balls and sticks, or cluttered with comfortable but tatty old loungers. The edges are strimmed like a rookie's head, the main area is raked and skelped and, hallelujah, the beds are as weed free as your back will allow.

Around and about the hammered-into-submission lawns, beds burgeon forth in a floral maquillage of the colour schemes presently in vogue. Your new trees, shrubs and roses exhibit labels from the country's ruinously expensive specialist nurseries that you 'forgot' to take off. You are absolutely broke and behind with the mortgage repayments, but your garden now abounds with household-engulfing old-fashioned shrub roses that only bloom once, the requisite 'in' perennials, exotic specimen trees and shrubs. (The number of native plants present will depend on your strength of character and the extent of the brain-washing inflicted by the local gardening bourgeoisie.)

In arbours made vicious by rambling roses sporting man-eating thorns your garden will sport rustic furniture, and Lutyens-style benches that the family complain are hell to sit on. Your patio or verandah is adorned with lashings of plants in hideously expensive containers. You decide it will soon look good enough to invite paying guests – to 'Go Public'.

You have created from your comfortable old back yard the grandchild of the Persian Paradise: the estatelet you will wreck your back on, devote all your 'leisure' hours to, buy shelves of books and magazines for, blue much of your salary on, and make greed-filled raids on garden centres for – come boom or slump.

On the subject of books, your shelves must contain books by Lloyd, Jekyll, Fish, Sackville-West, Verey, Hobhouse, Chatto and Scott-James. Other mandatory authors include Graham Stuart Thomas, William Robinson, Arthur Hellyar, Eion Scarrow, Geoff Bryant and Beverley Nichols. Your bible becomes Russell Page's stern and authoritative *Education of a Gardener*. Learning a few selected lines to quote will gain you much face.

Your metamorphosis from casual holiday weekend gardener is almost complete, but not quite: to win the desperately coveted title of Master Gardener you must graduate from the strict school of horticultural etiquette. This title is your passport to acceptability by ranks of the gardening élite. To gain it, you must acquire savoir-faire which, roughly translated, means know-how. You must learn which plants to grow, their names in English *and* Latin – *and remember them*.

You have made a good start, but you must also study which garden statuary and furniture to sneer at and avoid, which gardening books to quote from and decorate your coffee tables with, and which person and place names to drop. You must learn which tools to use, what gardening clothes to acquire, and which nurseries to be seen in. You need to make a lot of changes in order that your garden might hold its own in the gardendom hotbed of fashion. You must learn what is 'in' and what's 'out'; what is socially and horticulturally acceptable and what is not. You must study class in the garden. Help follows.

We perceive from English writer Nancy Mitford that class in the garden is no modern concept. In her novel *Love in a Cold Climate*, written in 1945, she is cheerfully waspish:

> … Planes was a horrible house. It was an overgrown cottage … furnished in neither good nor bad taste, but simply with no attempt at taste at all. The garden which lay around it would be a lady water-colourist's heaven; herbaceous borders, rockeries and water-gardens were carried to a perfection of vulgarity, and flaunted a riot of huge and hideous flowers, each individual bloom appearing twice as large, three times as brilliant as it ought to have been and if possible a different colour from that which nature intended. It would be hard to say whether it was more frightful, more like glorious Technicolour, in spring, in summer, or in autumn. Only in the depths of winter, covered by the kindly snow, did it melt into the landscape and become tolerable.[1]

English writer-gardener Jilly Cooper ensures that amateur gardener feet are led up the right garden path with the following guide to good taste in matters horticultural:

> The Englishman traditionally loves his garden. It needs cherishing and tending, but doesn't answer back. It is hardly surprising, therefore, that class distinction should be almost more rampant outside the house than in it. Once again, garden centres – like furniture shops – do a roaring trade because of snobbery. People are constantly ripping up the plants and paving stones of previous owners – 'Too ghastly, my dear.'
>
> I remember being mystified when a friend came to stay. 'You know, it's frightfully common to have 'Peace' in one's garden.' It was a few minutes before I realised she was referring to the beautiful yellow and pink rose next to the magnolia which flowers so gallantly and continually all summer. I can only suppose she thought it was vulgar because it is so universally popular.
>
> In the same way, Caroline Stow-Crat wouldn't touch gladioli, begonias and chrysanthemums, or fuchsias – except in the conservatory. Also on the

index would be gaudy bedding plants like petunias, French marigolds, calceolarias, cinerarias, calendulas, salvia, Californian poppies, zinnias, asters and yellow daisies, although Michaelmas daisies and white daisies are all right. Colour is also important: the white and green tobacco plants are much more upper-class than the red or mauve ones and dark red wallflowers better than yellow or mauve. Trails of blue lobelia are all right, but Oxford blue is very common, particularly when combined in military rows with white alyssum and scarlet geraniums.

Caroline would not be keen on any flower of a colour different from that which nature intended – blue roses, brown irises, pink forget-me-nots or daffodils. She hates tulips. If she had rhododendrons she would have not individual ones, but great clumps lining the drive. A friend once asked a West Country peer how he achieved his magnificent multi-coloured display.

'Oh, I move them around,' said the peer. 'When I want to change the colour scheme, I just get twenty men up from the factory.'

'Yellow and green should never be seen,' so Caroline would soon rip out anything variegated such as laurels or, even worse, privet and mother-in-law's tongue.

Some trees are more upper-class than others: one thinks of the great flat-bottomed oaks, beeches, limes and chestnuts, that look, as Taine said, as though they'd been tended for hundreds of years like the children of rich parents.

If you discount the cedars planted by Capability Brown, indigenous trees are considered much smarter than foreign ones, which is why the white double cherry scores over the imported pink one, and why the Stow-Crats tend to despise the silver birches and conifers of Surrey. Willow trees are all right growing naturally by a lake or stream, but would be considered the height of vulgarity in the middle of a suburban lawn, particularly if planted in a circle of earth.

The suburbs in spring, with their candy-floss mass of pink and white cherry, dark pink crab-apple, almond, laburnum and lilac, are quite beyond the pale. Pink hawthorn, although considered much more common by the upper classes than white, is for some reason acceptable in the suburbs.[2]

Soon you will be able to sneer with the best of 'em at the lower-class cultivators of screaming orange marigolds brawling with mauve lobelia, at petunias so puce they grab you by the jugular – at the 'backyard potterer', which (refined shudder) you were before your days of horticultural metamorphosis. And you can only benefit from our gardener's guide to despised plants, which follows.

Gardening writers are erudite in their perceptions of plants – particularly in the case of those they do not like. E.A. Bowles, an English writer of an earlier generation, vents his spleen admirably on a species of the *Lilium* genus:

*Helicodiceros crinitus* is the most fiendish plant I know of, the sort of thing Beelzebub might pluck to make a bouquet for his mother-in-law ... it looks as if it had been made out of a sow's ear for spathe and the tail of a rat that had died of elephantitis for the spafdix. The whole thing is a mingling of unwholesome greens, livid purples and pallid pinks, the livery of putrescence in fact, and it possesses an odour to match the colouring. I once entrapped the vicar of a poor parish into smelling it, and when he had recovered his breath he said it reminded him of a pauper funeral. It only exhales this stench for a few hours after opening, and during that time it is better to stand afar off and look at it through a telescope.[3]

And consider his portrait of a certain inoffensive species of crocus:

One little yellow crocus has an obnoxious trait in its character and is a little stinking beast, as Dr Johnson described the stoat. It is well named *graveolens*, and its heavy scent is generally the first intimation I get of its having opened its flowers. Sometimes I get a whiff of it even before I reach the crocus frame – an abominable odour of black beetles and imitation of skunk, or one of those awful furs with which people in the next pew or at a matinee poison you. A dried specimen of this crocus retains its scent for years, and so does the blotting paper it has been pressed in. I think it emanates from the pollen grains, and I suppose it must be of some use in its native country – perhaps attractive to some insect of perverted olfactory tastes.[4]

One may well think that all might not be hey-ring-a-ding-ding in Mr Bowles's garden in spring, but some of the blooms that come with summer incite his wrath to the point of violence:

I can admire and enjoy most flowers, but just a few I positively dislike. Collarette dahlias and those superlatively double African marigolds that look like India-rubber bath sponges offend me most of all. I dislike the cheap thin texture of godetias almost as much as I do the sinful magenta streaks and splotches that run in the blood of that family. I loathe celosias equally with dyed pampas grass; and spotty, marbled double balsams I should like to smash up with a coal hammer; and certain great flaunting mauve and purple cattleyas cloy my nose and annoy my eye till I conjure up a vision of them expiating their gaudy double-eyed wickedness with heads impaled on stiff wires like those of criminals on pikes, in a sea of *Asparagus sprengeri*, and forming the

*I am calmly extravagant about tulips.* —Hardy Amies

bouquet presented to the wife of a provincial mayor on the occasion of his opening the new sewage works.[5]

Mr Bowles can be quite eloquent when pressed:

Phloxes smell to me like a combination of pepper and pig-sty, most brooms of dirty, soapy bath-sponge, hawthorn of fish-shop, and meadow-sweet of curry powder.[6]

Gertrude Jekyll is equally articulate when it comes to plants with scents that do not please her:

There is a curious smell about the yellow roots of berberis, not exactly nasty, and a strong odour, not really offensive, that I personally dislike, about the root of *Chrysanthemum maximum* ... The only other hardy flowers I can think of whose smell is distinctly offensive are *Lilium pyrenaicum*, smelling like a mangy dog, and some of the schizanthus, that are redolent of a dirty hen-house.[7]

Bowles's contemporary, Reginald Farrer, is equally uninhibited in his verbal defamation of another plant, the humble 'mum':

... the chrysanthemum more almost than any other flower suffers from that megalomania which is the British gardener's sole ideal of beauty. All he cares for is to get a thing large; farewell colour, fragrance, elegance, so long as you have a vast draggled head that looks like a moulting mop dipped in stale lobster sauce. The result is a show chrysanthemum.[8]

Vita Sackville-West did not mince words on the unfortunates who have chosen to plant a hedge of rambling roses:

In a gracious, small and ancient town near where I live, someone had the imagination to plant a hedge of rambler roses. It occupies the whole of his road frontage, about 150 yards I believe, and in the summer months people come from all over the country to see it. I must admit that it is an impressive sight; a blaze of colour; a long, angry, startling streak, as though somebody had taken a long pencil and had scrawled dense red bunches all over a thicket-fence of green. A splendid idea; very effective, but, oh, how crude! I blink on seeing it; and having blinked, I weep. It is not only the virulence of the colour that brings tears to my eyes, but the regret that so fine an idea should not have been more fastidiously carried out. The hedge is made of 'American Pillar', a rose which together with 'Dorothy Perkins' should be forever abolished from our gardens. I know this attack on two popular roses will infuriate many people; but if one writes gardening articles one must have the courage of one's opinion. I hate, hate, hate 'American Pillar' and her sweetly pink companion 'Perkins'.[9]

There is one plant – the hapless rhododendron – that incurs the wrath of several eminent garden writers and is apparently beyond redemption. Rose Blight (alias Germaine Greer) mutters darkly:

> There lives an American person in Wadhurst, Sussex, who thinks there are not enough rhododendrons in the British Isles … To hear this gent, you would think that the gloomy, leathery, ubiquitous bloody rhododendron was in danger of dying out, instead of surrounding half the houses in England with grimy caves of hollow greenery. Take Frogmore, for example, a charming house, breathing the spirit of Augustan civilisation, which ought to be surrounded by plantings as graceful as itself. Queen Victoria was not content to dwarf it by the elephantine expression of her woe, Albert's mausoleum; she crushed it with giant causeways and Fingal's caves of grim shrubbery, featuring of course the ghastly rhododendron, which, when not dripping darkly, blazes briefly in mangled clots of egg, tomato and bacon colours … On gardeners' Sundays, the enthusiast is hard put to weed out of his itinerary those gardens which glory in 'massed displays of rhododendrons and azalea', where the sweet variety of English gardening has been flung aside for mountainous injections of peat upon which these gross vegetable aliens may consent to live darkly, sucking light from the air to fuel their annual pyrotechnics.[10]

Nigel Colborn also veers towards the vitriolic as far as rhodos are concerned, lamenting their introduction to the Britain by turn-of-the-century plant-hunters:

> It was during these big collecting years that Rhodomania caught hold of half the gardening population … rhododendrons began to smother the banks and glades of otherwise attractive gardens. Every day a new species or hybrid was introduced, usually from China. Luckily, many of us garden on limy soil and are able to escape them but there was a time when the leafier suburbs of London were in danger of disappearing under a neo-Himalayan understorey of gargantuan proportions. Every June, the most garish colours would scream out from every corner – flesh tones, purples, scarlets, whites, yellows and unimaginable bi-colours with speckles, streaks and blobs of colours in their throats. Then, for the remaining eleven months, the same suburbs would subside to a sombre, suicidal bottle-green … Rhodomania lives on to this day, but now the race is on to breed the smallest races from the yakushimanum hybrids – nicknamed 'yaks'- an ugly name, even for rhododendrons.[11]

If you yourself are a rhodophile, perhaps it would be a little more garden-correct to divert your affinities to a more deserving plant species.

The pen is indeed mightier than the sword.

# 16

# THE AVANT-GARDENER

*It is a common delusion among gardeners that their art is above the whims of fashion.*
—Anne Scott-James

Before embarking on our course of haughtycultural one-upmanship, it is necessary to be quite sure that one has a clear understanding of the term 'avant-garde'. The *Oxford Dictionary* offers 'innovative', 'pioneering', 'progressive', 'fashionable', 'up to the minute', 'an expert' and 'a leader in a given subject'. The desirability of attaining avant-garde status is emphasised by the terrifying antonyms that leap to mind to describe any gardener who isn't – 'conventional', 'traditional', 'conservative', 'ordinary' – in a word, dull and boring.

The objective, then, is to be referred to by the former adjectives, or in phrases such as 'a veritable leader/pioneer in the field of horticulture', 'an innovative and progressive gardener'... in other words, an avant-gardener.

Gaining this status is not merely a case of being able to refurbish your back yard with the rarest and choice of plant materials and the most expensive landscaping, designer furniture, statuary, tools and accoutrements, nor is it one of simple snobbery. This garden one-upmanship is a complex combination of fashion, taste, art and garden language, which instantly determines one's status in the circles of the gardening élite.

The stickiest wicket of all is that of garden design. Avant-gardens do not occur naturally, they are landscaped, preferably by well-known and ruinously expensive landscape architects, or by the blood, sweat and tears of the humble avant-gardener's back and brow.

A few years ago the (wild) cottage garden was all the rage and, pursuing Vita's policy of 'cram, cram, cram' and billowing informality, you could get

*My green thumb came only as a result of the mistakes I made while learning to see things from the plant's point of view.* —H. Fred Ale

149

away with a multitude of sins. The horticultural élite have made things more difficult by becoming more discerning in their ideas of what features constitute an avant-garden. Extensive plantings of natives, and of subtropicals (climate allowing), some topiary, expensive containers, statuary and furniture, and a certain amount of formality is now *de rigeur* in garden design. You can also forget your comfortable old vege plot. The edible garden must now be subjected to the same degree of formality and aesthetics as the rest of the garden, and you must create an ornamental and productive *jardin potager*. Rules for the edible garden are fully observed elsewhere in this volume.

If you live in a temperate area you can aim for a lush subtropical South Pacific rainforest design. It doesn't matter if your back yard is number 32 High Street. You must fill it with luxuriant foliage, flamboyant colour, plants of bold structure, shadowed canopies of ferns, palms and tangled climbers, opulent flowers and bold-leafed underplantings. A banana tree in a large and expensive container will gain you much face. It does not matter if your family need to take the machete to get to the garage, you can show off your subtropical landscaping to your cronies by idly passing them a sprig of screaming red bougainvillea and saying, 'Plants in the subtropical garden do not whisper, they make loud statements.'

If you can combine your subtropical design with an area of obscure native plantings you've got it made. Suitable remarks when showing off indigenous areas include 'It's essential to balance the exotics, my dear,' or 'We must not all plant mini-Sissinghursts, it is vital that we use our admirable native flora to integrate our gardens with their natural landscape.'

The fact that you absolutely hate the claustrophobic but avant-garde rainforest you've planted, consider the natives deadly dull and yearn for the good old days when your garden was a happy colourful jumble of sweetly scented roses and old-fashioned perennials is entirely beside the point.

If you opt for the formal look, here is a list of essential features:

• Walls of old red brick, or dark English yew enclosing everything.
• Paths that run straight as a die and intersect at precise geometric angles.
• An allee of pleached hornbeams or limes leading to an arbour or a statue (armless).
• Standardised shrubs and topiary specimens – everywhere.
• Beds must be bordered by low hedges of *Buxus sempervirens*, or evergreen herbs such lavender, rosemary or santolina. (It is less than avant-garde to whine that topiary and hedges are labour-intensive and you don't know how you'll find time to do anything else.) Do not even consider hedges of privet

or Leyland cypress, which are not only non-U but will turn a tiny sunny garden into a gloomy grotto in a couple of years.

- A summerhouse, gazebo or temple.
- All paths are to be made of old red brick, gravel or enormously expensive pebbles.
- Vast expanses of velvet lawn, hand-mown so that they have the striped texture so admired on the lawns of stately homes in Great Britain.
- A croquet lawn and a large pool (not the swimming kind) are nice optional extras.

You may find the essential features of the formal garden so daunting you will embrace the design concept of a South Seas jungle ambience with little less than religious fervour.

Whichever style you opt for, you must be well aware of the features that are horticulturally beyond the pale. These include:

- Rockeries (see Chapter 9).
- Rose/flowerbeds in the shape of lozenges, ovals or diamonds.
- Extensive plantings of annuals, especially those of pink, yellow, purple or orange.
- Groups of any plantings in the above colours.
- Crazy paving.

The rules are also uncompromisingly strict when it comes to choosing garden statuary and ornaments. Absolutely out are brightly painted grinning gnomes, cupids, Japanese lanterns, pagodas, buddhas (Japanese gnomery), plastic pots and containers, plastic hanging baskets, plastic anything, concrete Venus de Milos, pink flamingos standing on one leg, concrete bird baths, toads, frogs, ducks, cats or any other imitation animals, although you might just get away with one or two of the more expensive terracotta ones.

Beverley Nichols pulls no punches in his condemnation of vulgar garden ornaments:

I have a horror of those leaden cupids who illustrate so gruesomely the ultimate horrors of Bright's disease in many suburban pleasaunces. I cannot bear those grim terracotta pelicans which peer sharply from thickets of bamboos in the grounds of tasteless Midlands persons. I am depressed unutterably by those horrible little German manikins which some people scatter over their properties ... grouping them oh! so archly ... popping out of rhododendrons, or lifting their horrid heads from the lavender hedge. I wish one could deal with garden 'ornaments' as easily ...

But leaden cupids and little terracotta girls have a way of creeping into the gardens of even the strongest-minded people ... The city garden shops are responsible for these monstrosities ... before you know where you are your back garden will look like a Rhine maiden's grotto, and it will be so full of ornaments that there will not be an inch left in which to grow plants. You may weakly agree, at first, to buy one leaden cupid. The cupid will arrive, looking like a very horrible baby that has been petrified just as it was having an acute attack of wind. You think that perhaps if you get a quickly growing ivy you will be able to cover its revolting nakedness.

But you are mistaken. Your purchase of the cupid has caused your name to be entered into the books of the gardening firm as a 'sucker'. The proprietor will sit in his shop rubbing his hands, and licking his lips, and he will remember all the other horrors they have on hand ... that terracotta stork, for example, that was made in Czechoslovakia, and should have been allowed to stay there. It has green eyes and it stands on a cement log tinted, oh so cunningly, to resemble the real wood. And the bird bath, which is made of imitation marble, and has four wrought-iron sparrows perched on the brim (evidently about to be sick into the basin, if you will join me in a little coarseness).[1]

Mention of grottoes and frogs brings to mind the stinging retort made by the English physician-gardener Samuel Johnson when shown the ornamental grotto a gardener was making:

'Would it not be a pretty, cool habitation in the summer, Mr Johnson?' she said.

'I think it would, Madam,' replied he, 'for a toad.'[2]

Not all gardeners are so zealously damning about garden gnomery. Present-day Australian gardener Don Burke, although not personally over-enamoured, puts a case for tolerance:

The ultimate garden personality giveaway is unquestionably the acquisition and positioning of gnomes and other sundry statuary.

There was a time when bored or enterprising gardeners used to carve emus, kangaroos and balls out of living privet. Australia's urban railway stations boasted a whole menagerie of neatly clipped green elephants, flamingos and umbrella-like trees. Urban Transit Authority cost-cutting put paid to the brilliant topiary of generations past and now the most common garden ornamentation is the ubiquitous garden gnome.

Like coathangers in wardrobes, garden gnomes have a habit of breeding at an alarming rate, over-running gardens and spilling out onto driveways, paths and patios. As with any cycle of nature, a form of natural predation always seems to follow over-population. Gnomes have been kidnapped, beheaded or otherwise mutilated and many more have run off to join bands of marauding rogue gnomes ...

Some gnomes cause a lot of problems in a garden – every time you go to get your favourite pair of pliars they are missing.If you suspect your gnome is moving around at night, sprinkle talcum powder all around him on the ground. Check first thing in the morning for tiny footprints in the talc.

But the Australian concrete ornament craze has spread far beyond the humble gnome. A whole plethora of garden characters and animals now exist: cockatoos, emus, kookaburras, frogs, flamingos, kangaroos, eagles, crocodiles, swans, cats, ducks, lions, owls, donkeys and fish are all tended by assorted sleeping Mexicans and sundry Aborigines. Perhaps the strangest one of all is a little Japanese man who sits on the edges of ponds or in the middle of bridges involved in an act of indecency (or perhaps he once had a fishing rod?)!

But no matter what shape they take, all of these concrete mini-ornaments represent an aggressive statement from their owners: 'This is my garden and I'll do what I like with it!' – a bold statement of Australian individualism.[3]

Clearly a case, then, of selecting one's garden ornaments with great care because as Mr Burke concludes, 'one's man's gnome is another man's gargoyle.'

So to pieces that will be approved of in the avant-garden. Hand-glazed coloured pots and terracotta containers (the larger the better) ornamented with swags of grapes and garlands are eminently suitable, especially since both are hideously expensive. Rhubarb and seakale forcing pots and old chimney pots add a nice touch, but they must be well tucked into the vegetation, and you must resist the temptation to plant anything in them. Sundials and bird baths will pass, just, as long as they are not concrete; old metal watering cans and churns, stone troughs and sinks and wire hanging baskets are permissible as smaller *objets d'art*. Larger ornaments, including gazebos, pergolas, bridges and beehives (occupied or not), give a pleasant rural air even if you live a stone's throw from the motorway.

You have progressed through the avant-garden design and ornamentation test, but beware of complacency. Although you have purchased approved ornaments they must be discreetly and correctly placed, and care must be taken not to ruin the total effect by the selection of badly chosen furniture. Avant-garde bits and pieces set the seal on an avant-garden.

Furniture sneered at and best avoided includes supermarket folding chairs, loungers with excessive padding, all-in-one table and bench units, 'Olde Worlde' aluminium 'wrought-iron' table and chair sets, old sewing machine tables, and white plastic stacking chairs and tables – these last, absolutely the kiss of death.

Opt instead for Lutyens benches or Chinese Chippendale jobs, and old-fashioned deckchairs made from wood and canvas – tastefully executed reproduction ones will do, but genuinely antique ones are much better. If your budget can't stretch to these, select furniture fashioned from plain wood and steel; umbrellas to go with them must be of unbleached calico. Floral/jungle print anything is both vulgar and revolting.

You have all the correct trimmings and trappings in place – now to the nitty gritty of which plants to select. If you really can't take the formal, the subtropical or the native designs outlined above and are determined to have an avant-garde flower garden, it is possible, with due consideration.

Almost every season, certain plants are top of the avant-garde list while others become top of the hit list. You really need to be on your toes to keep up, but in general the élitist gardener can't get enough old roses – rambling, shrub or climbing varieties. Many achieve monstrous, viciously thorny growth and bloom for only a month of the year but they are desperately avant-garde. Lashings of silver foliage are indicative of extreme good taste, as are oceans of pinks, irises, foxgloves, delphiniums, nicotiana, ferns, lilies, violets and pansies, and *Alchemilla mollis*. For the water garden, *Gunnera manicata*, primulas, rodgersias and hostas are mandatory, and for nearer the house look for climbers such as wisteria and clematis, and any plant material with foliage that might be described as 'bold' or 'architectural'.

As you should have miles of brick walls to cover, climbing plants are essential. Naked brickwork or trellis, like naked soil, is to be avoided at all costs, and while on the subject of trellis, make sure you do not buy the bendy green or white plastic kind.

The avant-gardener employs climbers through old fruit trees, over gazebos and pergolas, over steel hooped 'temples', up rustic pole frames, over verandahs and on colonnades. Approved varieties of climbing plants include vines, especially *Vitis cognetiae*, single-flowered roses such as 'Wedding Day' and 'Mermaid', and aged wisterias.

There are of course many other acceptable plants that may be employed as climbers and as border plants, but they are too diverse to be listed here. The space is better devoted to what not to plant.

Beastly blooms include any salvias other than the perennial varieties, chry-santhemums, gladiolus, Afro-French marigolds, hybrid tea roses, begonias (es-pecially those ghastly waxen technicolour pink ones), bright pink flowering cherry trees, pampas grasses, calceolarias, and mesembryanthemum or portulaca daisies that come in colours so bright they reach out and grab you by the jugular.

Conifer beds are also non-U these days, according to gardening guru Christopher Lloyd:

> Those little squat figures sitting on rockeries are not always gnomes. Some of them are conifers doing duty. Most such are man-selected, not known in the wild, and doubtless they reflect man's hopes and aspirations in some kinky way. 'They provide full stops and vertical accents,' you will be told by those sufficiently articulate to put such claptrap into words.[4]

On the whole, beds are not approved of in the avant-garden. They smack too much of corporation planting schemes visited upon traffic island beds and public places crammed with bedding-out plants in vile shades of orange, magenta and bilious yellow.

The avant-gardener prefers 'mixed borders' rather than beds, and requisite plantings for these include, in addition to flowers from the desirable list, shrubs, the odd smallish tree, bulbs, annuals (discreetly chosen, even more discreetly placed), foliage and 'texture' plants, and drifts of perennials, all padded out with old-fashioned roses. Shrubs in the mixed border should not be allowed to be boring and to grow on their own; hybrid clematises romping through them provide added colour and interest.

If your choice of garden statuary is indicative of your true gardening personality, so too is your use of colour. This is a contentious subject among avant-gardeners and one on which you can be judged harshly and come horribly unstuck. We are forewarned by Germaine Greer on the use of plants of vibrant colour:

> Much could be done to mitigate the painful dazzle of the average suburban planting of polyanthus, aubretia, coleus, forsythias and prunus, if seedsmen would only leave off assorting the colours of their varieties. The eye aches at the mere picture of mixed varieties named 'Colour Parade', 'Illumination', 'Mardi-gras', 'Fiesta Gitana' and 'Bright Lights'. To see the plants themselves dancing in the summer sun is to experience the ultimate in restless visual blare.[5]

It is avant-garde to use bold colour, but you must do it according to élitist-gardener policy – that is, you should place all your 'hot' colours together in one border ('in' phrase: 'my brazen border'), and all your pastels in another.

If you lack confidence in your ability to handle colour you can bluff by planting a series of monochromatic areas, announcing sternly and authoritatively, 'One-colour planting schemes are so much more soothing and so much less distracting than multi-coloured ones, don't you think?' You will probably be very bored with your insipid soothing garden but it will be avant-garde.

Even the best of gardeners come unstuck with their colour schemes, and Australian gardener-writer Barbara Wenzel is no exception:

> Another careful plan that went astray was my colour scheme. It had been my firm intention to restrict my palette, apart from greens, to white, silver/grey and pale pink, with a frieze of blue provided by the lavender. The premise was deeply flawed from the outset; most grey plants have yellow flowers … The next defector from the grand plan was the lavender, which proved to have flowers of a deep and vivid purple instead of the azure haze I had in mind. It is quite extraordinary how many different hues can be adjudged by the writers of plant catalogues to be 'pink' or 'blue'. 'Pink' can be anything from the shrillest salmon (watch for the descriptor 'coral') to a magenta which induces a headache (a favourite euphemism is 'deep pink'). 'Blue' is almost never anything of the sort; the indigo-violet end of the colour spectrum is what they really mean. If you do get hold of a real blue like *Salvia azurea* it looks just awful with all the mauves and purples you will undoubtedly already have.
>
> On the whole, the clash between all the warring shades of pink was the hardest to sort out. Initially I spent a lot of time pulling out salmon dianthus, puce rose campion *Lychnis coronaria* and carmine cranesbills. Even my thriving clump of Japanese iris had to come out as they turned out to be mauve instead of white and were looking very sickly with the shell-pink 'Chaucer' roses behind them. I had a lot of trouble with the colour of all the irises I ordered. Some tall bearded white ones turned out to be most elaborately patterned with mauve stitches and frills and falls. Another supposedly pale pink iris opened in a glorious show of purple and brown … by dint of much clipping, moving and discarding, a reasonably coherent colour scheme emerged … all banished plants were replaced with white-flowered ones to avoid any potential clashes.
>
> There finally came a day when I laid down my shears and prepared to enjoy the painstakingly pastel picture I had laboured for. That was when the oranges and lemons began to ripen.[6]

An avant-garden will not be without a water garden. Top of the scale come large lakes. Large pools of classical design are tolerable, but beware a turquoise jelly-mould fibreglass job filled with bright pink waterlilies, which will bring instant life-long horticultural damnation.

If you cannot rise to a swan-studded lake or large ornamental pool and have to resort to the dig-a-hole-in-the-ground type, ensure that it is discreetly lined with black polythene or butyl rubber, and sealed at the edges by rocks, old bricks or costly ready-made paving stone.

It is important to remember that the avant-garden water feature is designed to show off the water, not a writhing tangle of oxygenating weed or duckweed. A few expensive waterlilies add a pleasing touch, but do not allow them to cover the entire surface of the water. Likewise, the pool must not become a seething mass of ravenous piranha-like bright orange goldfish; a few give the pool a nice sense of life and movement, but only a few. Try to resist the fancier goggle-eyed and hideously marked oriental varieties.

Every gardener will want some kind of statuary to enhance the water area. The same rules apply as for those ornaments throughout the rest of the garden. Fountains cast in concrete and figures of ill-mannered small boys urinating are in extreme bad taste. Anything made of bronze is highly acceptable, weathered stone permissible, and terracotta – just okay.

If garden space allows, the avant-gardener will need to give thought to the correct trees to plant. Approved favourites include Japanese maples, *Acer* species, Irish yews, silver birches, white-flowering cherries such as *Prunus* 'Tai Haku' (don't touch anything pink), the maidenhair tree (*Ginkgo biloba*), variegated tulip tree (*Liriodendron tulifera* 'Aureomarginatum'), and you can't go wrong with repeated plantings of the weeping silver pear (*Pyrus sacilifolia* 'Pendula'), or allees of lime, polar or hornbeam.

Tasteless trees for urban landscapes include pink-flowering cherries, (particularly *Prunus* 'Kazan' and 'Amanagawa'), golden weeping willows, Leyland cypress, weeping silver birches, purple-leafed *Prunus* 'Niger' and large conifer species. Small refined ones discreetly placed 'for accent during the colder barer months' are permissible.

The rules regarding fruit growing in the avant-garden are a little more relaxed, but features that will bring one much status are espaliered fruit grown against walls of antique brick; an orchard of ancient fruit trees through which clematis and rampant roses such as 'Kiftsgate' throw their stranglehold; grapevines, especially if gnarled and ancient; and tender fruits such as peaches or figs grown in a conservatory of Victorian design.

Last but not least is advice to the would-be avant-gardener who has only a small town section or courtyard. Lack of space? Rejoice! Less work, and the city courtyard, deck or patio garden is very 'in' and easier to run along avant-gardening lines than its large rural counterpart. You don't need acres of paddock or rolling park land – even a windowbox or a grouping of properly planted trendy containers constitutes an avant-garden.

All the basic rules discussed still apply to the city gardener but there are several refinements that can enhance tiny urban plots immensely:

- No-lawn areas – old flagstones, red brick, gravel or pebbles from which creeping thymes or camomile creep – are desperately *de rigeur*.
- Artificial window frames mounted on enclosing walls or trellises and backed by mirrors give a trendy *trompe d'oeil* look in addition to creating an illusion of size and space.
- A plethora of glazed or terracotta pots, or hypertufa containers planted with avant-garde approved selected dwarf trees (maples) and shrubs, bulbs in season, selected annuals, weeping patio (never miniature) roses, herbs and hostas. Ornamental New Zealand flaxes (*Phormium*) and cabbage trees (*Cordyline*) are the avant-gardener landscaper's dream, especially if your city garden is in England or Europe where they are gratifyingly expensive.
- If your pocket handkerchief is an awkward shape it is not done to try to attempt disguise. Avant-gardener philosophy embraces challenge. If your plot is long and narrow make a focal point of the shape by planting an avenue of English yews down both sides. In five years' time your garden will be steeped in funereal gloom and resemble an unkempt city graveyard, but it will be original.
- If you really feel avenues of yews might be a bit over the top you may substitute an evergreen framework of selected camellias and hebes – nothing too hectic in colour, though.
- Lashings of hanging baskets and windowboxes, but nothing plastic.

The rules for statuary and furniture with which to adorn the city avant-garden are subject to the same discrimination as rural gardens, except perhaps where a water feature such as a lion's head spouting water may be attached to an aged brick wall. An old church font is also an original feature, and though both may look as though they are providing holy water, they add a classy touch.

Features that absolutely should not be countenanced in the urban avant-gardener's plot include flashy red Hitachi/Hibachi barbecues, rotary clotheslines (disguise by training *Rosa* 'Mermaid' to cascade like an umbrella from its top, and dry all laundry in the dryer), mock balustrades, columns or fancy screen-block walling, crazy paving, rockeries, and Neo-Victorian street lamps or lanterns which, though they look pleasant, are considered to impart a certain artificiality.

The owner of an avant-garde city garden may well have enhanced one of his or her walls with a garden room or conservatory of Victorian or Edwardian design. If, when you purchase your property, there is one incumbent of aluminium or polythene have it demolished immediately in favour of one constructed of wood and glass. Do not even consider a kitset. Great kudos is gained by inviting other aspiring avant-gardeners to take morning or afternoon tea in your garden room, which should be chock-full of a mixture of plants in containers or narrow soil borders. Avoid flashy plants such as fleshy begonias, gloxinias and orchids, but incorporate tender subtopicals, rare ferns, palms, cycads and the odd African violet for a little restrained colour.

Approved furniture for the garden room is of wicker or natural wood, and all soft furnishings should be of pastel-coloured chintz; resist the temptation to have anything boldly patterned which could create a vulgar jungly effect. Do not countenance fringed and knotted macrame pot hangers, tanks of tropical fish, budgerigars in cages or parrots on perches. Smelly old dog baskets containing smelly old dogs and sleeping felines are traditional avant-garde furnishings. Wicker table tops should be littered with David Austin rose catalogues, Hillier's shrub and tree manuals, *Country Life* and *Home and Garden* magazines and RHS journals, even if your conservatory is in an inner-city location.

This guide for the aspiring avant-gardener is almost complete, but in addition to designing and planting the garden it is finally necessary to be aware of suitable clothing to wear. Lesser gardeners have been refused admittance to the ranks of the horticultural élite for turning out in the sort of garden attire worn by ordinary gardeners.

This includes any garments of vulgar and garish colours made of lycra, brinylon (including ski-pants), and mock parachute silk as in shell-suits. Anoraks with fake lambswool linings may be warm and practical but they are not trendy and therefore definitely non-U. The ultimate in bad taste for the female avant-gardener is a fleecy-lined jogging suit of peach or purple.

Skimpy shorts and swimsuits may not be worn by either sex. 'Bermuda' style shorts are acceptable in the hottest of weather as long as they are not of a multi-coloured jungle-print or 'life's a beach' type pattern, but of 'natural' fabrics in beige, dark green or navy blue. The same goes for all shirts and pants. Garments of denim are acceptable as long as they bear boutique designer labels and have not been bought in the local surplus store.

Headgear should comprise light panama or pure cotton hats in summer, and tweed caps or pure wool balaclavas in winter. Woolly bobble-hats are not permitted, particularly those with slogans across the front.

The avant-gardener wears fingerless or leather gloves. Like bobble-hats, woolly mittens are inexcusable. Pure lambswool is *de rigeur* for all sweaters, and though there is the small problem of their needing hand-washing every time you leave the garden, that is no excuse to defect to man-made fibres such as acrylic. Avant-garden persons may comfortably wear a jacket of oiled-green or a woollen Swanndri (of traditional colours) during the colder months.

Above all, do not think you can sneak out into the garden wearing a pair of gym shoes. This will damn you irrevocably if espied by a true avant-gardener. The only acceptable footwear for avant-gardeners is a pair of 'hunter' green rubber gummies or wellies in damp weather, and a pair of neat leather brogues in fine.

Congratulations! You have diligently studied class in the garden, adorned the plot with horticulturally approved plantings, furniture and statuary, and your person with suitable gardening attire. Go forth to your avant-garden as a truly seasoned avant-gardener.

# 17

# LES HERBES ET LE JARDIN POTAGER

*Rich chocolate earth studded emerald green, frothed with the white of cauliflowers,*
*jewelled with purple globes of eggplant, and the scarlet wealth of tomatoes.*
—Doris Lessing

An essential element in the avant garden is, of course, *le jardin des herbes*
and *le jardin potager*.

You can't fail planting herbs. Every single one of them is fashionable, regardless of how large or floppy they are, or how invasive their root systems. The
more obscure their origins, the more they are sought after. That they are more
or less useless on the home front for medicinal or culinary purposes is irrelevant
– they will do wonders for one's avant-gardener image.

When other gardeners call, family should be instructed to say: 'I think he/
she is meditating in the herb garden.' The herb garden has just the right ambience, as well as providing a fitting retreat for gentle gardeners of mature years.
It was, after all, in meditation among his peas and herbs that a certain monk
named Mendel discerned the laws of heredity that are the basis of modern
biological science.

French terms are mandatory when referring to one's *herbularis* – one is going
to grow only *fines herbes*, and *herbes pour le chef* – suitable for fragrant *bouquet
garnis*. The generally applauded *herbes* in this category include chervil, tarragon
(French, not Russian, which is supposed to have a coarse flavour – *entente* wins
over *detente*), chives and parsley.

It is necessary to cultivate at least four different varieties of chives since they
are reputed to sharpen the appetite and stimulate the kidneys. Garlic chives are
*de rigeur* in the organic herbalist's *jardin des herbes*, and used as companion
plants they are said to deter insect pests.

Parsley, though considered a common herb because of its misuse as wilted
sprigs of garnish, has an impressive medical history. Homer reports that the
charioteers used to feed it to their horses before going into battle to give
them strength, and modern medical science proclaims it an invaluable source

161

of vitamins A, B and C. Chervil is a must in any discerning gardener's soup. Among the more common herbs it is permissible to grow mint (at least four different varieties in an expensive container) and rosemary, since roast lamb without either is a culinary sin. Sage, thyme and oregano are approved for flavouring Mediterranean-type cuisine, which is very 'in' at the moment. All edible herbs must of course be interplanted with drifts of lavender, which is even more 'in'.

The manner in which you present your *fines herbes* is equally important – a sunny corner of the vege plot – ah, slip of the tongue – *le jardin potager* – won't do. They must be displayed in knot gardens of Elizabethan design that require several tons of old red bricks, or in geometrically precise parterres bordered by neatly clipped labour-intensive hedges of *Buxus sempervirens*. The construction of such elaborate gardens will require you to call in contractors, will take weeks and ruin you financially.

Firing in the mandatory unattractive vegetation will take only a few hours but you must give great thought to the construction of the herb garden. You should aim to recreate something on the lines of a grand medieval monastery garden. If you are fortunate enough to have a house with arched verandahs these will lend a distinct cloistered ambience. Take no notice of the neighbours' grins if you are transforming a modest plot fronting the main road in town. They are just the sort who would bung their herbs in the corner of the vege plot.

If the grandiose design sounds a bit like too much hard work, you can get by with plantings of herbs in trendy containers. Herb wheels or ladders are extremely acceptable – for these you must haunt expensive antique shops for ancient wagon wheels and wooden ladders (don't even think about using an old metal or aluminium one).

You should be aware that the selection of herbs the helpful garden centre staff recommend as mandatory will all have totally different growth habits and cultivational requirements. When first planted they all grow lustily and behave beautifully, then angelica, which requires shade and damp feet, will either burgeon forth glossy giant leaves or snuff it, according to whether your soil is damp or dry. Bronze fennel, beloved for the aesthetic appeal of its feathery plumes and its culinary benefits, will soar to six feet. The mints with sly stealth will indulge in a subterranean romp, pushing up healthy new shoots throughout the herb garden – and everywhere else. Herbs of more restrained growth habit such as rosemary, the sages, thymes and oreganos, which worship the sun, will grow pale and anaemic as they are overwhelmed by their lustier companions. In short, the 'recommended' selection of herbs will quickly outgrow their trendy spoke and rung confines, ending up in a sprawling, unsightly jumbled mass.

It is probably better, therefore, to confine the lusty treasures to individual containers, but the more eccentric or innovative these are, the better. Old boots, kitchen utensils, relics from the farm shed, old baths, wheelbarrows, boats, or even old lavatory pans and cisterns – any of these will be acceptable as long as they are 'imaginative'. A sensible collection of the herbs most commonly required for culinary purposes can also be grown in attractive terracotta pots just outside the kitchen door, but this might be considered just a teeny weeny bit boring.

It is absolutely not done to grow straight rows of spuds and carrots any more, and in any case such mundane edibles are out – designer veg are in.

The fads and fashions of gardendom decree that the erstwhile vege plot be referred to as *le jardin potager* and contain as many flowers and herbs as edible items. All must be grown together in as gloriously abandoned a mêlée as possible – never mind if you can't find the caulis and cabbages, as long as they are nesting there somewhere beneath the giant hairy leaves of the globe artichoke you are doing good, as the old saying goes. Accept now (and save yourself a lot of grief) that it is absolutely beyond the pale to indulge in plant discrimination or segregation in the potager.

The legendary and totally learned *Reader's Digest New Encyclopaedia of Gardening* defines '*potager* gardening' as 'edible landscaping'. In terms for the layman this simply means encouraging flowers and vegetables to be happy bedfellows – not a bad idea these days since many modern gardens often do not have the space for them to inhabit separate gardens. This is not a new concept – in the monastery gardens of medieval times the monks grew vegetables and medicinal herbs together, usually without incident, despite some of the latter being desperately toxic. Nor is the battle between the edible and the inedible in the heart of a gardener a new one:

> The garden was divided into four square beds bordered with box. Madame Magloire grew vegetables in three of them, while in the fourth, the bishop had planted flowers; there were also a few fruit trees. She had once said to him with gentle malice, 'Your Grace always makes the best of things, yet this bed produces nothing. Salads would be more useful than bouquets.'
>
> 'Madame Magloire,' replied the bishop, 'you are misguided. The beautiful is as useful as the useful – more so, perhaps.' — Victor Hugo[1]

Robert was an old Scots gardener who scorned all flowers together. They were but garnishings, childish toys, trifling ornaments for ladies' chimney-shelves. It was towards his cauliflowers and peas and cabbage that his heart grew warm. His preference for the more useful growths was such that cabbages were found invading the flower plots, and an outpost of savoys was once discovered in the centre of the lawn. —Robert Louis Stevenson[2]

So where did this word *potager* creep in? It comes from the French *potage*, a thick vegetable soup liberally laced with herbs. Seized by the élite of horticultural society, the word has been extended to *potager* as in the phrase, *le jardin potager* – the edible or cook's garden. It is an upmarket name for the backyard vege plot where designer veg have ousted useful items such as swedes, parsnips, carrots and turnips. Spuds are permissible as long as they are of the latest hybrid variety, but mandatory are any plants with names like 'mange-tout' (sugar-peas), ruby chard, *Lollo Rosso* 'Foxy' (auburn-headed lettuces) and bok choy (Chinese cabbage). Corpulent cabbages are only acceptable in the *potager* if they are purple and planted behind a dwarf hedge of box or golden *Lonicera nitida* for aesthetic appeal.

On the whole, the concept of the *potager* is more important than the produce, but to gain avant-gardener status it is essential not only to grow one's own vegetables but to be seen to do so in a fashionable manner. One must be able to join in intense and intensely boring conversations with other *potager* paranoiacs about the state of one's zucchini or kohlrabi.

If you have an orchard of ancient fruit trees (cascading old-fashioned roses rather than fruit) like that at Sissinghurst, you've got it made. Fruit trees herein must all be of the dwarf variety or espaliered. This is a method of pruning or training trees into rigid patterns by tying their branches to wire fences. Anyway, fruit, according to American gardeners Beard and McKie, is vastly overrated. It is defined in their *Gardening Dictionary* as the seed-bearing part of the plant which is eaten by birds or worms, drops off, gets funny spots, rots, isn't what was pictured in the catalogues, tastes like a glove or doesn't appear at all.

Messrs Beard and McKie note that everybody loves fruit trees, both for their delicious fruit and fragrant blossom, but:

> They are afflicted with hundreds of diseases and disorders, including trunk drool, root slobber, bark slime, stem drizzle, mush wood, limbsludge, twigfuzz, craptid, crud leaf, petal smudge, sprout drop, munge, dampcurl, bud custard, splotchblossom, devil's whiskers, lobe dropsy, creeping dinge, grey gange, sperl, flenge, munge, morbisy, and snet. The only practical preventive method is to dispose of the young trees immediately by burning or burying.[3]

The *potager* gardener certainly doesn't bother with apples or pears. He grows peaches and figs in a conservatory or against a 'warm wall' (preferably Elizabethan and of antique brick). A mulberry tree is also an extremely desirable feature, especially if it is ancient and is decorated beneath with lichen-covered rustic seats. A 'nuttery' is even more desirable and quite impeccably avant-garde. A soft fruit cage is a nice addition to the potager since it generally serves the dual purpose of also being a bird sanctuary.

Another must for the *potager* gardener is that all produce must be seen to be organically grown. The use of any chemicals is beyond the pale. Smile conde-scendingly when the 'spray everything that moves' tribe raise their eyebrows at the state of your home-grown produce.

True, it is pock-marked by flea beetles, scalloped by pea and bean weevils and riddled with wireworm holes, but you are happy to share the harvest of your modest *potager* with slugs, snails and everything that chews, creeps and crawls, as long as it is chemical free.

Get even with these philistine growers of unblemished but totally tasteless tomatoes by giving them some of your (blemished) but sweet, tasty organically grown varieties. The tiny cocktail varieties with names such as 'Sweet One Hundred', 'Sun Cherry', 'Tiny Tim', or 'Sweet Bite' are infinitely more fash-ionable in the *potager* than huge varieties like 'Beefsteak', 'Grosse Lisse' or 'Moneymaker' which, while they make a good job of feeding the wife and four kids, are large and vulgar.

Giant melons, pumpkins and marrows also come into this category. It is best to experiment with difficult-to-grow but aesthetically pleasing ornamental gourds, zucchini, capsicums, asparagus, and dwarf anything. Do not even con-sider cultivating whopping great crunchy lettuce; there are now so many hy-brids with frilly, coloured leaves that it is acceptable to use as them as ornamental border plants.

While on the subject of borders, the one place – the only place – where it is permitted to cultivate screaming orange and acid yellow marigolds is as compan-ion plants in the *potager*, where, like garlic, they are said to deter bugs. Similarly, every self-respecting *potager* gardener will present his or her vegetables threaded through with billowing drifts of edible flowers – nasturtiums, violets, calendulas, giant borage, pansies, violas, sweet peas, anchusa and others of their ilk.

Other unusual vegetables that should definitely have a place in the *potager* might include salsify and scorzonera, globe, Jerusalem and Chinese artichokes, aubergines, chillies, capsicum, chicory, celeriac, endive, ornamental spinach and seakale (the kids will loathe both) and stands of rainbow-coloured beet which they may eat out of sheer curiosity. It doesn't matter if you don't know how to pronounce, spell, cook or eat them as long as you are seen to grow them.

Vegetables to spurn include common or garden cabbages, swedes, turnips, Brussels sprouts and cauliflowers. Huge Spanish onions are out but dwarf onion sets are in – these are small onions which, planted in the soil one day, are transferred elsewhere by the birds the next.

Non-gardeners ( the supermarket set) may have the temerity to question the economic viability of growing one's own veges. You know in your heart that they have a point since each one of your tomatoes probably cost as much as a kilo of the supermarket variety, and each pea pod about a dollar, but no way are you going to admit it. Of course the cost of the little punnets of seedlings was negligible – it was the stakes and ties, fertiliser, and organic dust and toxin-free spray, not to mention the time and labour, and crop losses to diseases and pests, that shot the price up.

There are those who are reluctant to gather their harvests. Like the eccentric art collector who gloats over his masterpieces in a secret room, English vegetable gardener John Carey cannot bear his crops to be picked and eaten. He wants to grow and behold his vegetables as an aesthetic experience:

> As vegetable gardeners aren't primarily concerned with eating they harbour, like librarians, a tidy-minded dislike of anyone who actually wants to eat the commodities they're in charge of. To have to uproot cabbages, say, from a row, and hand them over for cooking, is always an annoyance. The gaps look unsightly, like snapped-off teeth. A stalwart, unbroken line of cabbages, on the other hand, with their hearts tight as fists and their purple outer leaves spread to catch the dew, raises your spirit every time you visit them.[4]

Other more plaintive views:

> Nothing discourages the amateur gardener like watching his family devour his whole garden at one meal. —Dan Bennett

> Gulp.
> I loved my vegetable garden.
> So here is my sad ballad:
> I nurtured it for months
> And ate it in one salad.
> —Arnold Zarett

There is, of course, the small problem of *glut* in the *potager* also, when every crop matures at the same time. A slave to fad and fashion, the 'grow your own' school, and to the feeling of romanticism engendered by your pretty and productive *potager*, you may be forced to crunch daily a hundred radishes, and accept that every lettuce and cabbage will come to maturity on the same day. Self-sufficiency may be defined as the method of growing vast supplies of the kind of vegetables one would never normally eat.

Your productive *potager* will force you to spend hours freezing, jamming, juicing, saucing, pickling and pureeing while the rest of the garden goes to pot. The trick is to turn this vulgar glut to your own advantage by being seen to do good works. Distribute your stringy beans, pock-marked peas and blighted tomatoes to various charitable organisations throughout the neighbourhood as 'wholesome, chemical-free home produce'. If you do not, your family will become vegetarian slave labourers who own a dozen chest freezers.

Some have become so discouraged they have thrown in the towel altogether. In 1970, in the days when a *potager* was still a common or garden vege plot, a despairing K.R. Flitscher wrote a heartfelt letter to the editor of *New Zealand Gardener*:

Dear Sir

Many periodicals, including your own, publish regular gardening features whose authors seem wedded to the idea that gardening is a worthwhile, even rewarding, pastime.

This is rubbish and I think it is time to hear the other side of the story. (Indeed, it seems that many of the hallowed traditions of New Zealand life deserve a second look and some detailed analysis.) I therefore offer for publication this summary of my own horticultural observations and reseaches in the hope that it may do something to restore a proper perspective.

Yours faithfully

K.R. Flitscher

## A PLACE OF TORMENT

Have you ever trodden on a garden rake? With the tines pointing upwards?

If so, you have suffered uniquely, for there are few weapons capable of administering punishment to feet and face simultaneously – but you spare little thought for such matters as the tines drive deeply into your flesh and the handle leaps upwards to catch your nose.

I happened to me recently and I believe it will prove a great blessing. During my convalescence, for the first time I thought logically about gardening. I calculated. I analysed. I remembered. And finally I came to a conclusion.

I shall withdraw from the ranks of the home vegetable gardeners. This archaic custom shall have no further part in modern life.

Since colonial times it has been tradition that the New Zealand male will, upon marriage, take spade in hand and dig a garden. The labour involved seems to be part of the bride price, which is not fully paid until complete paralysis sets in in the later stages of old age.

We have outgrown the need for this exhausting labour. Sir James Wattie, Lord Birdseye and others of their ilk have done mankind a service by providing us with a wide variety of readily available packaged foods. What we must do is recognise the gift they and refrigeration have conferred upon us. Then we must convince our wives.

This may not be so easy, so I have marshalled some of my own observations so that they may help you marshall your arguments. Then, next year, as you thin your carrots, you can try to decide where you failed.

My vegetable plot measures 40ft by 25ft – a fairly normal size. Digging it takes me six hours. This figure includes stoppages to roll a smoke (and smoke it), and occasional pauses for rest and contemplation. But this is unrealistic in that it does not include time spent in deciding to start, getting the tools out, putting them away because it looks like rain, getting them out again, going to town to buy a dozen beers to drink afterwards, and those horticultural discussions over the back fence which usually end up in the consumption of a dozen bottles of beer with a neighbour.

All told then, it takes me two full days to dig my garden. That is a whole weekend. And since I dig it twice a year, once in spring and once in autumn, I lose two whole weekends a year just in preparation.

But the time loss becomes far greater as I go through all the other motions (we must remember, of course, that at each stage the preparatory moves must be made – getting the tools out and so on). Sowing is comparatively quick, once I have remembered to buy the fertiliser and seeds, but my troubles are just beginning.

Weeds are far more prolific than vegetables. They germinate more quickly, grow faster and are more likely to survive flood, drought and pestilence. (Have you ever heard of blight attacking ragwort?) They must be removed manually. And the tragedy is that we cannot win. Each time I finish weeding my garden I am so confident that not one foreign body has escaped. Three days later the whole patch shows a flush of green and I must admit defeat once more.

I never cease to wonder at the powers of survival exhibited by those weeds. If I pass my hoe within six inches of a cabbage, I kill it. But I can pull a weed out by the roots, chop it in half, jump on it and generally maltreat it in a variety of ways, yet still it manages to live. In fact, it and the pieces which were separated from the main body during the torture test all manage to survive and create a healthy colony in the middle of my radishes.

However, by persistence, I can keep my weeds more or less under control. But having protected my fragile seedlings from the invading hordes, I am expected to turn around and destroy them. The illogic of this thinning process appals me. I plant the seeds reluctantly. Then I turn over a new leaf and coddle them, fertilise them, water them and weed them. And then I pull more than half of them out.

This is clearly absurd, especially as the justification I am given is that I am, in fact, increasing the yield. Pull out most of the plants to increase the yield? It is obviously a plot, hatched by the seed suppliers to make us use more seeds than necessary. This unethical behaviour has contributed to my decision to hang up my shovel.

But even more overwhelming is the brutality of the thinning process. The plants we leave in seem to wilt in sorrow at the passing of their brothers, but how many gardeners bother to spare a minute for the feelings of a bereaved parsnip? We give them a little water, but how many mourners at a funeral would consider hosing down to be a gesture of sympathy?

No true humanitarian can witness this wanton cruelty and remain a gardener. I, for one, refuse to do it again.

Recovered from my sorrow, I find that all is now routine. I continue to weed, I water, I spray, and I watch. But what has been the cost?

In terms of my time, the eventual harvest represents at least half of every weekend from September to May. This is a staggering waste of man hours, and I called my wife away from the dishes she was washing to tell her about it. She was unimpressed. In fact, she made several points quite forcefully. In order that you can marshall counter-arguments in advance, I summarise them here. She felt:

a) The time I spent in the garden was a good thing because it kept me out of the house;

b) If I would only get on with the job instead of merely pottering, my garden would be so successful that I wouldn't have to find excuses; and

c) It was hardly realistic to count time spent in the pub discussing gardens as time worked.

I tried to point out that if I spent more time in the pub I wouldn't have to get out into the garden to keep out of the house at weekends. She went away, muttering something about how much time she was able to get off from dishes, cooking, cleaning and so on to go out boozing with the girls.

The waste of time, staggering though it is, is only part of my case against gardening.

My accident with the rake finally convinced me that a man is a fool to risk his life among the dangerous assortment of weapons he is required to use to till the soil. I once impaled my left boot, narrowly missing my toes as I thrust a garden fork deep into the earth. And I vividly recall the occasion when the spade handle I was leaning on broke – as I fell I nearly ran myself through with the jagged end.

Not only are the tools themselves dangerous, but we do ourselves great harm in many indirect ways as we use them. How many blisters do you get each spring? I generally manage 10 – one for each finger.

During the early years of our marriage my wife knitted me a pair of fingerless mittens to protect the palms of my hands. I wore them until an acquaintance dropped around to see me one day while I was labouring among my vegetables. I felt that his mind was not on our conversation – his eyes kept wandering to my hands. He finally said that he admired my garden ensemble, which he felt was just right for a hot day in January – boots, shorts and mittens.

Since then, I have put up with blisters.

Muscular aches are another problem. A hard day on the end of a spade in early spring almost always means that I am confined to bed for a week afterwards. At such times I hear all sorts of snide comments from the kitchen about lack of fitness, but I show my self-control by continuing to read quietly.

Early summer brings a new problem. I like to get my shirt off; the sun's new heat feels pleasant upon my back. As I kneel to weed my beetroot I work slowly to avoid any recurrence of the muscular trouble from which I have just recovered. (Also, crouched behind the peas, I cannot be seen from the house, and it seems silly to waste such a situation.)

Thus, four hours later, as I near the end of a row, I begin to feel a slight burning sensation. Too late, I realise that I have fallen into another of the traps which await the home gardener – I am badly sunburned.

My wife is not sadistic, but I never have any trouble in persuading her to apply that icy lotion to my over-heated back. I think that she must feel glad at last that she can do something to help me. As I squirm and wriggle I feel that it might be better to endure the sunburn, but I don't think I could deprive my wife of one of her little pleasures.

Thus the physical dangers are quite obvious. But even more important are the psychological hurdles which the gardener must leap; particularly the deflation of the ego which invariably accompanies a comparison of my crop with my neighbour's.

I remember a late-night horticultural discussion with a friend. Inevitably, boasts were made, and some of his claims seemed to me to be rather exaggerated. Finally, the subject of beetroot came up. Gleefully, being very proud of my own crop, I challenged him to a weigh-in, confident that his humiliation would be complete.

The contest took place immediately. My largest specimen weighed in at 71b. Then I stood in the moonlight on my back lawn while he split his entry with an axe in order to fit it upon the scales. One needs a very stable personality to withstand traumatic experiences of this kind.

But we do not only suffer by comparison with our neighbours. Man is supposed to be the lord of the universe, or some such nonsense, but the gardener's ego takes another beating when he discovers that he is incapable of outwitting creatures reputed to be on a much lower evolutionary plane.

Dogs find my newly planted garden an admirable place to scratch and deposit their mangled bones. Cats find it an equally desirable place to bury whatever it is that cats bury at the dead of night. The net result is that my carefully planted seeds are hauled out in their thousands and lie helpless on the surface in the morning, an easy prey for those early birds which have defied our proverb by turning vegetarian.

It seems that there is no solution. I knew a man who tied a lot of tin cans to a string which he pulled from the kitchen window at regular intervals throughout the night, setting up a tremendous clanking din. He beat the dogs and cats, but the side-effects were too great. Loss of sleep, the nervous strain of peering into the darkness and wondering 'what's out there?' and the silence of the neighbours who had sent him to Coventry combined to bring about his downfall. As the ambulance took him away and the neighbourhood breathed a collective sigh of relief, I swear I saw a smirk on the face of a watching cat.

So where does all this get the gardener? He bears the scars on both his person and his psyche – raw hands and a brutalised disposition; aching muscles and a complete lack of self-confidence; a sunburned back; a perforated foot and a bruised nose. In return for which he has a superfluity of vegetables. Far more than he can ever use.

I began to realise the futility of it all last year when I decided to demonstrate my generosity by giving away what I could not eat. I packed a carton with two lettuces, a cabbage, a cauliflower, six beetroot and a large bag of peas, and set off around my neighbours to distribute my largesse.

Everywhere I was met by polite refusals. 'Sorry, we already have more than we can use.' After two hours of this I was beginning to get desperate, when I spotted an empty garage as I passed the home of the beetroot king. Quickly I scribbled a note: 'Sorry I missed you, but I thought you might need these,' dumped the carton on his doorstep and raced away before he could return and reject the offer.

Triumphantly I arrived home. There on the doorstep was a bag containing four lettuces, two cabbages, three cauliflowers, a dozen beetroot, and a gigantic stack of peas, beans and rhubarb. On top was a note saying: 'Sorry I missed you, but …'[5]

171

# 18

# HORTUS BOTANICUS LATINICUS

*I love to hear real gardeners talking, the Latin names rolling off their tongues,
sonorous and beautiful. I feel abashed when I take a sleeve and say, 'Do come and
see that pink thing over there.'*
*'Ah,* Centaura hypoleuca. *Very nice,' they say.*
*Never mind, it smiles the same for both of us.* — Pam Brown

Most leisure pursuits – computers, cricket, golf, sailing and horse-racing to name but a few – involve their participants in a jungle of impenetrable terminology. When it comes to gardening, there is a bewildering array of scientific terms to be learned by the novice. All plants are blessed with a scientific name, and many with more than one, and as though this weren't enough, the experts delight in changing them overnight just to keep us on our toes. It is this language of the garden – Hortus Botanicus Latinicus – that proves the biggest stumbling block for the novice avant-gardener.

For a dead language, Latin is doing very nicely. On a visit to an upmarket nursery the amateur gardener is plunged into a scenario where assistants and customers are speaking a foreign tongue and the labels on the plants need subtitles – in English. Nursery catalogues are just as bad, requiring a Latin-English dictionary at hand at all times. Amateurs discover that erstwhile gardening mates have begun to refer to their catmint as *Nepeta faasseni* or *N. mussinii,* leaving them to find their own way in the jungle of botanical Latin.

'Plant names in *Latin,*' you sob. 'I have enough trouble remembering them in English. The whole thing's impossible.'

And so to a crash course in botanical Latin nomenclature.

The scenario: a fashionable nursery which you are visiting with a new friend who is, of course, the coolest of avant-gardeners. The conversation between him and the assistant goes like this:

Avant-gardener. 'Have you a *Juniperis communis* 'Depressa Aurea'?'
Assistant: 'I'm afraid not, but we have *Juniperus squamata* 'Blue Star', which has a divine weeping habit.'
Avant-gardener: 'I am not keen on the common silver *Juniperus*. I prefer the 'Aurea'.' Then, horrors, turning to you he says, 'Don't you agree?'
    You mutter, 'Absolutely, oh, absolutely,' and before you can turn and bolt he is drawing you in again.
Avant-gardener: 'Well, failing the *Juniperus communis*, I simply must put in a *Prunus*. What do you think of *P. pendula* 'Shimidsu Zakura'?'
    'Magnificent!' you lie.
Assistant: 'We're temporarily out of those, but the other species people will kill for is *Prunus pendula* 'Kiku Shidare Zakura'. I think I've got just one left.'
    'Phew,' you think, 'saved by the assistant' – until your friend turns to you and says, 'Mmm, would you go for the 'Shimidsu' or the 'Shidare'?'

Do not despair. You don't have to learn the entire Latin language. From this terrifying dialogue you may notice that it's enough to pick out a few key words. Once these are understood you will be able to speak the lingo with as much savoir-faire as your learned friend.

Plant names are not difficult. They consist of two parts: the genus and species names (usually italicised) and the fancy hybrid or cultivar name. Genus simply means family but that is an untrendy word, so remember to use the former. For example, *Juniperus* covers the whole genus or family of conifers called junipers; '*squamata*' indicates the species of juniper; and the 'Blue Star' bit is the fancy hybrid or cultivar name.

Similarly, the word *Prunus* covers the whole genus of flowering cherries – the impossible Japanese words are their hybrid names. You can get by without remembering these tongue twisters unless you actually want to buy one, in which case you can swot it up beforehand and write it on a piece of paper – or on the palm of your hand so you can glance at it secretly if you want to play it really cool.

You need only remember the genus names to put avant-gardener techniques into operation in smart garden centres or when inspecting the plant materials in another expert's plot. Wave your arm languidly and say, 'That's a very fine *Juniperus/Prunus* you have over there.' Your host will immediately reply, 'Ah yes, *squamata* 'Blue Star' – quite delightful, isn't it?'

The word *pendula* (pendulous) is useful. It simply means weeping or downward-turned. Thus you can declare of any plant that looks the slightest bit droopy: 'The pendulas are so much more attractive, aren't they?'

The next trick is acquiring a few simple colour names to string together

173

with the species and hybrid names. To return to the original conversation and the good *Juniperus communis* 'Depressa Aurea'. The word 'Aurea' simply means gold, so you can point to anything of this colour in the garden and say: 'How attractive that 'Aurea' is.' Gratified by your admiration your host will eulogise over his acquisition, repeating its hybrid name so many times you will learn it easily. 'Alba' means white, 'Argentea' silver, 'Nigra' black or dark, and 'Rubra' describes plants with pinkish-red tones. Just point firmly in the direction of anything with white flowers or silver foliage, declaring: 'You just can't beat the Albas and Argenteas for giving a sense of coolness or freshness.' Never fails.

Common words such as 'lovely' and 'attractive', are definitely uncool and must be replaced with the word 'superba'. You can describe anything from a tree to an alpine (*Alpinus*) with this adjective. If you suffer a momentary memory lapse replace 'superba' with 'fine specimen', but never ever refer to any plant as 'pretty'.

You have now learnt enough key words to practise dropping them into phrases, for example: 'My word, is that a 'Pendula Superba' you have over there?' or 'I can't decide between a *Prunus* 'Pendula Alba' and a 'Rubra'' (any flowering cherry with either white or pink blooms and remotely drooping branches).

Many learned gardeners are passionate about natives and when they refer scathingly to 'those damned exoticas' you must sneer in agreement. A rival gardener will be vastly impressed if you study some insignificant clump of vegetation and proclaim appreciatively: 'A fine specimen of *Britannicus/Australis/Zealandia/Europeanus* 'Superba' – what a good choice.' He will not have heard this term before since we have just invented it, but you can't go wrong since he will be chagrined that he did not know the origin of the boring plant while you did. You will have put him at a distinct disadvantage in the Hortus Botanicus stakes. If you should have the tiny difficulty of his disagreeing with you and vehemently insisting that his *Europeana* 'Superba' is of New Zealand or Australian origin, simply bluff it out, saying: 'There is considerable controversy over the country of origin of the original genus, but it is believed to have been a native of …', naming again the country you chose first. This is called bluff and double bluff.

If you spy a plant you really adore and haven't a clue what its name is, bluff with panache, saying: 'Which one is this?', which indicates that you are perfectly cognisant of the genus but its particular species or cultivar name has temporarily eluded you. *Never* say 'What's this?', which implies you haven't a

---

*Anenome: Perennial herb imn the buttercup fanimly with amn extremenly amnoying mname.*—Henry Beard & Roy McKie

clue. This ploy has the disadvantage of sometimes leaving you to guess the genus, but the way round this is to stomp into the garden centre and ask for the plant just by its cultivar name. A good assistant will either know the genus or rush off obediently to ask someone else rather than lose face by admitting he/she doesn't know.

Your gardener's Latin is now so good it is time for a few final pointers. Again, just a few key words and a little guesswork is all you need. As an example we may take the Japanese maple tree, genus name *Acer*. Its leaves are often shaped like a hand, so they are described with the adjective *palmatum*. Often the leaves of this small tree are finely dissected, so top marks for guessing that the adjective to bandy about here is 'Dissectum'.

Advanced status in Hortus Botanicus Latinicus is gained if you can now interpret or string a colour word of your own at the end, for example, *Acer palmatum* 'Atropurpureum' just has to have leaves of purplish-red, while an *Acer palmatum* 'Dissectum Aureum', as you well know, would sport foliage of gold. Ambition, ambition – why stop at 'leaves'? – use *folius* instead.

*Florus* is Latin for flower, and a species described as *flore-pleno* will have many petals. *Floribundus* describes multi-headed cultivars that bloom freely over a long period.

A couple of satisfyingly impressive words are *grandifolius* and *grandiflorus,* the former meaning any plant with large foliage and the latter anything with a big flower. Words for the way a plant will behave in your garden? *Compactus* you guess immediately means it will (probably) stay small, while *giganteus* means whopping. *Sempervirens* ('always alive') is a useful word as it can be applied to anything evergreen. Useful words for general description include *grossus, horridus,* or *fatuus,* which you can apply to any plant material you don't like, and *elegantissimus* and *admirabilis,* which you can utter with gay abandon if you do.

British gardener and horticulturist Reginald Farrer is quite resolute about the need for Hortus Botanicus Latinicus:

> It is absolutely useless to ask any gardener to spare you Latin names, for the excellent reason that nine out of ten alpine plants haven't got any English name. Even our native alpines are very often as badly off as the newest Himalayan in that respect. They have no names except by the grace of science … At the same time, be candid, there are some botanical names that are

teasers. Where Polish discoverers or Russian explorers come upon the scene the result is apt to be an appalling jangle of horrors. Michaux, Stribnry, Przewalszky and Tchihatchew are responsible for some real jaw-breakers; and when it comes to *Michauxia tchihatchewi*, exhausted humanity gives up in despair. However, there is no help for it but to persevere. You cannot talk of these plants by any other name, because they haven't got any other name; so all you can do is to shut your eyes, blow your nose violently three times, and hope that you have sufficiently expressed that you mean Tchihatchewi.[1]

Christopher Lloyd takes the opposing view that, imprecise as they are, there is occasionally something to be said for using common names, particularly when it comes to night-scented plants:

> ... to give them their botanical names is to divest them of all magic. Reminiscing on frangipani-laden tropical evenings is evocative enough, and circumstances would seldom require the precision of *Plumeria acutifolia*-laden evenings.[2]

Exercise: test your etymological muscle. Make up a single sentence using all of the following words.

a) *pendula, compactus, rubra, Acer, cultivar, admirabilis.*

b) *giganteus, flore-pleno, aurea, genus, elegantissimus.*

c) *atropurpureum, grossus, sempervirens, folius.*

Hortus Botanicus Latinicus: plant names in dry polysyllabic mumbo-jumbo indulged in by bumptious plantsmen only? Only if you don't know what they mean or have not graduated in the art of bluff.

No sooner have you mastered garden Latin, than it dawns on you that even gardening phrases in English disguise a minefield of difficult colloquial and semi-colloquial terminology – not to mention double-entendre.

Our brief guide to horticultural hyperbole that follows will provide handy translations to useful phrases, which you will soon be able to bandy about with the best of them.

## BASIC TERMS

**Annual**: Any plant which, had it lived, would have flowered only once a year.
**Perennial**: Any plant which, had it lived, would have flowered year after year.
**Biennial**: Any plant which, had it lived, would still have died, but more slowly.
**Bed**: That in which the gardener thinks he spends his happiest hours.

**Cactus:** A plant that requires minimal attention, and in turn attracts none.

**Fruit:** Edible seed of a plant that appears in great profusion the moment you go away on holiday.

**Furrows:** Anguished lines disfiguring the gardener's forehead.

**Harrowing:** Gardener's experience that produces a furrow.

**Lawn:** Any flattish semi-green area covered with weeds, moss, kids, balls, dogs, sticks, rotary clotheslines, old cars, goats etc.

**Mulch:** Sound of a boot being removed from clay soil after the foot has stepped out of it.

**Plant sale:** Trestle tables groaning under the weight of geranium cuttings and spider plants.

**Rot:** Result of inappropriate gardening advice; affliction suffered by the roots of plants incarcerated in clay soils.

**Topiary:** The art of camouflaging a perfectly attractive shrub/tree to make it look like a deformed peacock or a one-legged giraffe.

**Patio:** Six stone slabs crammed with plants in containers.

## TYPES OF GARDENS

**Town garden:** Six stone slabs crammed with plants in containers surrounded by a fence.

**Country garden:** Two hundred hectares of paddocks devoted to rearing bulls.

**Bush/woodland garden:** Dense thicket intersected by muddy paths.

**Wild garden:** Bring your machete.

**Lakeside garden:** Bring your boots.

**Wild flower garden:** An out-of-control area engulfed by attractive native flora: creeping buttercup, bindweed, ground elder, oxalis, kikuyu and paspalum.

## ON A GARDENER'S LIFE

**'Gardening is so relaxing':** It's damned hard work and brutal toil.

**'It's such good exercise – keeps me fit':** My back and knees hurt and I am having cortisone injections in my wrists, elbows and shoulders.

**'Gardening is so creative':** I love heaving rocks, bricklaying, mixing concrete and laying paths, prising clay apart with a crowbar and tossing railway sleepers around.

**'Such an absorbing hobby':** I have to do something because I can't afford to go out, to the pub or on holiday.

**'It gives me shared interests with other gardeners':** I can grow anything better than him/just look at the state of his lawns/does he call those tomatoes?

**'Such an inexpensive hobby':** I am behind on the car repayments, embezzle from the housekeeping, and my children need new shoes.

**'I enjoy everything about the garden':** I live, eat and sleep the garden and am a crashing bore.

**'Amazing savings on growing my own veges':** In terms of time, labour, spray and fertiliser, my spuds cost $20 a kilo, my peas $5 a pod, and a cabbage head comes in at around $8.

## FROM ONE GARDENER TO ANOTHER

'I can't believe you look after all this by yourself': Man, what a mess.

'Your garden is so relaxed': It's wild.

'What delightful garden statuary': I love lumps of stone and broken concrete.

'What delightful rustic furniture': Not a patch on my Lutyens bench.

'How cheery those garden loungers are': All that floral print and padding would look great on a stage set for *Dallas*.

'It is so brave of you to open your garden to the public': You show-off.

'How clever of you to remember all those Latin names': You show-off.

'Mine is just an ordinary garden': I give it 12 hours a day, spend three-quarters of my salary on it and will kill myself if I don't win Gardener of the Year.

'I'm afraid my garden's nothing like yours': Thank God.

'I enjoy talking to other gardeners': I don't listen to a word they say because I'm so busy describing every nook, cranny and plant in my own.

'How quaint': You're kidding.

'Mine is an easy-care garden': I have a full-time gardener, a ride-on mower and I never go out.

'I love the tranquillity of your garden': Grey and white, white and grey, greyish white.

'Your garden is so restful': Boring.

'I'm just an amateur': I've been gardening for 35 years, have a degree in horticulture and have written 12 books.

'Such an interesting collection of shrubs': Look as if they all came out of the bargain bin.

'What a fine collection of silver-leafed plants': Yawn.

'A fine collection of hybrid teas': Blowsy and gaudy.

'Delightful, your old-fashioned roses': Wouldn't touch 'em with a barge pole. Grow into monsters in three months and flower for three weeks.

'I love to see old roses and wisteria together': Where is the house?

'Your plant combinations are just stunning': Fancy putting those in with those.

'What an interesting ground cover': Oxalis.

'Flowers always grow well for people who love them': Boy, you must hate yours.

'They grow like weeds for me': I have two spindly specimens under shade cloth which are fed and watered twice daily.

'You have such a fine display of exotics': It is immoral not to grow natives.

'Mine is a totally organic garden': The bugs are having a ball.

'Other people's gardens are so inspiring': I plan to find one I like and copy it to the last begonia.

'Your garden is so inspiring': I, too, could have a garden like this if I'm not careful.

New gardeners are particularly vulnerable to the language used in nursery and seed catalogues. Their best weapon in the line of defence against this poetic licence is the ability to interpret catalogue jargon correctly. A series of handy translations follow. (For an advanced course, see our Survival Guide, next.)

**Germination may be erratic**: One seedling appears every three months.
**Germination may be slow**: Don't expect anything to come up.
**Needs a sheltered spot**: A greenhouse.
**Grows best in full sun**: Requires a subtropical climate.
**Somewhat tender**: Guaranteed to expire at temperatures lower than 23°C.
**Bone hardy**: Will come through a cold winter but will expire in a wet one.
**Graceful**: Requires massive amounts of staking and tying.
**Arching stems**: Doesn't fall right over but allows flower faces to flop in the mud.
**First-class ground cover**: Rampantly invasive, has noxious weed classification.
**Delightful creeping habit**: As above.
**Vigorous**: Will strangle everything else in sight.
**Seeds freely**: A pain in the neck.
**Can be invasive**: A pain in the back.
**Good on walls**: Will only grow with the support and protection of a wall.
**Dainty**: Small and insignificant.
**Alpine**: Guaranteed to die at altitudes lower than 10,000 feet.
**Muted shades**: Insipid.
**Striking colour**: Unbelievably garish.
**An unusual colour combination**: Ugh!
**Subtle perfume**: Scentless.
**A plant of character**: Looks peculiar.
**Repeat flowering**: May offer a freak bloom or two in autumn.
**Indispensable and reliable**: Grown in every council bedding-out scheme.
**Choice**: Applied to any plant on which price inflation is required.
**Semi-evergreen**: Retains a few tatty leaves throughout winter.
**Hardy/easy-grow**: Will succeed if you can find the right combination of sun, shade, hot, cold, drainage and moisture.
**We are proud to be able to offer this new species**: We will be charging handsomely for this plant until rival catalogues get hold of it.
**We are proud to be able to offer limited stocks of this new species**: Same as above but three times the price.
**Seldom offered**: Difficult to propagate and even more difficult to keep alive.

Having got a grip on these key phrases, you are ready to begin deciphering the

179

innuendo of the main text. The hardest selling job will be done on plants that have lost their popularity, are of vulgar colour or, for any or all of the reasons above, the nursery still has in stock by the thousand. Some examples:

*Lavatera* 'Barnsley': **A truly spectacular shrub of unrivalled popularity, smothering itself in delightful pastel pink blossoms all season. One of the finest cultivars to be introduced in recent years:** There is not a front garden in the whole country that does not have one of these shrubs with their yucky pink flowers.

*Rosa* 'Rapture Red': **This rose caused a sensation when it was introduced last year. Its vibrant magenta colour a new and unique colour amongst roses – a truly spectacular hybrid:** This rose illustrates the depths of depravity to which commercial hybridists will sink in launching a plant of unbelievably hideous colour upon an unsuspecting public.

*Erigeron karvanskianus*: **An enchanting miniature daisy with pretty pink and white petals. Ideal for rockeries, paved gardens or walls. Hardy and easy to grow:** Correct on enchanting, but hideously invasive. Seeds everywhere, roots go down to China, impossible to remove once established.

*Meconopsis betonicifolia*: **A plant for the discerning gardener. A unique and mysterious blue poppy found in the Himalayas. We are delighted to be able to offer limited … An unbelievable cerulean blue flower with golden stamens. An aristocrat among plants. Deep-freezing the seed for six months will aid germination, which can be just a tiny bit slow:** We're only too happy for you to throw your money away. You'll need to order a bushel of F1 hybrid seed to get a few to germinate. Next to impossible to grow, and even if you succeed it expires after flowering once.

*Solanum jasminoides*: **A wonderfully easy climber which smothers itself with pretty white flowers throughout the season. Ideal for covering unsightly fences or walls:** Will smother any obstacle in its path, no matter how high or wide, including house, garage and trees. Reduces any garden regardless of size to a tangled wilderness of bolting stalks topped by a few scant flowers.

*Trillium grandifolium*: **An intriguingly unusual plant with dazzling white three-petalled blooms. Increases easily from underground offshoots. Enjoys moist soils and a little shade:** If you live in the middle of a forest on damp acid soil, this plant will grow like kikuyu or twitch. If your garden is anywhere else, you can slave over it for a decade without coaxing a flower out of it.

And finally, phrases *never* to use (in Latin *or* English) when speaking to plants:
Grow, you bastard.
If you don't flower, I'll kill you.
How would you like a long ride in the wheelbarrow?

180

# 19

# A SURVIVAL GUIDE CATALOGUES, GARDEN CENTRES AND NURSERIES

*Delph: Abbrv fr 'delphinium' lg shwy prnnl w bl flrs. Othr cmmn abbrvs incl 'mum', 'daff' and 'glad'. Ifu cn rd ths dfntn, u cn gt a gd jb at a nrsry.*
—Henry Beard & Roy McKie

The traditional retreat of the gardener in winter is beneath a warm blanket of mail-order catalogues. Catalogues may be defined as a form of light fiction written by seedsmen and nurserymen with the intention of selling their products. They are highly coloured, well written and utterly enticing.

They are also totally addictive and as winter progresses the gardener craves them more and more. Flushed and tingling like addicts near an opium den, we learn that the most valuable, the most gratifying, the rarest and choicest of plants are those which *we have not got in our garden*; that there are several hundred plants that are cultivars and hybrids offering 'amazing performance/absolutely new and magnificent varieties, surpassing by far any previous ones'. They are all on offer at 'never-to-be-repeated prices'.

Jonathan Cox offers the following thoughts:

There is a heady cocktail of joy, wantonness and guilt that only gardeners experience. You partake of it when, in spite of the fact that the bank has threatened foreclosure on the mortgage, and the garden is already crammed to overflowing so that to get anything else in will require the use of a shoe horn, and the children desperately need orthodontic work and new shoes – despite all this – you feverishly send off for another catalogue, fully intending to buy from it!

For some of us there is no longer any hope; catalogues have become an addiction. The words 'Rare – Few only' are guaranteed to have us rifling through our stationery drawers in a frenzy for the Fastpost stickers.

Cunning growers know that we can hardly wait for our next fix so they shamelessly include messages along the line of 'Anyone purchasing from this catalogue goes on our mailing list and will automatically receive our next two.' (As if we needed any encouragement ...)

Catalogue connoisseurs know that their favourite reading matter comes in all shapes and sizes, from lovingly handwritten and Xeroxed single sheets to the glossy-papered full colour forty-page Swane's rose catalogue, which measures nearly 30x30 centimetres and must have cost something akin to New Zealand's national debt to produce ...

From the latter I learn that a rose called 'Simplicity' has sales which total 18 million plants in the USA. 'Simplicity' was raised by Bear Creek Nurseries in California, which sounds delightfully rural, but with sales figures like that I bet they have long since dispensed with the bears and the creek and that now their royalty cheques go straight to a private box number in Beverley Hills.

Rose catalogues, in fact, make some of the best reading, for a variety of reasons. Their authors have long since run out of superlatives to describe fragrance in roses, which has now become 'huge', 'arresting' and 'penetrating'.

If Swanes are to be believed, one takes one's life in one's hands to sniff the potentially lethal 'Fragrant Plum', which they describe as having a perfume so strong it could carry you off.'

It is amusing too to note the particular virtues of roses named for the famous. I cannot decide whether Swane's have their tongues in cheek when they describe the rose 'Dolly Parton' as a 'voluptuous orange red with large shapely buds and huge many-petalled blooms.'

My one complaint would be that a catalogue like Swane's verges on the saccharine. Consider 'Perfect Moment', 'Pleasure', 'Sheer Bliss', 'Paradise', 'Dream Cloud', 'Misty', and so on. We need a change of mood from time to time in all this and I suggest a series of roses honouring famous villains, so that we could have catalogue entries like: 'Attila the Hun' (viciously thorny and very invasive), 'Long John Silver' (an extra tall grower which may need some support – thrives near the coast), and 'Count Dracula' (you'll go batty over this blood-red charmer who will put real bite into our colour schemes – garlic is not recommended for companion planting).

Overseas catalogues like Swane's are an irresistible drawcard for the catalogue addict. You see, the chances are that we will never actually be able to buy anything from them, so we are caught in an agony of longing which has all the hallmarks of unrequited love.

From time to time I torture myself by poring over overseas favourites. In the past I have lusted after *Viola* 'Devon Cream' (soft cream, slightly rayed and strongly fragrant) and *Clematis* 'Fair Rosamond' (white, flushed pink, with prominent purple stamens and the blooms have a pronounced scent – a blend of cowslip and violet) ...

Shortly afterwards I may be heard muttering 'quarantine regulations', 'fearful freight costs' and 'bankruptcy' to myself. For some reason, these seem to have a soothing effect on me.

Sometimes fate is kind to us and a much-coveted plant eventually becomes available via a New Zealand grower's catalogue. We shriek with glee, order three, and worry about where on earth we can possibly squeeze them in later ...

Trevor Griffith's catalogue of old-fashioned roses wth names such as 'Spinosissima Double Cream'; 'Spinosissima Irish Rich Marbled'; 'Four Seasons White Moss'; 'Rosette Delizy'; 'Marchioness of Londonderry', and so on ... is always a delight, not only for the charming descriptions of the roses themselves ('Sissinghurst Castle' – muddled, semi-double dusky plum coloured), but also for the pithy quotations liberally sprinkled throughout ...

You may find it comforting to remember these words of wisdom from his 1984-85 catalogue:

*We cannot do everything at once, but we can do something at once.*

The devotee can usually find something of interest in any catalogue no matter how humble, but there is one that is something else again: the Barnhaven Primrose Seeds catalogue is Art. Who else opens their catalogue with a selection of cries of rapture and poison pen letters from the punters? A sample from beneath the heading:

*To Barnhaven with Love and Hisses:*
*My doubles seed did nothing – despite my husband's home-made compost. Rubbish.*

Following these epistolary gems, the catalogue proper has the most wonderful potted histories, peppered with acute sociological insights, of the development of the polyanthus, *Primula sieboldii.*

*It was introduced to Britain in the 1860s and soon had Victorian hearts palpitating with rapture as it found its way into the mighty conservatories. There it sparkled in the lamplight and winked through the ferns at Ethne fanning away her after-the-ball vapours, and sucking violet cachous while predatory Gerald smoothed his moustache with a white-gloved hand so that his peck wouldn't prickle.*

And the gold-laced polyanthus:

*Enthusiasm was probably at its peak in the early 19th century. Shows were held in April in the local pubs and the supreme champion was awarded a copper kettle. Cherished plants were protected as they came into bloom with carboys cut in half, and a piece of slate over the opening kept out the rain. Competition was fierce. If you thought your neighbour's plant was better than yours, you could sneak out when the moon hung low and tip your chamber pot down the neck of the carboy.* 'Eckersley's Jolly Dragoon', 'Crownshaw's Invincible', 'Gillingham's Mantra', 'Bullock's Lancer', 'Nicholson's Bank Europe', 'Brown's Free Bloomer' – *champions all and gone to dust ...*

Catalogue-lovers need never feel alone, for their numbers are legion. Not only that, they are likely to be found in unexpected quarters. The novelist John Updike, for example, who has spent much of his adult life chronicling the madness that is America in the late twentieth century, shows himself to be a romantic at heart when he writes:

*The catalogue, that definitive naming of names, is the gardener's hymnal, whose music can be played all winter long … Much of the gardener's pleasure is in the head, in organisation and anticipation.*[1]

I, too, know no siren more seductive than a plant catalogue. But I accept that they are a necessary evil. Local garden centres are fine for punnets of annuals, spades, hoes and house plants, but they are a dead loss for unusual or interesting plants. For these one has to go to specialist nurseries.

These nurseries are almost invariably situated in some unheard-of location at the other end of the country so one must buy their treasures by post, a business fraught with hazard.

When compiling catalogues, nurserymen worth their salt use their literary skills and imagination to the full. Many nurseries make a fortune from catalogues alone and don't actually *sell* many of the plants listed at all (*Sorry, owing to limited supplies and huge demand …*). At large flower shows such as Chelsea or Ellerslie where the plants are not sold until the last afternoon, decent catalogues costing $3 plus can sell in thousands on the first and second days, making the plantsmen a tidy income by day three.

The catalogue opens with a friendly chat to soften you up for armchair spending. Self-congratulatory messages follow, to the effect that despite its being the worst growing season *ever*, their firm has an even bigger and better selection of plants to offer this year, and despite spiralling costs has managed to keep prices down to only a 40 per cent increase. They have an absolutely new selection of *unique* plant species to offer (only discovered recently in Tibet). The introductory chat usually includes a plug or two for plants they have vastly overproduced or been unable to shift, and concludes with a plea to get your orders in *early*. (At this stage the gardener of strong moral fibre relegates *all* catalogues to the bin.)

Plant descriptions follow. The elevated prose, strewn with adjectival hyperbole, quite puts some the best gardening writers' efforts into the shade. Downmarket nurseries resort to less elevated prose, concentrating instead on technicolour floral illustrations and featuring 'astonishing offers' and 'once-only specials'.

---

*Faith will never die as long as coloured seed and plant catalogues are printed.* — Anon

What distinguishes all mail-order catalogues is inaccuracy and exaggeration. As far as their photographic content is concerned some actually verge on the criminal. On big showy flowers like lilies and hybrid tea roses they're not so bad, but in the sections devoted to plants with small flowers the Hollywood treatment is taken to extreme. Every bloom is photographed with a super-zoom macro lens, both colour and size are grossly misrepresented, and fragile wee treasures appear with heads blown up to dishmop proportions. Gullible gardeners, like you and me, spend three-quarters of the year waiting for some costly shrub to burgeon forth the gigantic blossoms portrayed in the catalogue. When the plant finally blooms, the flowers are so small and inconspicuous we assume we have failed somewhere.

The nurseryman invariably hires a professional photographer to illustrate his catalogue, and in cohoots they are a formidable duo. First there's the 'pick and stick' ruse. That is, they will stick five luscious-looking blooms onto a stalk which, in the state nature intended, would bear only one. The plant is then described as being 'highly floriferous, bearing multiple heads of blooms', which is a bare-faced lie.

Misrepresentation of colour is also apparently the nurseryman's divine right – for 'soft lilac' read insipid mauve, for 'lavender' pucey-purple, for 'vibrant orange' screaming orange, for 'warm red' pillar-box red, for 'silver-blue' dirty lavender, and so on.

They cannot just say that the plant has flowers of clear yellow, blue, or pink etc. Even white doesn't exist. There is 'creamy white', 'dazzling white', 'snow white', 'purest white', but never just white. Why would a bloom be described as 'yellow' when it can be described as 'rich lemon', ' deepest gold', 'buttery' or 'brazen yellow'?

Literary fantasies are indulged to the full when it comes to blues: they are 'azure', 'Cambridge', 'amethyst', 'cornflower', 'delphinium', 'intense blue', 'ice-blue', 'baby blue', 'sapphire blue' – but never just blue. And this is far from being a modern phenomenon. As far back as the late 18th century the stern Miss Gertrude Jekyll was admonishing horticulturists on their misrepresentation of flower colour:

I am always surprised at the vague, not to say reckless, fashion in which garden folk set out to describe the colour of flowers … Flowers of a full, bright blue colour are often described as a 'brilliant amethystine blue'. Why 'amethystine'? The amethyst as we generally see it is a stone of washy purple colour … What, therefore, is the sense of likening a flower, such as a delphinium, which is really a splendid pure-blue colour, to the duller and totally different colour of a third-rate gem?[2]

Pastel shades bring forth a stream of verbal delicacy. They are: 'pale, 're-fined', 'soft', 'dainty', 'elegant', 'blushing', 'tinged' or 'tinted'. Finally, none of these colours is allowed to stand on its own – all must be preceded by the word 'gorgeous'.

An irate customer writing recently to a well-known gardening magazine about mail-order duplicity complained:

> One of the things that never ceases to astonish me about colours in garden-ing is the amazing description that nurserymen give them in their catalogues. You read of 'deep crimson tipped with mauve', and when the thing flowers it's simply purple.[3]

The only chance you have of getting to see the true colour and size of the plant in which you are interested is to actually see it growing in someone else's garden.

More heinous than exaggeration, misrepresentation or even lies is the rule of substitution. Many mail-order catalogues will send you the plant genus you ordered but will have substituted the hybrid form you desired with another. This ensures you end up not with the rarer cultivar but with the common vari-ety (freighted at your expense), which the local garden centre is giving away free with purchases over $3. Mail-order firms with slightly more scruples do ask for permission to substitute, but the end result is identical – you don't get the plant you want and may end up owning a plant you wouldn't normally touch with a barge-pole. This particular iniquity is again excused with the time-honoured ('limited-supply – overwhelming demand') catchcry.

Further skullduggery guaranteed to make me foam at the mouth is the *rule of refund*. For the (many) plants that are unavailable the refund comes not in the form of a welcome cheque (you are still sweating over the cost of your order) but as a generous little gift token 'which you may spend at our nursery at any time'!

Your money is already spent and gaining interest in the nursery's bank.

The final irony is that most mail-order firms have a minimum-order rule. This never ever equates with the amount on your refund token, and you end up spending *more* to bring it up to the minimum order price ...

A final word of warning. Never, ever, when perusing a nursery catalogue, succumb to the temptation to order a plant that has the words 'novelty' flashed below it. It is likely to be some hideous misbred hybrid that the nurseryman knows he will never sell after its first (disastrous) season. In catalogue termi-nology the word 'unique' carries similar connotations of misbegotten geneal-ogy.

Karel Capek knew all about it:

The hibernating gardener ceases entirely to be interested in what he has got in his garden, being fully occupied with what he has not, which of course is far more; he throws himself eagerly upon the catalogues, and ticks off what he must order, which, by Jove, must no longer be lacking in his garden. In the first rush he marks off four hundred and ninety perennials which he must order at all costs; after counting them he is a bit subdued, and with a bleeding heart he begins to cross off those which he will give up for this year. This painful elimination must be gone through five times at least, until only about one hundred and twenty 'most beautiful, gratifying, indispensable' perennials remain, which – on the wings of anticipated joy – he immediately orders.[4]

So you've done it. Your forms have been posted. The children must go barefoot to school, but you now await with mounting anticipation the arrival of your loot. The finale of the fiasco. The most disappointing part of all.

Months later, the day before you are due to leave the country for a holiday overseas, a courier van draws up outside the gate. But what's this? One small box?

'Yeh, thassit,' says the driver. 'Sign 'ere, mate.'

'These are live plants,' you announce stubbornly. 'The invoice says "check contents before signing".'

'Goddammit, mate, I got twennyfree more deliv'ries before tea – sign 'ere.'

You sign. You open the box. Inside are 30 of the 100 plants you ordered. Cryptic remarks are scrawled across the invoice: 20 are 'regret sold out', 12 have been 'substituted', eight are 'unavailable', and 'remainder of order to follow in autumn'.

(The substituted plants are so remotely unlike anything you would plant in your garden you subsequently spend long flight hours unable to sleep, trying to work out any possible similarity between the species you ordered and those with which you have been provided.)

You gingerly tease the pitifully small pots out of their cocoons of shredded paper. The plants inside are even smaller. The old-fashioned rambling roses (hitherto described as 'enthusiastically exuberant') with which, in your mind's eye, you saw your house festooned in spring, are no more than little bare sticks. Some of the 'well-established/well-rooted' perennials have hardly got beyond their second set of leaves. Other pots appear to contain nothing at all. You are magnanimous. You give the mail-order firm the benefit of the doubt and assume they contain species that are summer (?) dormant.

You distinctly remember ordering eight miniature *Dianthus* 'Little Gem'. As you unwrap the last pot, eight tiny divisions fall out. *Finis.* Your entire planting plan for the spring garden. You rush off to the greenhouse to repot the *Dianthus* fragments so you can get off on holiday and forget the whole damned business. 'I'll try a different nursery next year.'

Infuriated by the double dealing of mail-order nurseries you decide to hit back by growing your own plants from seed. You peruse one of the unsolicited glossies that found its way into your letterbox and it is immediately apparent that seedsmen's catalogues are rivalled in their use of euphemisms and superlatives only by real estate agents.

The first essential is to interpret the terms 'F1 hybrid' and 'F2 hybrid'. The former means that the product is priced *per seed* rather than per packet but is 'a superior strain producing huge yield'. The latter means ordinary well-tried and tested strains, or those that are not so big, bold and flashy.

Vegetable seed catalogues are especially ambiguous. Any variety not described as 'high-yielding' or 'heavy cropper' is a low yielder. 'Ideal for exhibition' means it will catch the judge's eye but is inedible. 'Delicate or subtle flavour' means tasteless. For 'tender' read stringy, 'succulent' read watery, 'firm-fleshed' read tough as. 'Crisp' means chewy, 'traditional texture' means like boiled cabbage, 'weather-resistant' – okay in a sunny sheltered place with good drainage. For 'striking flavour' or 'gourmet's delight' record family's comments. 'Nutritious' means it tastes foul but is good for you.

Anything described as 'novelty' or 'designer veg' means more or less edible and will look very pretty in the ornamental *potager*. 'For the discerning palate' – totally inedible. 'Disease-resistant' – the most brazen lie of all.

Untruths such as these, it seems, have been around for a long time:

> I cannot omit nor spare to deliver my mind, concerning the great and abominable falsehood of those sorts of people which sell garden seeds.
>
> A Gardiner, 1603

You can handle catalogues. You've got their measure. Take everything they say with a pinch of salt. You'll consign half of them to the bin as soon as they arrive anyway – well, one or two might just need checking out to make sure you don't miss anything *really* special … Garden centres are another matter.

---

*Seedsmen reckon that their stock in trade is not seeds at all … it's optimism. That's what they're selling you when you're seduced by that gorgeous picture on the front of the packet.*
— Geoff Hamilton

A garden centre has been defined as the only place where money grows on trees. Most garden centres are run along martial lines; their tactics are to instil blind panic and confusion with the aim of utterly demoralising one into premature unconditional surrender.

To outwit the nurseryman, a useful offensive tactic is to make an immediate purchase of a large and bulky plant from his bargain bin. He will be overjoyed to have found some poor fool of a customer to buy his hideous half-dead plant. Since your arms are now rendered inoperative, he will consider your further purchasing power not worth bothering about. A similar ploy is to stagger about hiding behind a large and disabling sack of potting mix.

Unlike the specialist plantsmen's nursery, in addition to punnets of annuals, potted 'mums' and obscure houseplants, the garden centre stocks barbecues, gimmicky tools, statuary and furniture, an impressive array of 'death from the air' toxic chemicals and 'feed your soil fertilisers' and much else besides.

Garden centres are usually alongside busy main roads, have huge parking bays and are easily accessible. The owners do not usually propagate their own plants but buy them in from wholesalers in container-loads. Many sport chic cafes serving upmarket day-long refreshments. The local horticultural cognoscenti may be seen in impassioned oratory here, their cafe latte and cappuccino going cold while they debate the merits or demerits of the stock.

Garden hypermarkets have wide aisles, and trolleys that are a cross between a pram and a concorde. It is possible to spend a good deal of time and a great deal of money in such outfits.

Garden centres are places where people who know next to nothing about plants flog what they think the public will want. To find your way it's important to speak their language. Here are some examples, with translation.

**It'll grow anywhere:** It's a weed.

**It needs full sunlight:** Doesn't stand a chance outside the tropics.

**It's meant to look like that:** It's meant to have yellow shrivelled leaves/be defoliated/be full of insect holes.

**You'll probably find it will die back a bit:** Don't blame me if you get it home and find it's dead.

**Try to give it a little shade:** Try to keep it where you can't see how unhealthy it is.

**Maybe you over-watered it:** I'm not blaming anyone, but it's your fault.

**Maybe you didn't water it enough:** I'm not blaming anybody but it's your fault.

**The plant DIED?:** I'm not blaming anyone, but there are only two people in this room whose fault it could have been and it's not me.

**Perhaps the soil was too rich/poor:** It's still your fault.

**It's meant to look like that:** Been in the bargain bin all season.

**It goes dormant in winter:** It's dead.

**It's the ideal present:** It's on clear-out.

**We offer a gift-wrapping service:** We use it to disguise/present/recycle plants that are rejects from the bargain bin.

The least helpful phrase offered by an assistant in a garden centre: 'Can I help you?'

It must be stressed that a garden centre has absolutely nothing in common with a specialist nursery. If you are bored with the brash begonias and petulant petunias in the local garden hypermarket and don't wish to suffer the slings and arrows of outrageous fortune involved in ordering from catalogues, you must go to source – the specialist nursery. To do this, it is essential to be a paid-up member of the AA, be a good map reader and be possessed of plenty of time.

A four-wheel-drive vehicle is also advantageous because the favourite habitat of the specialist plantsman is at the end of an inordinately long gravel road. As we have already determined, he (or she) is a reclusive specimen who chooses to perform his hybridisation and propagation in splendid isolation.

(Be advised here and now that you may be rewarded at the end of your 500km round trip with nothing more than a CLOSED sign. The specialist nurseryman does not feel obliged to let his public know when he needs to leave the property.)

Magnificent stands of exotic specimen trees and enormous shelter belts conceal his lair. After you have abandoned your vehicle and hiked the last two kilometres through the forest, an old wooden gate falling off its hinges leads you into the lesser jungle inside. It is evident that the specialist plantsman's collection has long outgrown his nursery space. There are containerised plants everywhere – some have outgrown their planter bags and have rooted in situ, rare orchids, bromeliads and tillsandias tumble out of trees, flamboyant climbers have engulfed the house in luscious embrace.

Every plant in this magnificent horticultural mêlée offers striking architectural foliage, subtlety of colour and exquisitely beautiful blooms. It is an impenetrable jungle of the rare, the unusual, the exotic – the *must haves*.

You despair. You consult your 'plants I would kill for' list. How will you ever find anything in the fabulous and fearful fecundity engulfing you? You fight your way towards the house in search of the nurseryman. This takes a long time as you stop often, trying to remember the exact location of this rare plant or that. The doors and windows of the house are all open. The remains of an uneaten sandwich and a mug of soup sit among a mountain of cuttings on the kitchen table.

You give up and wander around a bit more and, when utterly overcome by temptation, work your way over to a unique plant and attempt to wrestle it from the embrace of its neighbours. You clear a space and set about amassing yourself a pile of plants. Eventually, an eccentric figure wearing only an English panama hat, gumboots, shorts and fingerless mittens appears.

'Ah yes,' he says, eyeing your loot. 'Good choice.' And proceeds to tell you the Latin name, genealogy, history and hybridisation method, species and sub-species of each plant in precise detail. He will tell you he collected the original plant material for this hybrid from Kashmir in '46, and that he picked up the parents of the fern species that is your fancy from the swamps of the Amazon in '54. His mittened fingers will caress their flowers and foliage reverently and it is clear he will part with them with reluctance. He then spies your second pile – the plants you have been lusting after for years. They are sternly removed. 'Stock plants. Not on sale to the public for another two years.'

You ask if he has any similar cultivars. 'I have some, but they are not mature enough to go yet.' This probably means 'They're right over the other side of the nursery and I'm damned if I'm going to fetch them.'

You begin to realise that the nurseryman, too, has a supply of stock phrases for squashing customers who are a nuisance. Some examples:

**Would your children like to go and see the lambs in the paddock?:** Any chance of getting your brats out of my nursery?

**We've completely sold out of that hybrid:** I only grew 10 and am kicking myself for not having grown 100.

**It's not suited to your soil:** I'm damned if I'll let you have one of those.

*Salvia* **'Sissinghurst' is just right for your soil and luckily I have a few to spare:** Not one of my more successful hybrids.

The specialist nurseryman is a trifle testy when you ask prices because the truth is he doesn't actually want to part with any of his treasures. A figure is eventually agreed upon, but there will be no change forthcoming. He is not to be bothered with pecuniary trifles.

---

*Green thumb: common condition suffered by gardeners in which the skin of the thumb develops a greenish hue as the result of handling large amounts of currency at nurseries.*
—Henry Beard & Roy McKie

You will also be frowned upon if you ask to have one of the mountain of cardboard boxes or tomato trays mouldering everywhere in which to load your loot. He mutters irritably to the effect that he needs them all and shambles off.

You may not even be fortunate enough to meet the owner of the specialist nursery. As you leave you will find a battered old cashbox – an honesty box – on a three-legged table near the unhinged gate.

### NURSERYMAN'S LAMENT

Will it survive they ask?
Will it thrive they ask?
What about the frost?
What about the snow?
How does this plant grow?

Is it white or is it blue?
Perhaps the pink will do.
Does it like the sun?
Does it like the shade?
Thank goodness at last
A decision is made.

What about the insects and the bugs?
What about the snails and slugs?
Can I, should I prune it?
Can I, should I move it?
Fertiliser, which is best?
Those questions put me to the test.

As if this is not enough
Nature starts to do her stuff.
Hail, rain, snow and ice.
No, it isn't very nice.
Winds and gales, droughts and sun,
What a relief when the day is done.

How many times I ask
Why do I set myself this task?
Well, when you can look with pride
On customers well satisfied,
Then you would know this job's the best
If you can pass the customer test.[5]

# 20

# THE REVOLTING GARDEN

*Criticising another's garden does not keep the weeds from one's own.* —Anon

There is no tutor more learned, more creative in the art of the Revolting Garden than Rose Blight, alias Germaine Greer. Not for her the lavender-lilac languishing landscapes of old-fashioned roses and perennials – her preference is for a 'Lethal Garden':

> The London garden, dank, dark and filled with foul humours is, of course, under the influence of Saturn; ergo, plants of saturnine nature flourish therein. Most which seek obscurity and putrefaction for their habitat are poisonous in some degree, some so eminently so that they may do actual harm to pets (oh joy!) or children (alleluia!)
>
> Plant-men seem to guard this secret jealously, preferring to stress the benignity of 'Dame Flora', rather than to advertise to all and sundry that by buying their *Aconitum* the gardener is actually providing himself with the source of one of the most deadly narcotic alkaloids known to man. A casual touch of the leaves will irritate the skin and the pollen inflames the eyes. Planted where the neighbour's children jump into your garden, it will exact revenge a dozen-fold.
>
> *Aconitum napellus*, monkshood, is rather beautiful, although the blue flowers have the expression of a sort of frozen scream. Its steeples combine well with the flat, bat-shaped leaves of *Atropa belladonna*, deadly nightshade, whose brilliantly black berries are very attractive (and fatal) to children. This bedding scheme needs only the fine-cut and wonderfully poisonous leaves of *Conium maculatum*, hemlock, and the downy leaves and purple-veined flowers of henbane, *Hyoscyamus niger*, to turn your dreary lightwell or back area into a fascinating chamber of horrors.
>
> The lethal garden can be given further interest by tasteful plantings of hellebores *foetidus*, *viridis* and *niger*, all readily available, violently purgative and utterly poisonous. I have a soft spot too for *Caltha palustris*, the marsh marigold, who adores life in London and is quite poisonous; *Anemone nemerosa* (poisonous, acid and blistering); and other charming, venomous members of the *Ranunculaceae*, especially the celery-leafed buttercup, *Ranunculus scleratus*.

The crown of the murderer's garden is that most hypnotically horrible of vegetable phenomena, *Colchicum autumnale*, the autumn flowering crocus. Its luminous naked flower, the colour of anaemic gums, appears without leaves as the autumn light is fading and everything else is dying back. In its corms this vile thing harbours colchicine, an alkaloid which does not simply kill. The utterly diabolical gardener can try soaking his flower seeds in it to produce monstrous chromosomal mutations.[1]

If the idea of a lethal garden is not appalling enough, then perhaps a garden of macabre ambience might titillate your fancy. Ms Blight advises on which plants to choose:

As the Victorians well knew, some of the most repulsive gardening effects can be wrought with a minimum of effort – indoors. If you have a house which, like most others, is unevenly heated, poorly lit, full of spent gas fumes and draughty, you can torture almost any plant into truly wonderful contortions.

It is no use starting with a plant that, like the cyclamen, will defoliate, shrivel and turn up its toes in a matter of hours. The ideal torture subject is a plant like the philodendron, which will languish visibly but, limping and moaning, can be got to crawl along doggedly and painfully for years on end, stringing its limp dispirited leaves all about the room like the pennants of the *Marie Celeste*. Some demonic gardeners like to train their philodendrons round and round the walls of the darkest room in the house, especially dining rooms, wherein they loom over the table, craning like vultures in their permanent fruitless search for light.

For enthusiasts of the open-sore type of indoor gardening, the African violet, or *Saintpaulia ianantha*, is a great favourite. If grown in dry air and watered from above, it has a prodigious propensity to rot. In a good specimen, the merest touch will raise thousands of evil-smelling spores, to which nearly everybody is allergic. Some plant-haters have become so addicted to the drawn-out death throes of the *Saintpaulia* that they cannot function without three or four plants in various stages of moribundity about them at all times as they work.

*Gynura* repays poor husbandry with a rich display of small hairy orange flowers, which not only stun and horrify against the background of purple leaves, but instantly attract great scabs of aphids and crusts of whitefly. Even when not in bloom, the gynura is remarkable for its clumsy habit of growth and dredging action of the small purple hairs on its leaves, which comb every atom of garbage from the air and cannot be induced by any means to give it up.

If the higher pleasures of plant torture are not for you, you might, nevertheless, wish to call in the truly indestructible plants to help make some dull corner truly Stygian. *Rhoicissus rhomboidea*, often wrongly named kangaroo vine, has driven many a bedsit dweller to an early grave, while rubber plants, monsteras and aspidestras, especially if covered with dust and perpetually dormant, are perfect emblems of the futility of life.[2]

Another aspect of the Revolting Garden to be considered is best described as the Unpleasaunce. Visits to others' gardens offer satisfying proof that one is not alone in har-bouring a particular feature of garden slummery. Your hostess has shown you around her garden. 'Well, that's the lot – all there is to see. We'll go and have a cup of tea.' She is lying. You know perfectly well and so does she, that there is one more bit to see and that she doesn't want you to see it. It is that gruesome junk-filled area, the skeleton in every garden's cupboard: the Unpleasaunce. Every gardener has one, and one Unpleasaunce is much like another; they differ only in the size and variety of depressingly untidy things they harbour.

*Utilities*: At its best the Unpleasaunce is full of things the gardener has forgotten he owns: stakes, bamboo canes, decaying seedling boxes, solidified sacks of lime and fertilisers, pots and containers, rolls of shade cloth etc.

*Futilities*: The Unpleasaunce exists as the Mecca of the Unmentionables, largely comprising things the gardener hoards because he knows they will come in useful some time: mountains of plastic food containers, polythene bags crammed with black plastic planter bags (sizes all mixed up), bottomless polythene bottles with which to cover seedlings, condemned mouse traps, wobbly wheelbarrows, disemboweled dustbins, chipped bricks, senile secateurs that have lost their springs, other stricken tools waiting for repair, bald brushes, vast quantities of rotting pieces of (useful) wood, rusted kettles, coal scuttles, churns etc (absolutely *de rigeur* as imaginative plant containers but unused since they are welded to the ground by ropes of rank grass).

The Unpleasance harbours innumerable such gardening *objets d'art*, all aspiring to eventual recycling. In the meantime they give rise to clouds of biting midges at dusk, slimy gastropods at night, and places in the sun for squadrons of blue-bottle flies during the day. Bicycles the children have outgrown but refuse to part with impede access to the black plastic compost bins. Their lids are thrust skywards by barrowloads of weeds that are growing lustily and seeding themselves with profligate proficiency in the rich organic matter at the base of the bin because the gardener hasn't had time to fork it out and spread it on the soil.

*Flora*: Other things grow in the Unpleasaunce, of course. Old doormats sprout lush green grass quite unlike anything to be found on the lawns; pumpkin seedlings romp up old ladders and advance towards the rose gardens; forgotten crowns of rhubarb thrust evil red stems and bitter green leaves from a cracked forcing pot; weeds are legion, making an admirable job of self-sowing and populating all surrounding flowerbeds within a mile; jumbles of containers bearing dehydrated, weed-infested cuttings clutter a sizeable area.

*Fauna*: The Unpleasaunce is the abode of slugs, snails, slaters, mice and rats. Sometimes stray cats attracted by the vermin take up residence, which also makes it a good place to bring forth litters of kittens. There is often a wasps' nest or two because they know they may reside undisturbed since no one comes here. Clouds of fanged mosquitoes and the larvae of other biting insects breed in old watering cans and pots. Their presence greatly adds to the general unpleasant ambience of the Unpleasaunce and is a prime reason why the gardener visits only if he is desperate for a valuable item of debris.

*Architecture in the Unpleasaunce*: There may be historic garden structures in the more gruesome Unpleasaunces. Chief among these is the mandatory delapidated garden shed complete with rotting woodwork and broken windows. No one has the courage to venture inside, since it is crammed from floor to ceiling with much the same junk found outside, making entry impossible anyway.

Chief among gardeners' failed good intentions and New Year resolutions is to turn out the garden shed and chuck away every last item of useless old junk. There may be a scarred workbench or a trestle for chopping and sawing things on, and a three-legged potting bench awaiting surgical coupling of the fourth.

Lesser structures include clumsy home-made animal hutches and cold frames, these last outlawed because they are not aesthetically pleasing in the trendy new *potager* that used to be the comfortable old vege garden.

*Historical Exhibits*: The upmarket Unpleasaunce boasts a satisfying number of ancient artefacts, the relics of recent history waiting patiently for absorption into the soil. Larger period items include iron wringers and mangles, hand-mowers, old treadle sewing machines, cast-iron baths with claw feet, a large round washing machine complete with paddles, an Aga or Rayburn range circa 1920, gas or electric cooker also with claw feet (period uncertain), and brass bedsteads that were the pride of the gardener's ancestors.

These larger historical gems have remained in the Unpleasaunce because they are prohibitively heavy and because no one was ever found who could be bribed into removing them. Smaller artefacts include enamelled buckets, teapots and saucepans, galvanised hip baths, china bedpans, chamber pots and porcelain lavatory bowls, bottomless portmanteaux neatly boxing in a fine growth of slimy fungi, rusty milk churns and unidentifiable pieces of defunct machinery (period absolutely uncertain). Lurking in the stranglehold of the long grass that abounds in the Unpleasaunce are ancient rakes, saws and scythe blades, all with rusted teeth and prongs at the ready to inflict instant tetanus.

If the garden has been in the possession of the same family for several generations of ancestors who did not enjoy refuse collection courtesy of the council there will be disgusting heaps of old tins, bottles, chicken wire and barbed wire.

Almost all the period pieces in the Unpleasaunce would fetch a fortune on the antique market if the gardener could find the courage to hack his way into the interior and retrieve them.

*Aroma*: To complete the ambience of decay that permeates the Unpleasaunce it is necessary to have a garden bonfire site heaped with a vast pile of green plant material that it is impossible to ignite properly. This must be allowed to smoulder sourly for months on end, belching acrid black smoke, which will greatly enhance the total unpleasantness of the Unpleasaunce. Odours are important to its atmosphere of decadence and corruption. Heaps of decomposing dog bones and mountains of grass clippings in advanced stages of slimegreen putrefaction are *de rigeur*. Fungi, preferably poisonous, exude a satisfyingly damp stench of black rot. Decline and ruin is the milieu.

There are no fairies at the bottom of the garden. Just the Unpleasaunce.

# 21

# THE RELUCTANT GARDENER

*Most people who possess anything like an acre, or half of it, contribute weekly to the support of a gentleman known as a Jobbing Gardener. You are warned of the danger that he may prove to be Garden Pest No. 1.* — Lesley Phillips[1]

If you are a reluctant gardener, you have a little money, and you really do fancy fairies at the bottom of your garden, there is another option. You can pay someone else to do the heavy and the grubby, and keep the worst of the Unpleasaunce at bay.

The flaw in this otherwise admirable system is that finding good fairies or 'gardening treasures' is not so easy. Also, the modern jobbing gardener does not always wait to be offered his perks. Miles Kingston reveals his worst excesses in his 'Let's Parler Franglais' column in *Punch*:

### AVEC LE PART-TIME GARDENER

Monsieur: Bonjour, Twining.

Jardinier: Arrh.

Monsieur: Everything est lovely dans le jardin, then?

Jardinier: Arrh.

Monsieur: Bon, bon. Bon … Pourquoi la magnolia a disparu?

Jardinier: Pas disparu, monsieur. Je l'ai prunée un peu.

Monsieur: Vouz l'avez beaucoup prunée. Drastiquement. C'est maintenant un stump.

Jardinier: Elle aime le hard pruning. Elle adore ça.

Monsieur: Hmm … où sont mes dahlias?

Jardinier: Ils sont finis.

Monsieur: La semaine passé, elles n'etaient pas started.

Jardinier: C'est une saison désastreuse pour les dahlias.

Monsieur: Je ne vois pas mon flowering cherry.

Jardinier: Ce n'est pas flowering maintenant.

Monsieur: Je ne vois pas un non-flowering cherry.

Jardinier: Ah, well. Non. Le cherry n'aimait pas sa position. Il detestait le soil. Donc, je l'ai transplanté.

Monsieur: Transplanté? Où ça?

Jardinier. Dans mon jardin.

Monsieur: Dans votre … ?

Jardinier: C'est dans vos meilleurs intérêts.

Monsieur: Oh, well … Où est le lawn?

Jardinier: Lawn, squire? Oh, le patch d'herb. Je l'ai excavé pour y planter les oignons et les spuds, comme vous avez dit.

Monsieur: Moi? J'ai dit ça?

Jardinier: Absolument. Pas une ombre de doute. 'Ce damned lawn,' vous avez dit.

Monsieur: Et les chaises longues qui etaient sur la lawn? Et le croquet? Et le mower et la summer maison?

Jardinier: Tous en shocking condition. J'en ai disposé.

Monsieur: Correctez-moi si ja'i tort, mais dans la semaine vous avez remové les fleurs et les arbres, ruiné le lawn et auctioné ma furniture.

Jardinier: Je fais mon job. C'est tout.

Monsieur. Ha.

Jardinier: Il est tres difficile de trouver les jobbing gardeners, vous savez. *Tres* difficile. Especiellement pour peanuts. Si vous n'aimez pas mon travail …

Monsieur: Okay, okay. Sorry si j'ai été hasty.

Jardinier: J'accepte vos apologies.

Monsieur: Aujourd'hui, si vous faites seulement le tidying up …

Jardinier: Just laissez-moi à mes devices, okay, Squire? C'est tres difficile avec le criticisme constant.

Monsieur: Right. D'accord. J'apologise. Maintenant il me faut aller au travail.

Jardinier: Et moi aussi – la vie de jardinier c'est tres difficile …[2]

English gardener Nigel Colborn is distinctly uncertain of the advantages of inheriting an incumbent and reluctant jobbing gardener. He discovers that although you might share the same native tongue, you are still likely to suffer linguistic difficulties:

This won't matter too much because faithful old gardeners always know best and never do as they are told anyway. Some will go out of their way to obstruct you and even the most benign are as wilful as toddlers and a great deal more destructive. Matters are always worse if you are new to an area, particularly if you have bought the local crumbling manor or rectory. Buildings of this type frequently come with a trusty old soul who will arrive on an ancient bicycle and talk gibberish.

'The kitchen garden seems a bit overgrown,' you might say.

'Ooh! Aah! that wants more'n just a bit o'petherin.'

'I thought we'd plant potatoes to clear the ground.'

'Niver 'appen!'

'Sorry?'

'T'aint niver tate land. S'too clarty.'

'Well, what do you suggest?'

'S'up to you, really.'

'But what would *you* do?'

'Git rid o'nt.'

'But it's an ancient kitchen garden. It must have produced food for this house for a hundred years or more.'

'Ooh, aah.'

'So why not now?'

'Sick soil.'

'Sick?'

'Aah. T'aint no good for nothing now, only twitch and bellbine.'

All this means that he's damned if he's going to break his back forking the couch grass out of the vegetable beds or double digging, or any other strenuous stuff. However, if you're looking for someone to trim your edges, deadhead a few roses, train a dozen sweet peas a year and drink gallons of your Nescafe on interminable breaks, he's your man. When you have slipped a disc and developed a couple of hernias pulling the kitchen garden round to its original fertile state he will (a) take all the credit for the transformation, and (b) feed his and several other families on what he filches. You'll be left with the cabbage and turnips while the rest of the village enjoy petis pois, asparagus and fresh raspberries.[3]

Ralph Wightman, British naturalist and broadcaster, reinforces Nigel Colborn's reflections on the aberrations of the reluctant paid help:

> They turn up on the appointed day of the week whatever the conditions of rain, frost, snow or tempest. Only in April or May are they confined to their beds … Pruning, spraying, pricking out and every unpleasant job they avoid by saying 'I baint no gardener'. They will get rid of precious purchased dung at a colossal depth on a tiny area. In all matters connected with planting and

weather they are firm believers in the moon, and the moon is never in an auspicious phase ... [4]

The relationship between gardener and employer has always been tricky, often composed as it is of mutual bullying. Here is a case in point, where an English nobleman deplores and describes to a friend the predilection of his Scottish gardener for gravel paths:

'Angus McAllister,' said Lord Emsworth, 'is a professional gardener. I need say no more. You know as well as I do, my dear fellow, what professional gardeners are like when it comes to a question of moss ... Moss, for some obscure reason, appears to infuriate them. It rouses their basest passions. Nature intended a yew alley to be carpeted with a mossy growth. The mossy path in the yew alley at Blandings is in true relation for colour to the trees and grassy edges – yet will you credit it that soulless disgrace to Scotland actually wished to grub it all up and have a rolled gravel path staring up from beneath those immemorial trees!

I have already told you how I was compelled to give in to him on the matter of the hollyhocks – head gardeners of any ability at all are rarer in these days and one has to make concessions – but this was too much. I was perfectly friendly about it. 'Certainly, McAllister,' I said, 'you may have your gravel path if you wish. I make but one proviso, that you construct it over my dead body. Only when I am weltering in my blood on the threshold of that yew alley shall you disturb one inch of my beautiful moss. Try to remember, McAllister,' I said, still quite cordially, 'that you are not laying out a recreation ground in a Glasgow suburb – you are proposing to make an eyesore of what is possibly the most beautiful nook in one of the finest and oldest gardens in the United Kingdom.' He made some repulsive Scotch noise at the back of his throat, and there the matter rests.[5]

Eighteenth-century English writer Horace Walpole suffered similar difficulties with an elderly Scots retainer, and describes to his friend the Earl of Harcourt his attempts to encourage the latter to 'retire':

I am sensibly obliged, my dear Lord, by your great goodness, and am most disposed to take the the gardener you recommend, if I can. You are so good-natured you will not blame my suspense. I have a gardener that has lived with me for above twenty-five years; he is incredibly ignorant, and a mule. When I wrote to your Lordship, my patience was worn out, and I resolved to at least have a gardener for flowers. On your not being able to give me one, I half consented to keep my own; not on his amendment, but because he will not leave me, presuming on my long suffering. I have offered him fifteen pounds a year to leave me, and when he pleads that he is too old, and that nobody else will take him, I plead that I am too old too, and that it is rather hard that I am not to have a few flowers, or a little fruit as long as I live. I shall now try if I can to make any compromise with him, for I own I cannot bear to turn him adrift, nor will starve an old servant, though never a good one to please my mouth and nose. Besides, he is a Scot, and I will not be unjust, even to that odious nation; and the more I dislike him, the less will I allow my partiality to persuade me that I am in the right ... I will take the liberty of letting you know, if I can persuade the Serpent that has reduced my little Eden to be as nasty and barren as the Highlands, to take a pension and a yellow ribbon.[6]

Horticulturist and writer Alan Titchmarsh divides jobbing gardeners into two categories – 'treasures' and 'tolerables':

## THE TREASURES

They will cater for your every whim, thinking ahead and anticipating your gardening problems, fads and fancies. They know which plants you love and which you hate. They are quite good at recognising weeds. They are prepared to be flexible about hours and about their duties (they cope with children and pets when the occasion demands). They know the difference between weed-killer and insecticide. They work inside when it rains instead of going home. They will bring seeds and plants for you to try. They will listen to your requests and plant things just where you ask. They are capable of making their own cup of coffee. They are tidy. They clean their tools. They are rarer than blue roses.

## THE TOLERABLES

They are often inherited. They resent change. Their favourite flowers are chrysanthemums, dahlias, gladioli, scarlet salvias, standard fuchsias, orange French marigolds, and lobelia and alyssum. They love 'dot' plants. They have difficulty in recognising your treasures and pull them up as weeds. They insist on a manicured lawn. They will not allow you into the conservatory during working hours. The vegetables they grow will be their favourites, not yours. They don't hold with new-fangled tools/sprays/ideas. They dig beds where you don't want them and act on 'initiative' without asking if you actually want the orchard felling. They don't come to work if the weather's bad/ their corn is playing up/they put in twenty minutes' overtime last week and you forgot to pay them for it. They don't let you know when they're not coming in (it pays to keep you guessing). They manage to keep their jobs. But then staff are so difficult to find these days.[7]

The peculiarities of jobbing gardeners seem the same the world over.

In New Zealand, falling into the 'Tolerables' category is the countryman born and bred. He is a true son of the soil who has a lifetime of agricultural labour, farming or fencing behind him. He can 'turn his hand to almost anything' but in the evening of his years he has become so plagued by arthritis and other ailments or injuries connected with too much of the great outdoors ('me back, me knees') that he is slow-moving to the point of having become almost stationary. But he is still very good at giving advice.

His main virtue is that unlike his city colleague he is indifferent to inclement weather. He will potter about equally happily in scorching sun or torrential rain. He will not draw social distinctions between spreading manure or contentedly sowing flower seedlings.

The urban paid help will have come to the job by a different route to the son of the soil. His offer of assistance in the garden usually arises out of his desire to augment on a tax-free basis the amount of social welfare assistance made available to him by the state.

Employer/employee negotiations open on the 'cash in hand or cash cheques only' basis before he's your man. The main disadvantage of this type of employee is that he will almost certainly fall mysteriously sick, go on holiday, or disappear from the face of the earth just before the busiest times of year in the garden (with cash in hand).

The skills of this type of recruit to horticultural labouring sometimes include such unusual talents as having access to cheap supplies of costly herbicides, insecticides, tools and fertilisers which have apparently fallen off the back of a lorry, or have been 'acquired' by 'one of me mates'.

Someone so well connected in the right quarters also evidently has some sort of self-help arrangement with the Almighty, because he has a finely honed instinct for self-preservation. Whenever there are chores such as mowing, digging over the vegetable plot or excavating large holes for new shrubs and trees, the tasks may actually be begun (with caution), but they will almost certainly be curtailed by the weather 'turning real nasty' and remaining so for several days. By the time it clears you've had to get out there and do the job yourself. If he turns up at all during this period he will potter about mysteriously in the greenhouse, emerging only to collect his cash, expressing the pious hope that 'the weather will clear tomorrow'.

In the United States, Eleanor Perenyi, making a garden in Connecticut, found the jobbing gardener equally unsatisfactory. Only one out of a long succession of hired helpers grew to love the garden, in spite of which he earned the distinction of having never learned the name of a single plant.

When I look back at the long procession of incompetents, dumbells and eccentrics, young and old, foreign and domestic, who have worked for me, I wonder how I and the garden have survived their ministrations. I recall, for example, Mr R, a well-known figure in town because in spite of his shabby get-up he is said to be very rich, with large plantations in Brazil – or it may be the Cape Verde Islands. You see him moving at a rapid hobble along the street, on his way to some garden or other, usually belonging to a newcomer because we old-timers know that he brings death and destruction with him. Those he has worked for discuss him with tears in their eyes. The summer he gardened for me he killed two cherry trees, uprooted a plantation of Dutch iris and imparted crooked lines to the perennial beds from which they have never fully recovered …

It occurs to me that I attract the mentally unbalanced. Or perhaps their therapists have advised them to take up outdoor work? There was the beautiful Italian, a veritable Donatello with black curly hair and a bronzed torso we saw a lot of. He arrived in a Cadillac of immense size, did little work but talked a lot about trips he intended to make, businesses he meant to start, and often asked to use the telephone. He was eventually arrested for having tried to murder his mistress, and though he was given a suspended sentence, it seemed better not to have him around …

Not one of my helpers has ever had the slightest knowledge of horticulture, or even acquired it – not even my dear A.V., with me for five years, who truly did love the garden … but never learned to identify a single flower, bush or tree or any of the techniques associated with growing them.[8]

Garden writer Jason Hill has the last (scathing) word on the eccentricities of the reluctant jobbing gardener, concluding with the comment that he is prone to too much leaning on his spade:

Those who have employed a jobbing gardener will realise at once that 'contemplative', when applied to the gardener, is not purely a commendatory epithet.[9]

It is not, as Alan Titchmarsh reminds us, impossible that one might strike it lucky and find one of the 'Treasures' – someone who is devoted to both your service and your garden. There is one kind of Treasure who is to be valued above the price of rubies. He falls into a unique category, often rejoicing in the title of the Non-Gardening Husband. It is not generally realised what a priceless asset he is. I am fortunate enough to have one and I wouldn't change him for any green-fingered son of the soil.

The Non-Gardening Husband is happiest and feels most secure in a role of

Admirer of the Garden. He is not concerned with the difference between a camellia and a rose, but enjoys what I create, and takes his duties as chief of 'Oo-h and A-ah' very seriously. But NGH is also the one who, when he can make the time, gives me and the garden the gift of the brutal toil required to build retaining walls, rose poles and sleeper steps, move huge rocks, and perform all those tasks beyond my physical capacity. Reluctant gardener he might be, but it is he who translates so much of the female gardener's vision into reality with hard labour.

Imagine the horror of having a husband like Walter Fish, who was very definitely not a reluctant gardener. Margery Fish says he believed:

> Firmness in all aspects is a most important quality when gardening, not only in planting and pruning, dividing and tying up. Plants are like babies, they know when an amateur is handling them. My plants knew, but I didn't. Walter would not tolerate an unhealthy or badly grown plant and if he saw anything which was not looking happy he pulled it up. Often I would go out and find a row of sick-looking plants laid out like a lot of dead rats. It became something of a game. If I had an ailing child I was trying to bring round, I'd do my utmost to steer him away from that spot. It didn't often work and now I realise he was right in his contention that a plant that had begun to grow badly could never be made into a decent citizen and the only thing to do was to scrap it.[10]

Mrs Fish appears to have been dedicated to her Walter. Clearly she had her reasons. I should have considered such hard-hearted vandalism as *grounds* if perpetrated by any spouse of mine.

As it is, the the Non-Gardening Husband with whom I am blessed will never enrage me by demanding 'What the hell did you dig that bed there for?' or by making scathing remarks like 'Those daft herbs are throwing shade on my tomatoes'. If, like me, you are blessed with a Reluctant Treasure, cherish and nurture him – his worth is indeed beyond rubies.

# 22

# GARDEN REVELRY

*The best way to get real enjoyment out of the garden is to put on a wide straw hat, dress in thin, loose-fitting clothes, hold a trowel in one hand and a cool drink in the other, and tell the man where to dig.* —Betty Meredith

The garden must be more than a place of flowerbeds, shrubs and trees; it must offer outdoor living and entertaining areas where meals and drinks may be enjoyed *al fresco*. It must be a place where sacrosanct ritualistic seasonal traditions such as garden parties and the backyard barbecue may be performed.

I was reared in gardens of the northern hemisphere where a barbecue may perhaps be attempted twice a year as long as one is wearing thermal underwear, souwester and gummies (or wellington boots as they are called in England). When I moved to the southern hemisphere, things definitely looked up on the *al fresco* front. I discovered it was possible to sip one's Pimms and scoff one's steak wearing bikini, shorts or less, without risk of hypothermia or bronchial pneumonia.

I was vastly impressed to observe that all outdoor cooking appeared to be done by the man of the house. True, the chops were often a little overdone, and the chicken dangerously pink, but I was impressed. I thought that male gardeners in the Antipodes must also be the most splendid of house husbands. Until, with much rolling of the eyes heavenwards, their wives, who were extraordinarily articulate on the subject, put me right with all speed. Having attended three barbecue meals in as many weeks at which mein host plied me with gory slabs of dead cow, I was soon groaning and rolling my eyes with the best of them.

A male friend from England has been staying with us this summer. The only time I ever saw him cook was when his wife told him to put a pre-cooked Christmas pudding in the microwave for three minutes. I was so surprised I

*Barbecue: a form of ancient sacrifice, where meat is burnt on an altar to induce instant heavy rain.*

took a photograph. He is, you understand, the most beloved of male friends, but he is a chap so unreconstructed that, faced with hunger pangs and no one to cook for him, he will open a can of soup and consume it cold, rather than warming it in a pan. But invite friends round for a backyard barbie and he can't get out there quickly enough to help cremate the cutlets.

It appears that as soon as the sun comes out, men are seized by the urge. In gardens all over the globe, rusty ironmongery is dragged out of the shed and dusted down. Mountains of otherwise edible chops and sausages are frazzled on the outside while remaining dangerously raw inside.

While chops, cutlets, drumsticks and other desperately expensive choice cuts are being ruined on the barbecue, bonhomie has evaporated by the time the food is served – two hours late. On the Richter scale of domestic disruptions, a barbecue must run neck and neck with joint attempts at interior decorating. Marital breakdown may only be avoided by adopting a dumb uncritical attitude of appreciation as your spouse does it all wrong.

Wives ponder why the hideously expensive labour-saving equipment that could microwave, grill, roast or bake the party meal stands idle in the kitchen, while their husbands stomp round cursing, performing CPR on a heap of unresponsive charcoal briquettes. You know summer has come when the supermarket shelves are stocked with enough barbecue lighting fuel to blow the ozone layer apart. What this does to the taste of the food is something else again.

My best gardening friend's theory is that men think of barbecuing as part of the great outdoor scene, healthy and masculine. The reality of course is somewhat different. An entire industry exists to give them the feeling that they are at home on the cooking range.

'Let's ask the gang round,' says the man of the house. 'We'll just have a simple barbecue.' Groan. Simple for him maybe, but mega-hassle for the rest of the family. Everyone must fetch and carry for the maestro as he cremates pieces of dead flesh or brews cultures of salmonella bacteria. 'It will give you a day off cooking,' he declares generously, neglecting to mention the four hours you will spend clearing up afterwards, as he quaffs ale with his cronies.

The illusion that Dad is a *chef de cuisine* on the barbie must be maintained at all costs in front of the children. Early burnt offerings must be smuggled back into the kitchen for frantic more thorough cooking, or the chicken portions surreptitiously partially precooked before they hit Father's flambé machine.

In all fairness, some men do know their limitations on the culinary front and invest in grand electric plug-in or gas-fired contraptions, which are indeed capable of spit-roasting an ox.

Most, however, regard this as cheating and wimpish in the extreme. If Og and Mog could barbecue a beast for their families on the floor of a cave over a few smouldering sticks, then so can they.

Perhaps the urge to barbecue is rooted in men's most primitive instincts. You only have to look at the barbaric array of accessories – Ivan the Impaler forks, torture-chamber skewers, flesh-tearing pincers and red-hot pokers (not the botanical kind) – to suspect that this is suburban man's attempt to reacquaint himself with some not very civilised urges. Sure, the chicken and chops may come in plastic packs from the supermarket, but it's man the hunter and provider searing them in a magnificent mêlée of smoke, flame and grease beneath the sky. He may be choking and cursing, but behind the conflagration of his sacrificial altar he is the splendid primitive omnipotent male.

I am moved by golden flower-scented evenings washed in lavender and rose. I am moved by the happiness of relaxing with friends in the garden, sipping a glass of chilled wine. I am not so moved by the macho barbecue scenario and the ash-encrusted offerings sacrificed on the altar of the Hibachi. This seasonal ritual insisted upon by the male gardener can only be said to give the female of the species the opportunity to demonstrate her astonishing capacity for forbearance and wifely condescension.

When he utters those dread words ('simple barbie lunch party') you can always pray for rain. The garden needs it anyway.

The so-called garden party is one of the major annual rituals associated with gardening. It has, however, little to do with the garden and can scarcely be called a party.

It comes in at the top end of the horticultural social calendar and its main function is to allow the gardening élite to see, to be seen, to make useful business and social contacts and to exchange the latest in green-fingered gossip. The party may well be presented in the guise of a fundraising charity event, with proceeds going to such worthy causes as the Restoration of the Cathedral Roof Appeal, or to the Benevolent Fund for Impoverished Retired RHS Gentlefolk. Either way, it will cost you.

The garden party originated as an essentially British tribal tradition that was eventually extended to colonial acquisitions in far-flung outposts of the Empire. They ranged from the grandest of them all, the Royal Garden Party, to the much more modest affairs held in most shires and counties. You really do have to be an example of eminent personkind to be invited to The Garden Party - that held each year at Buckingham Palace by HM Queen Elizabeth II.

Just you and 8000 other eminent personalities trampling the most noble lawns of all, and inspecting the most noble herbaceous borders of all.

The theory is that you take afternoon tea with the Queen, but in that mob one usually has to slum it by eating one's cucumber sandwiches with lesser members of the 'Upper Grasses', such as dukes and duchesses, earls and marquis, or, if you are of fairly lowly social prominence, with the odd Honourable and his missus.

Unlike garden parties held for more philanthropic reasons, the Royal Garden Party is of financial benefit only to those firms that hire out morning dress or 'worn once only on the catwalk' gowns from *haute couture* fashion houses.

If you have any eminence in the horticultural world at all you are more likely to be invited to a smart but more parochial affair in a well-known garden. In addition to its social significance, the garden party will undoubtedly be in aid of a major charity event – usually identified on the front of the gilt-edged invitation card. The startling figure it is going to cost you is announced in small print on the reverse, but the piece of vellum will look very handsome on the mantelpiece or propped up on top of the tele. It will also enhance your status enormously if you display it prominently when gardening cronies call and mutter vaguely, 'I suppose you're off to the party at the lodge next month?'

Hazards to be negotiated at the more socially ambitious or Upper-Grass garden party include:

• Vehicular one-upmanship

• Choice of what to wear

• Refreshments

• Conversation

• The weather

• Garden bores

If you are genuinely concerned to promote your avant-gardener status, borrow a decent car for the occasion – the 'take the kids to school' family runabout will not do. The parking lot at the Old Rectory, Mansion Manor or Historic Homestead will look as though the charitable funds are to be raised by an auction of Range Rovers, Land Cruisers, BMWs and Volvo Estates. I remember my acute embarrassment on the occasion of one Upper-Grass garden party when my husband Brian rang to say he had been unavoidably detained. I would have to take myself off to the horticultural thrash in the family heap. With nearly two decades of Anthony history attached (including teaching young persons to drive), my elderly, battered but much beloved Honda hatchback had to serve as Cinderella's carriage. I did not even have time to attempt to hose off its usual crust of mud and manure.

The next question is what to wear. This is enormously important because sartorial elegance is the very essence of the garden party. You can forget about comfortable old gardening gear here, or even avant-garde trendy denim gardening gear. Silk is *de rigeur* – silk shirts, ties, frocks, handkerchiefs and scarves, along with neatly creased pants, well-polished shoes – and of course if you are the female of the species a hat as enormous and eye-catching as you can manage.

Fake flowers on one's hat are okay – just – but in the good taste stakes your status will be considerably enhanced by a hat dripping with the best freshly picked blooms your garden has to offer that day. The flowers in your host's garden take second place to the ambulatory specimens at a garden party, because once the initial excitement of seeing who is there has worn off, everyone sizes up what everyone else is wearing.

It is a foregone conclusion that, having spent your all on sartorial finery that will not let the side down, you will find your outfit totally unsuited to the weather on the day. Most horticultural thrashes are held during the summer months, often in the late afternoon or early evening. This means you may be lucky and have a hot sunny day, in which case you will come off with no more than a case of third-degree sunburn and madly wilting flowers on your hat.

But more likely is that you will step out in your flimsy frock to find the ordained day cold and wet. Having been caught this way once too often and staggered home frozen to the bone, I decided at a recent garden party to wear a full set of thermal underwear under my ankle-length summer gown: long-sleeved vest and longjohn underpants – the lot. Smugly congratulating myself on being one of the few female guests present whose conversation was not taking place through chattering teeth, I received my come-uppance when the heavens opened and heavy rain not only moulded the flimsy white gown to my body in a socially unacceptable manner, but rendered it totally transparent also, starkly outlining the vestments beneath.

It's best to accept that you just can't beat the weather at a garden party. An hour into the grand affair, if, as it normally does, it has rained, one's beautiful hat will have collapsed in a sodden heap (on one memorable occasion the rain was so heavy the dye ran out of my hat, streaking my face and neck with rivulets of bright turquoise). The high heels of smart shoes (worn against one's better judgment) will have sunk deep into your unfortunate host's lawn, and one or both will have fallen off altogether. This causes you to spend the rest of the party trying to shift unobstrusively from foot to foot, maintaining a curious stalk-like gait because you have one leg longer than the other. The smartly creased pants and silk gowns will be spattered with mud around the hems and up the backs.

If the rain gods have decided not to water the host garden, it is a reasonable supposition that there will be a freezing wind. In addition to making you paralytic with cold, this will mean that both your hands will be occupied hanging on to your grand hat rather than pushing desperately needed alcohol and nibbles into your mouth.

Which brings us to the next great anomaly of the ritual. Unless you have honoured a lower-echelon do with your presence (in which case the eats are of the curled white bread, egg or tomato sandwich and shop-bought pastry variety), the 'refreshments' served will be absurdly unsuited to an occasion when one must eat standing up in a huge crowd in inclement weather.

In fact, one must be possessed of a high degree of manual dexterity and have excellent co-ordination of hand and eye if one is to down any food at all. One hand is devoted exclusively to clutching a precious glass of punch, Pimms, strawberry cocktail or champagne (depending on the grandeur and pocket of the hosts). The remaining all-purpose hand must be free to shake hands with the horticultural personalities one has always wanted to meet, while somehow at the same time clutching a plate of food and conveying portions of it to one's mouth.

If your host is practising petty economies ('more proceeds for the cause') the food may be served on paper plates. This is a disaster because they crumple or fold up seconds after you have piled them with delicious titbits, which then cascade to the ground all over your new shoes. Plastic plates are marginally more supportive, but their surfaces are generally so glossy that the food slithers off instead.

Hosts with a more finely developed penchant for watching guests suffer will put on a banquet of strawberries and cream. These, and those mouth-watering little tartlets heaped high with fresh fruits and cream are traditional garden party fodder. I have never once managed to actually consume any while at the same time clutching a drink and maintaining a conversation, without spilling the whole lot over my person or, agony of agonies, over the distinguished gardener to whom I have just been introduced.

Worse than any of these, though, are dips. Why in the name of gardendom must a culinary curse as absurd as a runny dip be served in this particular situation? Smiling slaves press them upon one, and so delicious do they look (the dips, that is), that one cannot resist trying to scoop up a liquid splodge of curry or seafood dip with a minuscule carrot or celery stalk. Both curry and seafood flavours seem to contain colourings that are especially ruinous when applied to good clothing.

I am vastly impressed with anyone who manages to eat anything at all at a garden party.

For reasons such as these, garden parties do not call for sparkling conversation or witty banter. Most of us settle for being seen by the maximum number of other important guests, meeting gardening celebrities, and not letting the side down by making spilled food-or alcohol-induced gaffes during a satisfyingly high-powered horticultural discussion with an eminent personality.

Sometimes a garden party will not require you to cast about in your mind for any conversation at all, because you may have the ill fortune to be pinned firmly in a corner by the inevitable garden bore. I hasten to add that there is something of this fellow in all of us, but on the whole we are all interested in what the other chap has to say, and more than willing to listen and learn. Try clapping an anguished hand to your brow ('a migraine coming on – do excuse me'), or to your heart ('Lord, I must get my angina tablets from the car – do excuse me'). Or just come out with, 'So fascinating talking to you, but I absolutely must head for the loos – do excuse me.' If all else fails, just switch off from the monotone about antirrhinum rust and let snippets of other people's conversation entertain you.

If the thrash is in the northern hemisphere it may go something like this:

'Jeremy, how marvellous to see you, and without Arabella – the kids have chickenpox, I hear.'

'Yah, fortunately we're insured.'

'What, against chickenpox, isn't that desperately expensive?'

'Of course, but I'm in the city now. Banking. Company fronts up.'

'What about your nurseries and gardens?

'Got a manager in – God, there's Priscilla Prominent, what is she wearing? It looks like a fertiliser sack – Priscilla darling, how divine to see you, gorgeous outfit, makes you look so slim.'

'Giles, thought you'd be here, that your new Porsche in the lot?'

'Yah, how's Henry?'

'Made a heap in importing irrigation systems from Hong Kong. Going to retire, lucky sod.'

'Retire? He's only 25!'

'Yah, quality of life and all that – going to hybridise spider plants.'

And in the southern hemisphere:

'Blue, Gidday mate, bit toshed up, eh?'

212

'Yeh, bloody uncomfortable, eh?'
'Whaddya doing here?'
'Bought a little sheep station in Central Otago. Joker who specialises in shelter-belt trees popped an invite.'
'Bit of land with it?'
'Yeh. Bit. 2000 acres.'
'For real?'
'Whaddya doing here yerself?'
'RHS invited us. Tarted the homestead and gardens up orlright – gonna be in the best Kiwi gardens guide this year.'
'Good on yer, mate.'
'Could do with a beer.'

When other people's conversations pall and you finally escape from the garden bore, you must seize your chance to take a token turn about your host's flower borders in the company of one of the famous gardeners present. In this case, with any luck he or she will do most of the talking, and if you have read, marked, and inwardly digested the sections on Hortus Botanicus Latinicus and avant-gardenership, you will be able to demonstrate that although you are giving him your absolute attention, your own knowledge of all things horticultural is profound.

'Ah,' you say, breaking off the discussion. 'A prime specimen. 'Viennot' is one of the best of French women.'

The personality will either be so impressed with your knowledge of roses that he or she will maintain a respectful silence, or be so mystified as to prompt you to launch into a detailed airing of your superior knowledge. Think of the mileage you can get out of a line such as 'Course, Rupert picked my brain on obscure French hybrids at the party last month ...'

The end result of the ritualistic garden party may be that you have a chill/sunstroke/indigestion/ruined your clothing/been bored mindless, but you will have stood up and been counted in the ranks of élite horticultural society.

The garden has always been a place for more than public revelry: it is the perfect setting for romance, and besotted young swains and moustachioed villains have lured sweet young things into the shrubbery from time immemorial. No book of garden humour would be complete without an extract from Tennyson's immortal poem 'Maud': the line 'Come into the garden, Maud' must be one of the best known in the English language. The reply from English comedienne, Joyce Grenfell, sums up the age-old battle of the sexes ...

213

# COME INTO THE GARDEN MAUD

Come into the garden, Maud,
For the black bat, night has flown,
Come into the garden, Maud,
I am here at the gate alone;
And the woodbine spices are wafted abroad,
And the musk of the rose is blown …

Maud replies …

Maud won't come into the garden
Maud is compelled to state.
Though you stand for hours in among the flowers
Down by the garden gate.
Maud won't come into the garden,
Sing to her as you may.
Maud says she begs your pardon
But she wasn't born yesterday.

But Maud's not coming into the garden
Thanking you just the same.
Though she looks so pure, you may be quite sure
Maud's on to your little game.
Maud knows she's being dampening,
And how damp you already must be,
So Maudie is now decamping
To her lovely hot water b.

Frankly, Maud wouldn't dream of coming into the garden
Let that be understood,
When the nights are warm, Maud knows the form,
Maud has read 'Little Red Riding Hood'.

Maud did not need much warning
She watched you with those pink gins,
And bids you a kind 'Good Morning'
And advises two aspirins

You couldn't really seriously think that Maud was going to be
    such a sucker as to come into the garden.

Flowers set her teeth on edge,
And she's much too old for the strangle hold
In a prickly privet hedge.
Pray stand till your arteries harden
It won't do the slightest good,
Maud is *not* coming into the garden,

And you're mad to have thought she would![1]

An absolutely indisputable case of 'Do not heed him gentle maiden ...'

# 23

# THE FLOWER SHOW

*In eager queues we gardeners trot*
*To see the prizes we have got,*
*And swell the chorus of dissent*
*That roars and rattles round the tent*[1]

The flower show is the single most popular ritual of every garden season. It is an advanced survival course for only the hardiest of gardeners. Size and scope range from Chelsea/Ellerslie, where almost a quarter of a million people compete to see if they can fit into the marquees and knock them over, to small rural community affairs with the ubiquitous sausage sizzles, strawberry and Devonshire teas, amusements for the children and a brass band, and everyone goes home with a prize.

Times are changing, though. Everyone used to dress up for the show, but apart from the squire and his lady and the community hierarchy (instantly recognisable in their Lakeland/Country Life knitwear, oiled green waterproofs and green wellies or brogues) both sexes now turn up in fluorescent stretchy lycras, black leather motorbike gear, denim with everything, or jogging suits. The band has been abandoned in favour of a disco, or country and western, which can be heard as far away as the next town, and there as many commercial stands to part you from your money as there are genuine exhibitors. The prizes have the same monetary value as they did in the 1950s and the cups and medals are veritable antiques.

A horticultural paradox on the show front which I have yet to fathom is the syndrome called 'The Country Show', which takes place seemingly at any time of the year in most big cities. For eager townie gardeners who flock to a day in the 'country', this means sharing a few hundred metres of battered local park with 30,000 other 'country' lovers.

At the 'country' show you can buy 'country' artificial flowers and helium-filled glitter balloons, run the gauntlet of salespeople brow-beating you into buying a water filter to purge your filthy city water of pollutants, browse through stalls selling 'country' mugs and keyrings with your name on them, or wooden plaques on which an obliging 'countryman' will burn the name of your house and garden for a considerable fee. Should you have need of a 200-horsepower tractor, or a ride-on lawnmower for your inner-city plot, this is the place.

You can dine on wholesome 'country' food, too – rural crabsticks, burgers, sausages, pizzas and fish and chips. The country candyfloss is especially good. Plastic sandwiches which have long succumbed to cling-film asphyxiation and dehydrated 'meat' pies are three times the price of those in the snack bar just outside the gates. To avail yourselves of rural fare you must queue with the other 30,000 folk whose stomachs are collectively growling. It is cheaper to have the local delicatessen make you a flash picnic hamper than to feed the family at the 'country' show. If they whine that they are thirsty you have two options: suck in your teeth and meet the extortionate price demanded by the punk 'countryman' with rings through his nostrils who is selling cans of luke-warm Coke, or point out to them the sinuous coils of the queues for the loos.

If you decide a spot of collective starvation will do your family no harm at all there are always 'country' entertainments in the showring to placate them. These range from dancing displays by scantily clad cheerleader (country) wenches, aerobatics displays by rural aeroplanes and parachute drop teams, and dog handling by the (rural) metropolitan police.

Tucked away right at the back of the park will be a few plant stalls run by staunch city/country women. For sale on the trestles is all the rubbish the impetus of the show has finally made them pull from their gardens – spider plants and geranium cuttings by the hundred, and wodges of ground cover which continue, despite the adverse conditions, to multiply before your eyes. Any vegetative treasures will have been bought by the countrywomen before the grounds opened to the public. There will be a couple of small tents exhibiting floral art and flowers, all gasping piteously in the heat or blown to pieces by the gale-force winds that are also doing their best to uplift the marquees.

If it is pouring with rain as well you have the bonus of being up to your ankles in mud and in danger of impaired vision as 30,000 umbrellas whip up and down.

'The Country Show' as presented in the city is a myth perpetuated by commercial enterprises for the sole purpose of parting the townie from his money.

At the very bottom of the annual horticultural social calendar comes the true country show, the village fair, or the grand charity events staged in local gardens. Intense rivalry and inter-village politics go on in rural communities in order to secure the honour of having one's garden chosen by the parish as the venue for the annual fruit 'n' flower bash. I have discovered the honour to be a dubious one, although the kudos and status of being the host garden and having rural folk come from miles around to view are undoubtedly enormous.

Essential and comprehensive advice on how to survive the critical eyes of gardening neighbours from across the county is given in the section of this volume called 'Going Public'. We deal here with the physical trauma inflicted upon your plot by the erection of marquees and stalls, and of several hundred feet tearing up your lawns.

The 'entertainment' to really draw the line at is pony rides – their sweet little hoofs are synonymous with instant baldness of the greensward. They also eat everything in sight when not employed giving rides to screaming toddlers. Resist also any 'entertainment' that tends to make people rowdy, for example an inter-village tug of war event. If the committee slips this one past you, be prepared for razed herbaceous borders and to reseed the entire lawn in autumn. Fight to the death any plans for a beer tent, or quaint medieval pastimes such as baby shows, coconut shies or water ducking. The latter involves beefy 18-stone countrymen being hurled into the water by guffawing 'friends', and the venue for this sport is among the hybrid waterlilies in your classical ornamental pond.

There is nothing you can do about inter-village rivalry over the fruit and flower exhibits – they have been at it for generations. Accept that the feuds fought over pots of jam, fairy cakes and the size of marrows, potatoes and beetroot will make that between the Montagues and Capulets seem like a minor tiff. Once away from their fruit and veges they are really quite good friends (and all related).

One of the worst experiences I have ever suffered in my long and chequered career as a gardener was to play host garden to a major rural fundraising fête on a cold, wet, and windy day – a fête worse than death …

From Maud Peters, The Hall, Ditton-Bishop, to her sister:

My Dear, as usual the flower show was a huge success and William actually managed to collect six firsts! You'll never guess who came down for it. Penelope Masters! It was actually her first real flower show. Naturally she'd been to the

Chelsea one, but that hardly counts, does it? None of the fun there is at ours. I don't think dear Penelope quite realised the kind of clothes to wear. If it had been fine – of course it never is for the flower show – her suede shoes and lovely Ascot frock would have been most appropriate. But it just chanced to be rather wet and I really don't know where Penelope thought one has flower shows, but she seemed a bit upset when she found we had to go right across the vicarage fields to reach the ferns.

I had my brogues and burberry and William was really very good about holding an umbrella over Penelope. Once we got inside she seemed quite interested in the peas and beans, and she was really quite amusing about the marrows, though I was rather glad that the rector couldn't quite catch what she said. Of course I'm thoroughly broad-minded myself, and marrows have sometimes struck me as being rather coarse. Penelope must have been rather overdoing it with all those nightclubs because, just as we were talking about potatoes, she suddenly clutched my arm and said, 'My dear, I'm afraid I'm going to faint!' Of course I offered to go home with her, but she said it was just through being shut up in the tent, and might William drive her home? It meant poor William missing my judging but he was very good about it.

Penelope Masters to her cousin:

Sylvia. If ever your life depends on going to a flower show, just die. It's quicker. My dear, can you imagine it? I thought the wretched affair was in the town hall! I did wonder why Maud wound herself up in her old burberry, but you know what she is. Of course it was raining, but I thought that going by car and being indoors it would rather cheer up the squires and people to see some clothes that weren't home-grown. Well, we'd only gone a little way when the car stopped. Maud shouted in that dreadfully hearty way of hers, 'Here we are!' and I found we had to squelch our way over the most enormous field.

I nearly lost both my heels and I was smothered in mud and simply soaked. William thought he was holding the umbrella over me, but being him it just dripped. At last we got to a floppy tent. My dear, you never smelt such a lot of hot, wet people mixed up with earth! Crowds of women in tweeds with faces like horses and not a lick of paint between them – just as God and the weather made them! Why do they call it a flower show?

There were little piles of vegetables and the most obscene-looking marrows. Well, my dear, we counted every pea and measured every bean, and Maud told me some tale about Pike having no business to have won the first prize for cottage potatoes because he grew them in his master's bed. As if I'd have cared if he'd grown them in his pyjamas! Anyhow, William seemed to have won every other prize and no one could call The Hall a cottage. When

Maud started talking about another tent it finished me. I looked all googly-eyed and said I was going to faint. William drove me home. When we got there we sat by the library fire, and he didn't seem at all in a hurry to get back! Really, my dear, the woman's an imbecile! *Quelle vie*!

Yours,
Penelope[2]

In almost any country, at the very top of the scale is the national flower show in spring, which is the first major spectator sport of the horticultural season. It may exhibit the finest display of blooms anywhere, but the ambulatory species are equally fascinating. Their foliage is distinctive, their ground cover spectacular, and each is a hardy annual.

Bowing low over the begonias are weather-beaten ladies from rural parts who do heavy spade work and open their gardens annually for grand charity events; sniffing the rose exhibits are immaculately groomed matrons from the cities who have never seen a spade; they are fawned upon by equally immaculately groomed garden landscapers who know that gardening will make them money; they are all despised by stern retired specialist plantsmen and nurserymen who view the whole idea of garden design as 'pansy'. Then there are those who are just there to be seen and admired like the prize-winning exhibits. Expensively scented, vigorous climbers and the result of careful propagation, they think hybrid teas are something accompanied by scones and cream.

The following specimens are easily recognised:

*Specialist Plant/Nurserypersons (retired):* Fierce. Plants stand to attention when they see them coming to avoid being poked about by the walking sticks they carry – a cunning device to give their owners a fragile appearance. In fact, they have an indomitable physique honed in the life-long bracing conditions of their country homes. The low-flying bosoms and stooped backs are the result of years of bending over recalcitrant vegetative treasures.

Elderly plantspersons have been members of the Royal Horticultural Society since birth. They despise modern roses, garden designers, garden centres and foreigners. They attend the flower show on days restricted to the media and RHS members, when they may commune with tweedy souls with similar prejudices. They know their onions – and their hybrid cultivars, their grafted fruit trees, and the history and genealogy of any plant on display. If they honour one with conversation they will elaborate (at length) on how they discovered a better strain of this or that hybrid in Nepal in 1948.

*The Exotic Bloom*: Ms Exotic Bloom has heard somewhere that wallflowers are something fabulously expensive printed onto silk wall-hangings. She has had an ensemble adorned with the same flowers made especially for the show so that she can compete with the botanical species. She likes to be dressed correctly for the occasion and to stand out in a crowd, in the hope that she may just have the good fortune to secure a retired horticultural plantsman with a good fortune.

Her laquered talons indicate that bedding out is not actually the sort of bedding she does. She has managed to secure a date (prior to pursuing her well-heeled plantsman) with the male horticultural celebrity who declared the show open. Her object is to persuade either of them to place upon her delicate little paw a ring containing a rock so large you could grow alpines in it.

*The Con Man*: The horticultural con man scarcely knows a rose from a rhododendron but he runs a successful landscaping business, using a combination of old Oxford/King's College bluff. He employs jobbing Australian and New Zealanders to service gardens from London to Auckland. In addition to 'Avant-garde Design' he pushes, among other things, *objets d'art* such as antique Ming and Ching 'investment' pots that fell off the back of a ship from Hong Kong. One of his more devious ploys is to present them ready planted with 'special' plants bought as a job-lot from a wholesale plant market. These will expire as soon as their owners get them home. When he is called to explain himself, his devastatingly charming grovel will ensure that he leaves the gardener's property with a signed contract to come back and totally refurbish it.

In addition to his pecuniary ventures, the secondary reason for the con man's solitary prowl around the flower show is for the purpose of picking up girls. To facilitate this he wears the latest in trendy denim gear, a rakish leer, and hair cascading over the back of his turned-up collar like trailing alyssum. The cad is a social ground cover, vigorously invading the pockets of those whose idea of a landscaped plot is a bought-in 'Insta-Garden'.

*Mr and Mrs Oddbod*: They are the very backbone of gardening society. They belong to camellia and rose societies, enter glads and mums in every local competition, boost their veges with Miracle-Grow and edge all borders with lobelia. They love a good 'show' and to ensure maximum visual impact plant beds of annuals of pink, orange and yellow mixed. The National Flower Show – Chelsea, Ellerslie or wherever – is their nirvana.

Mrs Oddbod is enchanted with the water gardens and is determined to purchase a Cupid peeing into a shell, despite Mr Oddbod's roars of how the *#**! do you think we are going to get that home on the coach?'

He likes to keep an immaculate garden that is a tribute to his ongoing war against slugs, snails, greenfly, caterpillars, whitefly, blackfly and mildew. His mission at the grand show is to discover what new horticultural napalm is on the market. He is also kept busy assessing instalment payments on every new gardening gadget being demonstrated by wide boys from the cities. On the last evening, when everything at the show is put up for sale, he and Mrs Oddbod stagger out clutching as much (wilting) loot as they can carry.

If you do not fit into any of the categories of ambulatory specimens outlined, it is certain that you are a keen gardener or a true plantsperson of less mature years. You attend the shows because you have a deep love of your craft and all things associated with it, and a deep respect for and devotion to the plants you grow.

The one fatal flaw in your otherwise admirable gardening character is that you suffer from the compulsion to show them. There are several reasons for this disability. You may suffer from the delusion that your plants are bigger, better and brighter than anyone else's, and if you are a nurseryman as well as a keen gardener, your plants may sell well enough at the show to allow you to retire and devote the rest of your life to hybridising obscure weed-suppressant ground covers. If you are a budding avant-gardener you may wish to enhance your reputation by consorting and exhibiting with the country's leading gardening nobs. It is also possible (just) that you want to exhibit your plants for the love of them. Whatever your motives, the path to the prize-winning bloom or exhibit is long and hard.

To show successfully you will need a hide as thick as an ox, a constitution as strong as an ox, a sense of humus, a strong back, and last but not least, an iron bladder. You will also need a heated greenhouse. It is given that 50 per cent of the displays at the national show are plants that are out of season. If you decide to go the whole hog and exhibit a garden design scene in addition to individual blooms, the drama unfolds something like this.

You decide to create a little 'cottage garden in spring' scene using scented perennials and roses. You have to organise all these plants in the greenhouse during the previous autumn. You bring them out of doors in early spring to harden them off and, given enough warm sunny days, you are confident that they will be in bud in time for the show. In your mind's eye you see the gold medal award card propped up against your display, which is a carpet of colour and fragrance.

You fantasise … cameras flash, the media jostle to get near enough to hear the self-deprecating statements and black lies that fall modestly from your lips

('I put in very little effort – the plants did their thing so well'). The reality is that a humdinger of a late frost will come to carry them all off, or scar them irrevocably, or you will have to hack them out of frozen ground with a pickaxe and return them to the greenhouse. The elements might, of course, go to the other extreme and deliver an unseasonally warm and sunny spring, in which case your embryo display is indeed a sheet of carpet of colour and fragrance – a month before the show.

Even if the vagaries of the weather together with the trauma of the process itself don't terminate forever your aspirations towards showing, and supposing your blooms are actually looking good enough to exhibit, there is the problem of transportation. You decide to do a trial run and cram the family hatchback with plants and display materials similar to the ones you are going to use on the day. You haven't gone two kilometres down the motorway before you admit:

1. Peering into rear-vision mirrors that reflect only foxgloves and delphiniums is definitely dicey.
2. Peering through a front windscreen full of gypsophila is definitely dicey.
3. The need to take fewer blue delphiniums next time so that you can see the blue lights on the police car.
4. It will take 10 trips in the family vehicle to get all your display props – pieces of ancient gnarled wood, outsized rocks, concrete bird baths, sundials, watering cans, tree branches, labelling equipment, half a ton of peat, plants for sale – to the site.

You decide to buy a van. Naturally your finances are stretched and anything like a four-wheel-drive Range Rover or Land Cruiser is out of the question. After eschewing the various clapped-out wrecks bereft of warrant of fitness documents advertised in the local paper, you hear of a large van, a 'bargain', through a friend. It seems like a sturdy vehicle and (allegedly) has only 3000km on the clock. You have no way of knowing whether it is on its second or third way around, but you can only buy what you can afford.

Older vans were designed for the enjoyment of having the engine actually inside the cab. This way you can appreciate the burning oil smell, and throaty roar of the engines better. You discover that foxgloves don't like fumes, and that earplugs and a fully stocked vehicle repair tool kit are essential.

By the time you have loaded all your gear, the van is groaning at the springs. A heartbreaking pruning of the gypsohphila allows you to see your way ahead fairly clearly and the wing mirrors do give you some rear vision, but there are total blind spots involved when driving a van. You begin to understand the suicidal philosophy of other van drivers on the road – what they can't see won't hurt them.

Finally, deaf and exhausted, you arrive outside the showgrounds. Every parking meter has a shroud over its head, and there are more 'No Parking, No Loading' signs than flowers on your gypsophila. You recklessly double-park and invite hernias as you lob your fragile treasures inside the main gate, bribing an itinerant labourer to keep an eye on them while you park your vehicle. You tell him you'll be back soon, but you forget to say which day. The exhibitors' carpark is 3km from the main show marquee.

A stroke of good luck allows you to commandeer a small trolley that another exhibitor has left unattended for a moment, and you pile your gear on and fight your way into the show tent. The scene inside is one of epic nightmare. The heat, the noise, the mess are horrendous; there is no one in sight to direct you to your allotted space, and you are bumped and jostled by other exhibitors feverishly erecting their displays. Only the thought of the expenditure on the van and the distance of the carpark from the show tent gives you the strength to carry on.

The first thing you discover when you've finally found the tiny space that cost you a bomb is that staging your display takes twice as long as you anticipated, and that the plants involved in your display are definitely wilting. When you've tweaked, watered and coerced them into some semblance of your original design, you creep wearily back to the van to negotiate the city traffic to wherever you are going to stay for the night. Like many exhibitors, even seasoned ones, you may be so exhausted by this point (or the first repayments on the van may have rendered you so penniless you can't afford accommodation) that you throw yourself amongst the plant litter in the back of the vehicle and doss down there, emerging weary, unwashed or unshaven next day.

The day of the show: judging at 9.30, gates open to the public at 10.30. You observe miserably that your cottage delphiniums are definitely looking faded, and someone has bumped your stand so that the large rock has rolled onto your cutesy little pansies. You realise that your exhibit now bears little resemblance to that you spent long hours designing and planning on paper. You spend a frantic half hour trying to hammer the plants, rocks etc into submission and are then commanded to leave as the god-like procession of judges appears.

You decide to go and stoke up on black coffee at the refreshment tent, but so has every other nail-biting exhibitor. By the time you've had your caffeine fix the public has been let in and you have to fight an impenetrable mass of excited humanity to get back to your stand.

When you do, the placard in the middle of your pansies does not announce gold, nor silver, not even bronze – but you have a highly commended. Ignoring what appears to be the entire membership of the Country Women's Institute at the front of your stall, all grabbing trays of your hybrid foxglove seedlings, you can't even be excited by the thought of the financial return until you have read the judges' comments scrawled across the rear of the card.

You have been downgraded because the bit of moss you had tucked in at the base of your dead tree trunk had not been labelled with its full botanical name. You have long since given up trying to understand either the criteria for judging or the rules of the show, but you curse yourself for this oversight because you do know that the judges are sticklers about correct labelling. Yours is not to reason why but to obey. You have been praised for your design layout, but downgraded again for overblown plants. The fact that they were tight buds when you loaded them into the van only yesterday, and that the appalling heat in the tent is responsible for this, is apparently entirely beside the point.

At this stage you learn also that you are going to stand nine hours a day for the next three days answering the same questions and running the gamut of public approval or disapproval. You wonder quietly whether a dash of whisky from the hip flask you had the foresight to bring along might not shake your delphs out of the grand wilt that is a prelude to premature demise. You resist the temptation to take a swig for yourself because the loo queue is impossible and any attempt to relieve yourself will leave your stand unattended, which is against the show rules. There is no answer to this one except to have bullied a long-suffering partner or relative to come with you, but you didn't because you had to place your 10kg display rock in the passenger seat.

The reaction of the public is the next hurdle. Some are delightful, telling you that your display is 'lovely' and takes them right back to their granny's old cottage garden; some unnerve you by just stand staring and say nothing; while others are quite forthright and say 'Pity about your foxgloves', or 'Musta looked really nice yesterday'. On the plus side the pansies you have spent years hybridising are selling well, but you agonise because you hadn't been able to cram more into the van.

By the end of the show you will have pushed mind, body, bladder and patience to the limit of their endurance. You are half starved and dehydrated and have been living on adrenalin, but you will certainly have met many of the horticultural hierarchy and it has been good to compare notes with them (you can name-drop shamelessly back home). You will have seen the best plants and garden design the country has to offer, and made vital contacts with other specialist plantspersons, all of which will help your own career as a leading horticultural expert or avant-gardener.

It is the last afternoon and the show is drawing to a close. In spite of everything you are on a high, feel in a party spirit and decide to have a swig from the hip flask after all. You are brought down to earth with a bang as the sale of the exhibits is announced. In your naiveté you did not realise that the crowd that had been eyeing your wilting display with such gratifying concentration were actually waiting to claw it to pieces with their bare hands. Suddenly they all converge on you, grabbing everything, even the plants that were too special to sell and were to have gone home with you. 'That's not for sale!' you roar at a determined-looking old lady who has lifted your best hybrid delphinium and is attempting to cram its four-foot stalk into her shopping bag. A few bolder spectators climb onto your stand and grab the props – the rocks, and dead half tree trunks. You give up and simply grab the money from those who are actually offering any.

Eventually they slip away and all that is left is a tent that looks as though a typhoon has passed through. You have to pack up and attempt to negotiate your way through the several hundred exhibitors intent on the same process. You begin to feel glad you 'sold' most of your display as you stagger to the final tape – the crowded route to the carpark and the roads to the motorway, which are jam-packed solid with the trucks and vans of exhibitors who effected escape before you.

But as you are leaving, several well-known gardening personalities wave their hands cheerily at you and yell, 'See you next year!' If you were able to think of anything but hitting the first pub off the motorway for a pint of ice-cold shandy and a large meal, and that if ever you exhibit at a national show again you will show only individual blooms, you'd realise, albeit through baptism by fire, that you have been accepted in the ranks of the nation's leading exhibitors and horticulturists.

If you have had the wisdom to choose to remain a spectator at the show rather than an exhibitor, essential points to remember are:

1. The day of the flower show will be wet. Take waterproofs, boots and umbrellas.
2. The carpark and entrance gates to the show will be a minimum of 2km apart from the marquees. Take a stick.
3. Take iron rations and thermoses. Imbibe the contents of the latter carefully for fear of having to join the loo queue and miss half a day of the show.
4. Resist the temptation to buy anything until the last hour, especially tall perennials, because two large poly bags will handicap you horribly as you try to view the exhibits and fight your way through the crowds. If you have to go home on public transport, they will be decapitated anyway.

5. Accept that you will be unable to see many of the stands because you will be swept past them in a tide of sweating, jostling humanity.
6. Before you leave home, set out a herbal footbath.
7. On the way home purchase a takeaway.

The show? We wouldn't miss it for the world.

## THE GARDEN COMMITTEE

Oh give me your pity, I'm on the committee,
Which means that from morning to night
We attend and amend and contend and defend
Without a conclusion in sight.
We confer and concur, defer and demur,
And reiterate all of our thoughts.
We reverse the agenda with frequent addenda,
And consider a load of reports.
We compose and propose, we suppose and oppose,
And the points of procedure are fun!
But though various notions are brought up as motions,
There's terribly little gets done.
We resolve and absolve, but never dissolve,
Since it's out of the question for us.
Where else could we make such a fuss?

—Anon

# 24

# THE UNKINDEST CUT

*Gardens should be like lovely, well-shaped young girls: all curves, secret corners,*
*unexpected deviations, seductive surprises and still more curves … —H.E. Bates*

One's garden on tele? Glamour, fame and public adulation? Why not? All it takes is ten and a half gruelling hours in burning sunshine, keeping one's wits about one, remembering the name of every plant in Latin, trying not to repeat oneself, pretending to speak naturally (and authoritatively) with a giant camera and a film crew a few feet from one's face. Ten and a half gruelling hours for ten minutes' television time.

However, our moments of glory are brief in this life and to have the humble plot on tele is undeniably a great honour. The filming process is something else again …

The crew is delightful, full of fun and enthusiasm, but you dither about, gabbling nervously, worrying about the forthcoming ordeal and how you are going to cope. The size of the TV camera is astonishing and, contrary to expectations, you are told not to look at it – to try to ignore it, and to look only at the vegetation you are describing. You are only too glad to try to ignore it, but since it is barely a few feet from your face, this is a little difficult.

Behind the cameraman is a high-powered director, an audio technician who secretes microphones up one's jumper, and the dazzling, totally charming female TV personality who will conduct you around your garden. She will show you places and plants you never knew you had, and fire obscure questions about them, leaving you to bluff, lie or gabble incomprehensible gobblygook which you know is going to haunt you forever.

Delightful though the film crew are, they have two things in common: they all have size 12 feet and punctuate every other sentence with the command 'Cut!' This is the word with which, when you have already struggled through a speech five times and have totally forgotten the original theme, they will interrupt you mid-flow, again *and again*. This is the word which, when you actually know the answer to the question and are responding with a brilliant piece of oratory, they will suddenly and inexplicably hurl at you. It is the word which, when your throat is hoarse, you are utterly addle-brained and exhausted, your feet are balls of fire, and you have forgotten the names of the commonest of plants, they will utter nonchalantly while you are praying through clenched teeth, 'Oh, please, not again ... ' Cut.

After 'cut' comes the phrase 'One, two, three, *take!*', which is the signal for the sequence to be reshot, that is – you've got to do it again. By the time you have rehearsed it five times, your voice comes out totally unlike your own because all spontaneity and naturalness evaporated on take three. At first the one, two, three count before the 'take' command lulls you into a false sense of security. You *think* you have time to *think* – to mentally phrase an authoritative, informative, clear and concise answer to the question. The flaw in the system is that since the original question was asked 20 minutes ago, you have forgotten what it was.

If you have a large garden, some of the more inventive presenters may want to take shots from the tops of ladders. It is your duty to stride off and lug these out of the garden shed, which is at the furthest point from where the filming is taking place. This will mess the trendy denim garden gear you blued a month's salary on especially for your TV debut. Since the noonday temperature has soared to 30°C it also ensures that you will be presented on the screens of the nation sweaty and dishevelled.

The dynamic director, contrary to one's expectations, is a happy relaxed personality, but his creative genius may dictate that he requires his cameramen to crash about through your woodland glade as though he were on location in the rainforests of Brazil. He may want to film you knee deep among the lilies and *Iris kaempferi* in the water garden or grappling manfully with the giant foliage of *Gunnera manicata* as though he were on location in the swamps of Sumatra. This sort of film sequence on the small screen has recently been pioneered in New Zealand by plantsmen like David Attenborough and the results can be quite realistic, even in a garden in the suburbs of Auckland.

The technique is as follows: you are told where to stand while the cameras get hoisted on top of the ladders in the shrubbery and the presenter climbs into your best specimen tree. At the command 'Take!' he crashes down onto the most fragile of your best dwarf maples. Smiling with breathless charm at the camera, he announces: 'We have here a rare and precious *Acer* specimen – as discovered by that reknowned plantsman David Attenborough in remotest China.' This is absolutely a black lie since the specimen in question is two a penny down at the garden centre. Furthermore, your little tree has acquired a strange contorted habit and does not now resemble any *Acer* species at all.

229

The bubbly lady TV personality invites you to announce its cultivar name; you obey and outraged viewers plague you with abusive phone calls for days afterwards to tell you haven't a clue what you're talking about, or to make such offensive remarks as 'Wot, call yerself a gardener?'

The director briefly loses control when the cameraman says the take is no good anyway because twigs got stuck in the lens.

Filming is thirst- and appetite-inducing work. Film crews must be fed and watered regularly and copiously – by you. For six months before the show you have worked yourself to the bone and wrecked your back transforming your back yard into something you think viewers would like to see. You have fallen behind with the mortgage repayments buying *interesting* and impossible-to-rear plants. For three days before the arrival of the crew you have sweated over a hot stove baking and cooking goodies good enough for august TV personalities, delighted to extend them the best hospitality you can provide. They fall upon the banquet with gratifying appreciation while you dash about filling innumerable tea and coffee mugs. You have time to neither eat nor drink.

The crew are kind and forbearing about the worst of one's bloopers. Mistakes only result in the sequence being cut and refilmed two, three, or four times or until you get it *right*. Dazzling dynamic lady presenter turns to self in rose garden: 'What are the names of those three beautiful white roses?'

Self: 'They are my trio *par excellence* – *Rosa* 'Iceberg', *R*. 'Frances Phoebe' and ...' (deepest darkest horticultural amnesia ). Cut!

At the poolside, spouse has launched into impressive verbal pontification (having, against his better judgment, been persuaded into speaking by delectable damsel) when along comes fat lady labrador, launches herself into water and ruins take. Emerges and shakes muddy water all over lady TV personality wearing designer fashion. Cut!

The hitherto tranquil and patient sound technician freaks out because the neighbouring orchardist has decided today is the day to spray his citrus using his tractor. All speech sequences have to be squeezed in according to whether man and machine are at the far or near end of the orchard. Spouse and director drive off to see the orchardist in an attempt to save sound technician's sanity. The orchardist is unimpressed with garden television, tells them he's got work to do and invites them to *!*#! off.

Mid-afternoon and the sky darkens, the heat becomes more oppressive and the thunder clouds roll in. Rain lashes down, but the resilient crew remain undaunted and as fresh as daisies. Time for (more) coffee and cakes – it will clear up soon and the day is yet young. You are sent to brush your hair and put on some 'lippie' while they refresh themselves.

They think the trellis draped with old roses is very nice, and by way of a diversion decide to shoot some film there as a promotional sequence for the next series. Lady TV personality takes one's secateurs and, smiling into the camera, proceeds to deadhead one's precious old rose in full bloom. Tractor roars to end of paddock – cut. One, two, three, take! TV personality stumbles over words. Cut. One, two, three, take! The blooms on the rose are disappearing. One two, three, take! The wind whips TV personality's sunhat off. Cut. One, two, three, take! There is not a bloom left on your magnificent rose. 'We'll take one more sequence to be sure,' announces the director. Your rose has had a midsummer pruning to end all prunings, but at least you can impress your gardening mates by name-dropping: 'Of course (name of famous TV personality) pruned my *Rosa* 'Buff Beauty' beautifully when she was with us the other day.'

The terrible day finally ends and you retreat to bed with a bottle in fit of despair, emotionally and physically drained, vowing Never Ever Again. *Ever.* You indulge in self-flagellation as you try to remember what on earth you said – and *why*. When is the programme going on? How long will you have to dread it? You try to arrange to leave the country the day before the screening but funds are not forthcoming. The doctor has said he does not think you need any valium.

Come the evening of the show you are gibbering wrecks. The gorgeous lady TV personality sets the ball rolling by announcing that your garden will be on *last*.

You groan and sweat your way through the whole nerve-wracking scenario, refusing to believe you really look that old/bald/fat/ugly or sound like *that*. The crew have presented the garden beautifully – it looks like a million dollars and you can hardly believe it is your humble plot. You alternate between loud cries of self-congratulation and anguish. Then the programme is over and the telephone starts ringing. Abusive calls from outraged specialist plantsmen aside, it seems you have become an unofficial phone-in horticultural advice service for the nation – *for days*. Mrs Watkins from Whangaparaoa is livid because she wants to know the-name-of-that-yellow-plant-by-the-birdbath-on-the-telly and you haven't a clue. You receive mountains of begging letters scrounging seeds and some folk even enclose SAEs demanding you send them cuttings of your best plants.

Ten minutes on television? The unkindest cut of all.

# 25

# GOING PUBLIC

*You must not any of you be surprised if you have moments in your gardening life of such profound depression and disappointment that you will almost wish you had been content to leave everything alone and have no garden at all* ... —Mrs T.W. Earle[1]

Nine years ago when I began the brutal toil of creating a garden from a wilderness of paddocks waist high with rank grasses and weeds, nothing could have been further from my mind than ending up with one that would be open to the public. Had I known then what I know now, I should probably have abandoned gardening altogether and joined the Ladies' Embroidery Circle.

At that time Open Gardens were usually large and well-known public properties. The idea of welcoming private guests into ordinary everyday gardens and using them for fundraising events was quite a novel and daring concept.

Going Public has probably been the steepest learning curve upon which I have ever embarked.

In the early days of hacking my way into the interior to make gardens at Valley Homestead, I was contacted by the local Country Women's Institute, whose good ladies 'had heard that I was making some interesting gardens' and could they come and have a look?

Somewhat perplexed I agreed, and before I knew it a steady trickle of visitors poured onto my earthworks (looking aghast or fascinated according to personal inclination) to observe the progress of my labours. I began to be summoned from my epic digs to answer telephone calls that went something like this:

'Good morning, Diana Anthony speaking.'
'Is it you who's got that open garden?'
'Well, sort of, I guess.'
'This is the Townswomen's Herb Circle. Our members would like to visit the garden next year. When does it look at its best?'
'October and November when the roses and old-fashioned perennials are in full bloom.'

'Oh dear. That's inconvenient. We've got a coach trip to the national show then.'

'Well, I'm trying to create a garden for year-round interest. You are welcome to come at another time.'

'How about an evening visit in July? Give us an excuse to go out for a meal first.'

'Will you be happy to see the garden in the dark? I don't have floodlighting.'

'Oh, of course, dark evenings then. Perhaps a coach trip to the carpet factory would be better ...'

Few gardeners can have any concept of how opening their garden to the public will change their way of life and, in advanced cases, their personality. Every avant-gardener or horticultural expert who has allowed their gardens to enslave them will fall into the trap of holding open days at some time or another, if only to keep them in money to support their habit. If you are going to do it properly, the first step is to get between the pages of a national 'Gardens Open to the Public' guide.

This sets you the exercise of describing in 30 ruinously expensive words the irresistible style and contents of your garden. Study other gardeners' prose before you commit yourself, viz:

Lawn Acres, Upper Crust
Lord and Lady Lawnatic
Immaculate lawns, fine herbaceous borders. Extensive lawns, old roses and perennials. Velvet lawns. Visitors not allowed on lawns. Proceeds to Grass Hybridisation Society. Plants for sale. Paper money only. No change given.

Cutesy Cottage, Coseycot
Miss Maud Maudlin
Sweetest little cottage garden dripping with roses and forget-me-nots. Heirloom flowers inherited by Miss Maudlin from her granny, well-known author of Reminiscences of a Gardening Granny. No children or dogs, but cats are welcome. Tussie-mussies for sale. Entrance: free.

The Old Rectory, NewlyRich
Mr and Mrs NewMoney
This historic vicarage and garden have been refurbished and renovated in the most daringly avant-garde style. It is now landscaped with the best of sub-tropical plantings, notably giant banana palms, succulents and stainless steel sculptures which contrast elegantly with the quaint old Tudor rectory. The

*piece de resistance* is the Tropical Man-Eating Plant House. The old-style herbaceous borders and sweeping lawns have been replaced by swimming pools, saunas and a home gymnasium. Visitors may avail themselves of these facilities for an immodest fee. Entry: megacash. Donated to Millionaires' Maintenance Fund.

42 High Street, Anytown
Bert and Lil Watkins
Comfortable wee city garden specialising in extensive annual bedding schemes and hybrid tea roses. An eye-catching spectacle in spring with clumps of bold yellow King Alfred daffodils beneath the fluffy pink blossoms of Japanese flowering cherry 'Kanzan'. This is followed by a summer blaze of purple petunias, orange marigolds, standard fuchsias and mauve lobelias, stunning against the red brick walls of the villa. Handpainted gnomes and windmills for sale. Entry: donation to Anytown Garden Club, or swap seeds and cuttings. OAPs and children free.

The Old Mill, Riwaka
Jade and Jonathan Greenee
Give yourself a great outdoor experience and visit our wildlife, wildweed and wildgarden sanctuary. All organically managed. Children and dogs welcome, but their safety is the responsibility of their owners and, regretfully, we cannot be held accountable for their loss. Bring compass, survival blankets, iron rations, distress flares and binoculars. Durable clothing and footwear is a good idea. Entry fee: subscription to *World Greening* magazine, available from sales shed near protected weed paddock at bottom of sanctuary.

Joking apart, my first step onto the learning curve indicated that keeping a garden to the standard expected by the public costs money. As the gardens slowly matured, visitor numbers continued to spiral. It was apparent that I would need to trade in my old mower for a modern, greater-horsepower model, and pay for a few hours of help with the mowing.

The dilemma of whether to charge an admission fee resolved itself. I had decided I would prefer an 'admission by donation' rather than an embarrassing collaring of guests with hand outstretched. Half the proceeds would go to a major charity and half to Diana's mower and mowing fund. This naive idea never worked because even after several coachloads of visitors there would scarcely be a few coins in the donation box. One evening after a particularly well-heeled group left it contained the grand total of sixty cents. That same evening an unknown rose cutting from the side of the road bloomed and we promptly called it 'Sixty Cents'!

One of the many eccentricities of the general public is their reluctance to part with the ridiculously small admission fees charged for garden entry. For the few dollars involved they could scarcely buy a sandwich or cuppa in a cafe – a newspaper even – yet they resent handing over this pittance for spending a pleasant morning or afternoon in a beautiful garden. Occasionally driven into a waspish mood by the tight-fistedness of my guests, I have muttered darkly about the cost of constant maintenance of a public garden (renewing of foot-path materials, reseeding of lawns, restocking of borders, replacing ornaments damaged or broken by unsupervised visitors' children etc).

Responses recorded to date include: 'They only charge $2 at Dunroamin' and their garden is much bigger than yours', '$3 is a lot to just look at a garden', 'The weather's turning nasty and we think we'd better go, can we have our money back?', 'We've been before, do we have to pay again?', but the visitors who win hands down for sheer audacity are the ones who ignore the 'Garden Closed' sign which is displayed after hours and ruin a family meal to ask, 'As it's after hours, do we need to pay?'

A final word to aspiring open gardeners: when you accept a telephone booking from a coach or group, learn, as I have, to arrange for their leader to have the admission fees collected in an envelope or paid by cheque beforehand. If you do not, you spend the entire visit attempting to extract the fees from the individual visitors while at the same time answering a thousand questions. Some guests won't pay at all, and no one, but no one, will 'have change'.

I learned fast in those early days. Balancing the time spent showing visitors around the garden and answering their questions with the amount of mainte-nance required to keep the garden to a standard acceptable to the public kept me haring round like a madwoman. So an admission fee was set, even if it meant prising it out of visitors' paws with a crowbar.

Another major hurdle on the economic front at this time was the necessity to provide a public toilet. Would we have enough visitors during the months the garden was open to justify the considerable expense of erecting an outdoor lavatory? At first I was possessed of divine faith that for the short time guests were in the garden they would 'manage'. This school of thought demonstrates more than anything else before or after, my incredible naiveté on the open garden front. I had reckoned without small boys, old ladies, coach parties from afar, and the 'simply curious', who will get indoors and do an 'open home' job despite all one's efforts to prevent them. The end result is that no matter how nice the visitors are or into which category they fall, the privacy of your family and home will be invaded by total strangers wishing to avail themselves of lavatorial rights. One broiling hot summer afternoon the results were almost disastrous.

We live in an old New Zealand homestead, and all our doors are of solid pit-sawn kauri wood and fitted with old-fashioned locks to which large metal keys must be applied. On the fateful day, for some reason the key jammed inside the lock on the lavatory door and the unfortunate lady inside was unable to effect exit. The full horror of it was that she was not missed until the rest of her party were back on the coach. A furious red-faced driver panted up our long steep drive, perspiring profusely, to announce in dark tones: 'One of me party's missing.'

As we searched the gardens without success a horrible suspicion began to form. Sure enough, agitated thumpings and cries emanated from inside one of the bathrooms. We were unable to open the door and the key was too firmly jammed for the incarcerated to extricate it and slide it under the door in the time-honoured tradition. Fortunately, our villa is single-storeyed and although our windows are set fairly high they were open because of the heat, and I was able to climb into the bathroom from outside. The lady inside was old, but neither frail nor sweet. The key was absolutely jammed in the door and I couldn't remove it either. She gave me a tremendous earful and did not appreciate my efforts to help her climb out through the window, despite careful and helpful placement of stools and chairs.

In the end the coach driver, even more red-faced, this time from embarrassment, had to go back down to the coach and beg the assistance of more ladies, and between us all we released the prisoner from her stalag by lifting her bodily through the window and down onto the verandah outside.

The party was now so late for the next highlight of their outing they would have to give it a miss. I was the ultimate persona non grata among the hostesses of the Open Gardens world.

I knew then I would have to wait a bit longer for my new lawnmower and invest in an outdoor loo. But I had reckoned without the combined forces of the council and planning authorities.

We have a large garden in a totally private rural area without another dwelling in sight. I had on offer at least six discreet, well-lit, well-ventilated sites for a small outdoor lavatory cum-washroom. We planned an attractive small building in natural wood with shingled roof, well screened by shrubs.

The council rejected both the design for the building ('inappropriate') and all six possible sites ('too far from the main dwelling', 'too near the main dwelling', 'insufficient foot access', 'drainage will be a problem', 'too obstrusive', 'inadequate lighting and ventilation facilities', 'structure too big for site'.

The definition of bureaucracy offered by my dictionary reads 'any administration in which action is impeded by unnecessary official procedures'. To this day, we still do not have an outdoor lavatory.

At the height of the garden season we now manage with a discreetly positioned portaloo rented from a local hire firm who deserve an award for services to mankind. In retrospect, if I had had the faintest inkling of the lavatorial requirements of the general public – that is, that there is no stronger stimulus to the bladder than the absence of a lavatory – my garden would not today be a member of the Open Gardens scheme.

Adhering strictly to one's chosen opening times is important. You can bet your bottom dollar that if you are five minutes late opening the gates, there will be at least two cars of frustrated customers glowering through their car windows. But deprive yourself of half an hour's lie-in on a Sunday morning and not a soul will turn up until midday.

You may have learned, as I have, that it is more convenient to admit the public by appointment only. This gives you some time to scoot madly round in the early mornings and evenings and get the maintenance done. It also prevents the family starving because you daren't go to the supermarket in case visitors come.

Most guests are considerate and keep to within half an hour either way of their appointment, and compensate for those who, having arranged a time, do not turn up at all. I try to be charitable and imagine that some dire domestic catastrophe has befallen them to prevent their coming. But the guests calculated to give me apoplexy are those who do not make an appointment and just turn up.

They roll up outside the front door full of *joie de vivre* just as you are about to serve the family a meal, or are halfway through tackling the most filthy job in the garden. 'We didn't make an appointment,' they announce, 'but we hope you won't mind us having a look round now that we are here!' I do mind. I mind terribly and desperately.

One of the sore points between me and my garden guests has become their attitude to labels. As the host of an open garden one is regarded as a bit of an expert and will be called upon to identify every plant therein. Many guests demand to know why you haven't got labels on everything in the garden, 'then we wouldn't have to bother you with asking'. The simple truth is that I learned that even if one spends the entire winter sticking labels under every plant, each and every one disappears by mid-spring.

This is because guests rarely remember to bring notebooks with them, and if they cannot get to you to ask the plant's name, the obvious answer is to swipe the label.

I am immensely comforted to know that that great guru of English garden-dom, Christopher Lloyd, has just the same problem:

> Label-pickers are a terrible nuisance. I do believe in the importance of a garden that is frequently being opened to the public being properly labelled, although I seldom have mine that way. It's an expensive and time-consuming business but it is important and I have label blitzes in the winter (sometimes masses get written but there's no time to put them out!). All those I use are of the stick-into-the-ground type, as mine is not essentially a tree and shrub garden. Visitors, who mostly have bad eyesight, will pick them out whether of the ground or of a pot … will they stick them back again properly? Almost never … it won't even go back in the same pot or in front of the same garden plant because by then her (or his) attention has moved on to something else, or she's talking volubly the while, to a companion.
>
> Thus do garden labels get scattered all over the place and this is almost as disheartening as when they find their way into the occasional dishonest gar-dener's pocket or bag.[2]

Like me, Lloyd must have learned never to stick a prominent label halfway into a bed or border, because the less sensitive visitor will not hesitate to amble in to read or fetch it, mindless of the havoc his or her feet are causing.

I can find it in my heart to forgive the label-pickers, frustrating though they are, because I have often longed to know the name of a magnificent unlabelled plant in another garden, but the guests who are absolutely infuriating are those who will bring the flower or plant to you, rather than taking you to the plant. They sidle up clutching a great handful of torn-off flower heads and foliage for which they demand identification.

If you are bold enough to hazard a 'What a pity you picked it', through clenched teeth, they will be vastly offended and retort, 'I've only taken off tiny pieces.' They retreat in high dudgeon when you tell them that they are the tenth person to bring you 'tiny pieces' off the unfortunate specimens that day.

---

*Gardeners who think they know everything are annoying to those of us who do.* —Anon

The most brazen visitors of all are the ones that will tear off a piece of a prized plant and take its label as well. When they get home and stick the greenery into the ground, do they write on the reverse of the label details of the scene of the crime, i.e. *Cheiranthus* 'Bowle's Mauve'/Purple wallflower, swiped from Anthony's place, July 2?

It follows that an ensuing hazard is the garden guests who will attempt to stock their own gardens with seedheads, or cuttings, or in some extreme cases with whole plants, from yours. Quite recently I apprehended the proverbial 'dear little old lady' who had uprooted an expensive catalogue-bought foxglove. When asked politely for its return, she removed it from beneath her armpit, hurled it at my feet and hissed, 'It's only a wild one!'

On another occasion I was honoured by a visit from an eminent garden personality. He appeared to be bending double to tie a shoelace, but I found him slipping cuttings up his coat sleeve from a dainty ground cover beneath his feet. I do not know which of us was the more embarrassed. What puzzles me is that these cuttings collectors, who would not dream of nicking stuff from the shops, just don't see their habit as theft, and in many cases will boast quite openly that they 'grew it from a cutting I nabbed from old Perkins' garden'.

English gardener Nigel Colborn has made a study of the professional plant kleptomaniac:

People build up their plant collections in different ways. There are few gardeners who can say with a clear conscience that they have never snitched so much as a cutting or a few seeds ... However, there are those who carry plant stealing beyond the realms of this minor pinching into the realms of serious larceny ... One of our most famous gardens was allegedly stocked with loot swiped over a lifetime from friends, rivals, national institutions – anywhere the owner could operate without fear of retribution. His style was impressive – it seemed the more obvious and daring he was, the more he got away with it – literally! Even when he was visiting gardens with a group, he would hang back from the main body to fill his pockets with whatever he fancied ...

For dedicated kleptomaniacs, certain items of equipment are essential. In public gardens it pays to have a large badge that says 'Seed Collector'. Wearing one of these enables you to browse away to your heart's content, not only taking as much seed as you like, but also lifting cuttings, bulbils and seedlings from under parent plants. Without a seed collector's badge, you will have to resort to stealth. You will need to carry a number of polythene bags, have a coat with deep pockets, or carry an umbrella which is closed but unclipped so you can drop plant cuttings into it. If it begins to rain, whatever you do, don't open the umbrella. The embarrassment of standing under a sudden rain of plant shoots has to be experienced to be believed.

You will also need a sharp knife – the small red Swiss army types are good because they stay sharp and the more expensive ones have tiny 3-inch saws for woody cuttings. Carting loppers around the garden is likely to raise suspicion and, although secateurs will fit into large pockets, it isn't half painful when you forget they're there and sit on them in the tearoom.[3]

Lady Maconochie of Inverewe Castle in Scotland became so incensed at garden visitors' outrageous and perpetual thieving of cuttings from treasured plants she invoked a curse upon their heads:

> Awake my muse, bring bell and book,
> To curse the hand that cuttings took,
> May every sort of garden pest
> His little plot of land infest
> Who stole the plants from Inverewe,
> From Falkland Palace, Crathes too,
> Let caterpillars, capsid bugs,
> Leaf-hoppers, thrips, all sorts of slugs,
> Play havoc with his garden plot,
> And a late frost destroy the lot

I have learned also that in every party there is always one, perhaps two, person(s) who will sidle stealthily up to one and say in tones of extreme virtue, 'I'm asking you while no one else is looking, but could you give me some cuttings from your pelargoniums?' You reply as tactfully as you can, 'I'm sorry, no, I can't, because that would not be fair to the rest of your party. If I give to you I feel I must offer cuttings to everyone else too, and I wouldn't have a plant left.' He or she will stalk angrily away, muttering to the effect that they 'will never come to this garden again'. An intriguing and fascinating code of misplaced morality.

One learns quickly that, as with any group of people, 90 per cent are wholly delightful, but there will always be the minority who will make you foam at the mouth.

Going public means becoming hopelessly addicted to the weather forecast, and living in a state of complete neurosis about what the weather is or is not going to do. Of knowing that it is a foregone conclusion that the wind and rain will (again) devastate the garden into which you have put so many hours of hard labour for a large charity event. If it does not pour torrents and blow gales the day before (when the lawns have to be mown come hell or high water) it will certainly do so on the day. It is equally certain that the day after will be calm, dry and, of course, sunny.

Indelibly engraved upon my heart is the week before a television crew came to film the garden. Spring had sprung, rosebuds were bursting, the weather was warm and settled. Everything in the garden was lovely. I broke the cardinal rule and allowed complacency to steal into my gardener's heart. Two days before the film crew were due, the weather changed dramatically, bringing torrential rain and gale-force winds. The taller perennials, cut down in their prime, lay face down in the mud. The sodden lawns were ankle deep in rose petals; whole flower heads whirled through the air like a multi-coloured snowstorm. As I raced around demented, trying to tie up canes heavy with blooms, three hardy lady visitors strolled along the storm-stricken rose walk saying, 'Oh, isn't this romantic – walking ankle deep in rose petals!'

I hid around the corner. Crying.

Going public means not only remembering all the plant names in two languages, but cultivating a memory for people's names and faces as well. So often garden guests stroll up with a jovial smile and greet you like a very dear friend. They have obviously been to the garden several times, but perhaps the last time was a year ago, and several thousand guests have passed through since then. You haven't a clue who they are, even though you might have conversed at length with them on some occasion.

Christopher Lloyd puts it this way:

Such visitors don't always make it easy for you. 'Well', they say, 'you know me,' or 'Who am I?', and are quite disinclined to help. Can you ever deceive people by pretending to recognise them, wreathing your face in welcoming smiles while you gaze confidently at them and start a carefully worded conversation that will at the same time not give your ignorance away but perhaps throw up the clue so that the blessed moment of revelation arrives? I must admit to being a bad actor on these occasions. I'm so preoccupied with racking my brains that my unhappy condition is only too apparent.[4]

This incurring of the wrath of regular visitors is not confined to the garden. People collar one in the supermarket and start a matey gardening conversation. It suddenly dawns on them that you are looking a bit vague and not showing much interest in what happened to their tomatoes after that awful attack of blight. They say, 'You haven't forgotten us, have you? You remember, we came at Easter, and then we came back with Aunty Marg and Uncle Ted only last month and you told us about pruning roses.' All of which makes the situation far worse because by now you have even less of a clue who they are.

I have been accused of being snooty by offended visitors because not only

241

have I failed to recognise and greet them instantly, I have failed also to acknowledge that I might once have spoken to them, and have subsequently walked right past them in the street.

✦

During peak season the guests with notebook in hand who pin you in a corner while others require your attention are sanity-threatening. They either require one to design and plant an entire garden for them on paper, or belong to the Intense Questioner tribe. They are oblivious to the queue of other guests and insist on involving you in a detailed discussion of the finer points of tissue culture, but more usually on riveting subjects like why you think their roses have downy mildew.

Now in the fourth year of being an Open Garden hostess I have learned that verbal fencing is an integral part of the horticultural scene and that one must cope with it as best as one can. Visitors are mostly just tactless, but sometimes the verbal slap in the face comes from surprising sources such as benevolent-looking old ladies or jolly middle-aged matrons who can be astonishingly vitriolic. They will assault you thus, guide book in hand:

'It says you've got lots of rare plants. Where are they?'

'Most of the beds contain unusual species. The new hybrid *Lilium* 'La Toya' is just behind you.'

'Why is it unusual?'

'It is an intense deep purplish-red and has wonderful gold stamens.'

'Bit over the top for my taste. My friend's got a carnivorous plant that eats spiders. That's more unusual than anything you've got here.'

Candida Lycett Green had this to say about conducted tours:

When I take first-timers around the garden they fall into three categories. There are those who go round chattering about something else completely, and pass each specially prepared view with unseeing eyes, even walking over a brand new bridge without so much as a 'My, oh my!'. They are the ones who take gardens for granted.

Next there are the recently converted enthusiasts, who never stop asking questions and telling you about their own gardening problems: 'How exactly do you grow begonias from seed?' and 'When are you meant to prune ceanothus?' As I don't know the answers to any of these questions, the journey around the garden becomes fraught as opposed to serene.

The last category are the old hands who walk around in virtual silence. When they pass an evidently glorious display of tulips, they do not say 'What wonderful tulips' but 'What are you going to follow those tulips up with?'

Then, when walking around the carefully contrived vegetable garden they say, 'If you want to see a really beautiful vegetable garden, then you ought to go and look at Rosemary Verey's.'[5]

An artist would probably lay down his brush forever if his work were described as 'pretty'. Bitter experience has taught me the equivalent in garden visitors' condemnatory adjectives are 'interesting', 'unusual', 'unfortunate' and 'strange'. 'That's an unusual way to prune *Lonicera nitida* (your best topiary specimen trained over 10 years).' 'What an unfortunate colour combination (your carefully colour-coded bed of apricot *Nicotiana*, *Rosa* 'Abraham Darby' and salmon foxgloves).' 'Interesting, your use of those tall salvias at the front of the bed instead of at the back.'

I have learned (almost) to cope with remarks such as: 'Of course, in a cottage garden situation such as yours, you just bung everything in and it all looks after itself.' The vision of the impenetrable jungle it would all become overnight without constant care and attention has to be allowed to flit silently through one's head. Jaw-clenching is mandatory when a visitor who has studied one's treasured collection of silver-leafed plants with gratifying thoroughness announces: 'It will look quite pretty when you get some colour in there.'

Then there is that question most often asked by visitors: 'Are your gardens finished now?'

English gardener and writer H.E. Bates would reply: 'The garden that is finished is dead.' I think so too, Mr Bates. I think so too.

Going public means never being able to put off until tomorrow what needs doing today – even if it means weeding when you're half dead with flu or mowing until midnight. Visitors have high expectations and 365-degree panoramic vision when it comes to sickly plants, unpruned shrubs and weeds. They do not want to see a bed of roses desperately in need of deadheading. (This can be quite a relaxing chore by moonlight.) There is also the visitor who will prowl around the garden and eventually, in front of all the other guests, triumphantly present you with a weed so huge you have mistaken it for a shrub.

One of the nicest things about having the garden to oneself again when the

*One of the great things about gardening is that when the huge wave of summer does finally break, and its leaping curve of green flings into every garden a marvellous iridescent spray of petals, in colours our language hasn't caught up with yet, its joyful and indiscriminate tide lifts everyone off their feet – both proper gardeners and people like me.*
—Paul Jennings

visitor season is over, is that one can sink into the very depths of garden slummery. The lawns can be left until tomorrow – next week even, the wheelbarrow can take root in the middle of the drive, and the rubbish pulled out of the borders can be left in heaps until you feel inclined to shift them. Bliss.

Above all, going public has meant learning to listen – and many visitors are immensely knowledgeable plantspeople from whom you can learn a good deal. More trying is to listen and try to learn from guests expounding personal gardening philosophies that are the absolute antithesis of one's own; to listen to detailed descriptions of every nook, cranny and plant in someone else's garden, of their prize-winning begonias, or the splendour of their perennial borders, while they are critically eyeing yours.

Going public has meant learning to listen to guests without once saying 'I', 'me', or 'mine'. This is an advanced lesson. Christopher Lloyd sums up:

> Being visited by strangers is, as an occasional experience, enjoyable. Most of them are well behaved and appreciative and they leave you with the feeling that the effort was worthwhile. Of course you may be among those who consider admittance to their gardens of the public an invasion. Basically this is because you are selfish and arrogant and look down on them (or would like to feel you can look down on them) as, in various ways, inferior to yourself. 'Thank God that's over!' you exclaim, as you punctually lock the gates a few moments before time, possibly raising your voice so that you can be heard by the last departing guest.[6]

Going public has not been without its pitfalls but the satisfaction of knowing that sharing one's garden with others is giving pleasure, raising funds and making a positive contribution to the community far outweighs the pain. Going public is the best possible lesson in how to behave in other people's gardens.

Gardeners are renowned for their generosity and to compensate for the 'cutting collectors' are the delightful many who will turn up with plant treasures you have lusted after for years tucked under their arms. If you have been honoured by visits from eminent horticulturists the result is often an invitation to visit their gardens and exchange cuttings etc, and new friends made.

From a strictly economic point of view, in proportion to the time and labour involved, opening your garden to paying guests will never make a second income, but it will pay for a few hours' help with maintenance per week, with perhaps a little to spare – which goes straight back into the beds, of course.

But my open garden has brought through the gates hordes of delightful knowledgeable gardeners whose passion is my passion, and whose pleasure is my pleasure. Nothing has been more satisfying than to share the fruits of my labours with like-minded souls. To bask in their appreciation, which, in spite of the often scurrilous tone of this discussion, has undoubtedly been one of the nicest aspects of opening the gardens at Valley Homestead.

If, as an aspiring avant-gardener, you are considering opening your garden to the public, or merely continuing to pursue the time-honoured art of gardening, hang on to your sense of humus and never forget that all gardeners know better than other gardeners!

Happy gardening.

Before you put this little book away
Please promise me you will never say
'You should have seen my garden yesterday.'
—Reginald Arkell

# CHAPTER NOTES

**1. The Gardener**
1. Karel Capek, *The Gardener's Year*, George Allen and Unwin, 1929.
2. Vita Sackville-West, *In Your Garden*, Michael Joseph, 1951.
3. Christopher Lloyd, *The Well-Tempered Garden*, Allen Lane, 1983.
4. Sir Frederick Moore, letter to the *Gardener's Chronicle*, 13 March 1937.
5. Richard Monckton Milnes, Lord Houghton, *Monographs*, 1873.
6. Beverley Nichols, *Down the Garden Path*, Jonathan Cape, 1932.
7. Gertrude Jekyll, *Wood and Garden*, 1874.
8. John Evelyn, *Directions to the Gardiner at Says-Court*, 1664.
9. Karel Capek, *op. cit*
10. *Ibid.*
11. Margery Fish, *A Flower for Every Day*, Studio Vista, 1965.
12. Beverley Nichols, *op. cit.*
13. *Ibid.*
14. *Ibid.*
15. Laurie Lee, *Cider with Rosie*, Hogarth Press, 1959.
16. Elizabeth von Arnhim, *Elizabeth and Her German Garden*, Macmillan, 1898.
17. *Ibid.*
18. *Ibid.*
19. Karel Capek, *op. cit*

**2. Tough Cookies, You Lady Gardeners**
1. Elizabeth von Arnhim, *Elizabeth and Her German Garden*, Macmillan, 1898.
2. Sackville-West, Vita, *In Your Garden*, Michael Joseph, England, 1951.

**3. The Trouble with Gardening**
1. Jonathan Cox, 'According to Plan', *New Zealand Gardner*, August 1995
2. Barbara Wenzel, *Painting the Roses White*, McCulloch, 1989.
3. Georges Duhamel, 'In Sight of the Promised Land' in *The Gardener's Quotation Book*, Robert Hale, England, 1991.

**4. Garden Attire**
1. Lee Bailey, *Country Flowers*, Clarkson N. Potter, 1985.
2. Theresa Earle, *Pot Pourri from a Surrey Garden*, Smith Elder & Co, 1897.
3. Shirley Ernest, Whakatane, New Zealand.

4. Valda Paddison, 'Throwing Down the Gauntlet', *New Zealand Gardener*, September 1995.

5. Lady Seton, *My Town Garden*, Nisbet & Co, 1927.

6. Audrey le Lievre, *Miss Willmott of Warley Place*, Faber & Faber, 1980.

7. Louisa Johnson, *Every Lady Her Own Flower Gardener*, 1840.

8. Eleanor Sinclair Rohde, *The Scented Garden*, Medici Society, 1931.

9. Jonathan Cox, 'Garden Attire', *New Zealand Gardener*, July 1993.

**5. The Answer Lies in the Toil**

1. Karel Capek, *The Gardener's Year*, George Allen and Unwin, 1929.

2. Thomas Hill, *The Gardener's Labyrinth*, 1586.

3. John Evelyn, *Directions to the Gardiner at Says-Court*, 1664.

4. Samuel Reynolds Hole, *A Book About Roses*, Edward Arnold, 1870.

5. W.C. Sellar and R.J. Yeatman, *Garden Rubbish*, Methuen & Co, 1936.

**6. The Vast Eternal Labour**

1. John Evelyn, *Kalendarium Hortense*, 1664.

2. Vita Sackville-West, *The Garden*, Michael Joseph, 1946.

3 Reginald Arkell, *Green Fingers Again*, Herbert Jenkins, 1942.

4. Cassandra (Sir William Connor), 'A Ray of Sunshine', *Daily Mirror*, 14 May 1963.

5. Beverley Nichols, *Down the Garden Path*, Jonathan Cape, 1932.

6. W.C. Sellar and R.J. Yeatman, *Garden Rubbish*, Methuen & Co, 1936.

7. Karel Capek, *The Gardener's Year*, George Allen and Unwin, 1929.

**7. Laying Down the Lawn**

1. Karel Capek, *The Gardener's Year*, George Allen and Unwin, 1929.

2. Rumer Godden, *An Episode of Sparrows*, Pan Macmillan, 1956.

**8. A Thorny Issue – the Rosarian**

1. Sir George Sitwell, *On the Making of Gardens*, reprinted by permission of David Higham & Associates and Frank Magro, England, c1942.

2. Elizabeth von Arnhim, *Elizabeth and Her German Garden*, Macmillan, 1898.

3. Germaine Greer (alias Rose Blight), *The Revolting Garden*, Andre Deutsch, 1979.

4. David Austin, 'English Roses', *New Zealand Gardener*, June 1996.

5. Vita Sackville-West, *In Your Garden*, Michael Joseph, 1951.

6. Beverley Nichols, *Garden Open Tomorrow*, Heinemann, England, 1968.

7. *Ibid.*

8. George Orwell, article in the *Tribune*, 21 January 1944.

9. Samuel Reynolds Hole, *A Book About Roses*, Edward Arnold, 1870.

10. *New Zealand Rosarian*, Spring 1993.

11. Jonathan Cox, 'My Last Rose', *New Zealand Gardener*, March 1995.

## 9. Gardening on the Rocks

1. Reginald Arkell, *Green Fingers*, Herbert Jenkins, England 1934.
2. Reginald Farrer, *My Rock Garden*, Edward Arnold Publishers, 1907.
3. W.C. Sellar and R.J. Yeatman, *Garden Rubbish*, Methuen & Co, 1936.
4. Beverley Nichols, *Down the Garden Path*, Jonathan Cape, 1932.

## 11. The Stress of it All

1. H Beard and R. McKie, *A Gardener's Dictionary*, Workman Publishing Inc., New York, 1982.
2. Karel Capek, *The Gardener's Year*, George Allen and Unwin, 1929.
3. Jonathan Cox, 'Horticultural Horrors', *New Zealand Gardener*, October 1993.

## 12. A Plethora of Pests

1. Justin Richardson, 'Parasite's Paradise', *Punch*, July 1947.
2. Elizabeth Pack, 'Cabbage White', publication unknown.
3. Douglas Sutherland, *The Art of Gentle Gardening*, Breslich and Foss, 1984.
4. Germaine Greer (alias Rose Blight), *The Revolting Garden*, Andre Deutsch, 1979.
5. A.P. Herbert, *Look Back and Laugh*.
6. Vita Sackville-West, *The Garden*, Michael Joseph, 1946.
7. Celia Thaxter, *An Island Garden*, Houghton Mifflin, 1894.
8. Hessayon, D.G., *Armchair Book of the Garden*, PBI Publications, 1986.
9. W.C. Sellar & R.J. Yeatman, *Garden Rubbish*, Methuen & Co, 1936.
10. John Carey, 'The Pleasures of Vegetable Gardening', *Sunday Times*, 24 February 1980.
11. Germaine Greer, *op. cit.*
12. *Ibid.*
13. *Ibid.*

## 13. Animals in the Garden

1. John Evelyn, *Kalendarium Hortense* 1664.
2. Germaine Greer (alias Rose Blight), *The Revolting Garden*, Andre Deutsch, 1979.
3. Anon, *The Complete Florist*, 1706.
4. Ursula Bethell, *'From a Garden in the Antipodes'*, from *Collected Poems*, Oxford University Press, 1985.
5. Gertrude Jekyll, *Wood and Garden*, 1874.
6. Barbara Wenzel, *Painting the Roses White*, McCulloch Publishing Pty, Australia, 1989.
7. Vita Sackville-West, *In Your Garden*, Michael Joseph, 1951.
8. Celia Thaxter, *An Island Garden*, Houghton Mifflin Co, 1894.
9. Fanny Burney, *Diary and Letters of Madame d'Arblay*, 1800.
10. Elizabeth von Arnhim, *Elizabeth and Her German Garden*, Macmillan, 1898.
11. Celia Thaxter, *op.cit.*

12. Stanley Roger Green in *The Countryman Gardening Book*, David and Charles Holdings, 1994.
13. *Ibid.*

**14. Children in the Garden**
1. Dylan Thomas, *Under Milk Wood*, J.M. Dent & Sons.
2. Germaine Greer (alias Rose Blight), *The Revolting Garden*, Andre Deutsch, 1979.
3. Elizabeth von Arnhim, *Elizabeth and Her German Garden*, Macmillan, 1898.
4. *Ibid.*
5. *Christchurch Star*, letter from F.Y., reprinted in *New Zealand Rosarian*, 1983.

**15. The Education of a Gardener**
1. Nancy Mitford, *Love in a Cold Climate*, Hamish Hamilton, England 1977.
2. Jilly Cooper, *Class*, Eyre Methuen, 1979.
3. E.A. Bowles, *My Garden in Spring*, T.C. & E.C. Jack, 1902.
4. *Ibid.*
5. E.A. Bowles, *My Garden in Summer*, T.C. & E.C. Jack, 1914.
6. *Ibid*
7. Gertrude Jekyll, *Wood and Garden*, 1874.
8. Reginald Farrer, *My Rock Garden*, Edward Arnold Publishers, 1907.
9. Vita Sackville-West, *Vita Sackville-West's Garden Book*, Michael Joseph, 1968.
10. Germaine Greer (alias Rose Blight), *The Revolting Garden*, Andre Deutsch, 1979.
11. Nigel Colborn, *This Gardening Business*, Cassell, 1989.

**16. The Avant-Gardener**
1. Beverley Nichols, *Down the Garden Path*, Jonathan Cape, 1932.
2. James Boswell, *Life of Samuel Johnson*, 1781.
3. Don Burke, *The Lazy Gardener*, Horwitz Grahame, 1983
4. Christopher Lloyd, *The Well-Chosen Garden*, Elm Tree Books, 1984.
5. Germaine Greer (alias Rose Blight), *The Revolting Garden*, Andre Deutsch, 1979.
6. Barbara Wenzel, *Painting the Roses White*, McCulloch Publishing, 1989.

**17. Les Herbes and le Jardin Potager**
1. Victor Hugo, *Les Miserables*, Dent, 1909.
2. Robert Louis Stevenson, *Memories and Portraits*, Chatto & Windus, 1920.
3. H. Beard & R. McKie, *A Gardener's Dictionary*, Workman Publishing Inc, 1982.
4. John Carey, 'The Pleasures of Vegetable Gardening', *Sunday Times*, England, 24 February 1980.
5. K.R. Flitscher, 'A Place of Torment', *New Zealand Gardener*, 1970

**18. Hortus Botanicus**
1. Reginald Farrer, *My Rock Garden*, Edward Arnold Publishers, 1907.

2. Christopher Lloyd, *The Adventurous Gardener*, Allen Lane, 1983.

## 19. A Survival Guide to Catalogues, Garden Centres and Nurseries
1. Jonathan Cox, 'The Joy of Catalogues', *New Zealand Gardner*, March 1994
2. Gertrude Jekyll, *Wood and Garden*, 1874.
3. J.F. Leeming in *The Garden* (Australian magazine), 1973.
4. Karel Capek, *The Gardener's Year*, George Allen and Unwin, 1929.
5. Jean Simmons, 'Nurseryman's Lament', *New Zealand Gardner*, 1996.

## 20. The Revolting Garden
1. Germaine Greer (alias Rose Blight), *The Revolting Garden*, Andre Deutsch, 1979.
2. *Ibid.*

## 21. The Reluctant Gardener
1. Lesley Phillips, *The New Small Garden*.
2. Miles Kingston, 'Let's Parler Franglais', *Punch* 1981.
3. Nigel Colborn, *This Gardening Business*, Cassell, 1989.
4. Ralph Wightman, *A Book of Gardens*, Cassell, England, 1963.
5. P.G. Wodehouse, *Leave it to Psmith*.
6. Horace Walpole to the Earl of Harcourt, *Letters Vol VI*, 1771.
7. Alan Titchmarsh, *Avant-Gardening*, Souvenir Press, 1984.
8. Eleanor Perenyi, *Green Thoughts*, Allen Lane, 1982.
9. Jason Hill, *The Contemplative Gardener*, Faber & Faber, 1940.
10. Margery Fish, *We Made a Garden*, Faber & Faber, 1983.

## 22. Garden Revelry
1. Joyce Grenfell, 'Maud Can't Come into the Garden', reproduced by Vivien Green, Sheil Card Associates, England.

## 23. The Flower Show
1. Reginald Arkell, *More Green Fingers*, Herbert Jenkins, 1984.
2. *The Countryman Gardening Book*, David & Charles Holdings, 1994.

## 25. Going Public
1. Theresa Earle, *Pot Pourri from a Surrey Garden*, Smith Elder & Co, 1897.
2. Christopher Lloyd, *The Adventurous Gardener*, Allen Lane, 1983.
3. Nigel Colborn, *This Gardening Business*, Cassell, 1989.
4. Christopher Lloyd, *op. cit.*
5. Candida Lycett-Green, 'Mrs Rupert Lycett-Green's Garden', *The New Englishwoman's Garden*, Rosemary Verey and Avilde Lees-Milne, Chatto & Windus, Random House, England, 1987.
6. Christopher Lloyd, *op. cit.*

## ACKNOWLEDGMENTS & BIBLIOGRAPHY

The author and publisher gratefully acknowledge the following for permission to reproduce copyright material in this book. Special thanks to Julian Matthews for allowing reproduction of material that first appeared in the *New Zealand Gardener*. The author has attempted to contact all copyright holders of material quoted in this book, regrets any oversights and omissions, and welcomes approaches from any copyright holder she has been unable to contact, especially in the case of quotations from antiquity.

Anon, *The Complete Florist*, England, 1706.

Anthony, Diana, *Seven Summers at Valley Homestead*, Godwit Press, New Zealand, 1994

Arkell, Reginald, *Green Fingers*, Herbert Jenkins, England, 1934.

Arkell, Reginald, *More Green Fingers*, Herbert Jenkins, England, 1938.

Arkell, Reginald, *Green Fingers Again*, Herbert Jenkins, England, 1942.

Austin, David, 'English Roses', *NZ Gardener*, June 1996.

Bailey, Lee, *Country Flowers*, Clarkson N. Potter, Australia, 1985.

Beard, H., and McKie, R., *A Gardener's Dictionary*, Workman Publishing Inc, New York, 1982.

Bethell, Ursula, 'From a Garden in the Antipodes', from *Collected Poems*, Oxford University Press, 1985.

Blunt, Wilfred, *In a Gardener's Dozen*, BBC Publications/ Royal Horticultural Society, England, 1980.

Boswell, James, *Life of Samuel Johnson*, England, 1781.

Bowles, A.E., *My Garden in Spring*, T.C. & E.C. Jack, England, 1902. Reprinted by permission of Thomas Nelson & Sons, England.

Bowles, A.E., *My Garden in Summer*, T.C. & E.C. Jack, England, 1914. Reprinted by permission of Thomas Nelson & Sons, England.

Burke, Don, *The Lazy Gardener*, Horwitz Grahame Pty, Australia, 1983.

Burney, Fanny, *Diary and Letters of Madame d'Arblay*, England 1800.

Capek, Karel, *The Gardener's Year*, George Allen and Unwin, England, 1929.

Carey, John, 'The Pleasures of Vegetable Gardening', *Sunday Times*, 24 February 1980, England.

Cassandra (Sir William Connor), 'A Ray of Sunshine', Daily Mirror Syndication International, England, 14 May 1963.

*Christchurch Star*, letter from F.Y., reprinted *NZ Rosarian*, 1983.

Cobbett, William, *Cottage Economy*, England, 1828.

Colborn, Nigel, *This Gardening Business*, Cassell, England, 1989. Reproduced by permission of Laurence Pollinger, England.

*Countryman Gardening Book, The*, David & Charles Holdings, England, 1994

Cooper, Jilly, *Class*, Eyre Methuen, England, 1979.

Cox, Jonathan, 'Garden Attire', *New Zealand Gardener*, July 1993.

Cox, Jonathan, 'Horticultural Horrors', *New Zealand Gardener*, October 1993.

Cox, Jonathan, 'The Joy of Catalogues', *New Zealand Gardener*, March 1994.

Cox, Jonathan, 'My Last Rose', *New Zealand Gardener*, March 1995.

Cox, Jonathan, 'According to Plan', *New Zealand Gardener*, August 1995.

Cran, Marion, *The Garden of Ignorance*, Herbert Jenkins, England, 1912.

Culpeper, Nicholas, *Complete Herballe and English Physician*, J. Gleave & Son, England, 1826. Reprinted by Magna Books, England, 1992.

Earle, Theresa, *Pot Pourri from a Surrey Garden*, Smith Elder & Co, England, 1897.

Ellacombe, Henry, *A Gloucestershire Garden*, England, 1895.

Ernest, Shirley, 'Plea for Gloves', *New Zealand Gardener*, June 1996.

Evelyn, John, *Directions to the Gardiner at Says-Court*, England, 1664.

Evelyn, John, *Kalendarium Hortense*, 1664.

Farrer, Reginald, *My Rock Garden*, Edward Arnold Publishers, England, 1907. Reprinted by permission of Hodder & Stoughton Publishing Co, England.

Fish, Margery, *We Made a Garden*, first published W.H.L. Collingridge 1956. Revised edition Faber & Faber Ltd, England, 1983.

Fish, Margery, *A Flower for Every Day*, Studio Vista, 1965.

Fletcher, H.L.V., *From Purest Pleasures*, Hodder & Stoughton, England, 1948.

Flitscher, K.R., 'A Place of Torment', *New Zealand Gardener*, 1970

French, Marion, 'Gardener's Complaint', *Round and Round the Garden*, Angus & Robertson, Australia, 1993.

*Garden Lovers' Quotations*, Exley Publications, 1992.

Gerard, John, *The Herball or Generall Historie of Plantes*, 1597, reprinted by Senate, an imprint of Studio Editions Ltd, England, 1994.

Godden, Rumer, *An Episode of Sparrows*, Pan Macmillan, England, 1956.

Greer, Germaine (alias Rose Blight), *The Revolting Garden*, Andre Deutsch (Private Eye Publications), England, 1979.

Greer, Germaine, *News from Stump Cross*, Aitken, Stone & Wylie, England, 1992.

Grenfell, Joyce, 'Maud Can't Come into the Garden', reproduced by Vivien Green, Sheil Land Associates, England.

Hazlitt, William, *Why Distant Objects Please*, England, 1821.

Herbert, A.P., *Look Back and Laugh*

Hessayon, D.G., *Armchair Book of the Garden*, PBI Publications, England, 1986.

Hill, Jason, *The Contemplative Gardener*, Faber & Faber, England, 1940.

Hill, Thomas, *The Gardener's Labyrinth*, England, 1586.

Hole, Samuel Reynolds, *A Book About Roses*, Edward Arnold, England, 1870.

Hugo, Victor, *Les Miserables*, Dent, England, 1909.

Jekyll, Gertrude, *Wood and Garden*, England, 1874. Macmillan Papermac edition, 1983.

Johnson, Anne, 'Squitch Grass', *The Countryman Gardening Book*, David & Charles, England, 1973.

Johnson, Louisa, *Every Lady Her Own Flower Gardener*, England, 1840.

Kingston, Miles, 'Let's Parler Franglais', *Punch*, 1981.

Lawson, William, *A New Orchard and Garden*, England, 1618.

Lawson, William, *The Country House-Wife's Garden*, England 1700.

Lee, Laurie, *Cider with Rosie*, Hogarth Press, England, 1959.

Leeming, J.F. *The Garden*, Australian gardening magazine, 1973.

Lessing, Doris, *The Habit of Loving*, MacGibbon & Kee, England, 1966.

le Lievre, Audrey, *Miss Willmott of Warley Place*, Faber & Faber, England, 1980.

Lloyd, Christopher, *The Well-Tempered Garden* , first published William Collins, 1970, revised edition Viking, 1985.

Lloyd, Christopher, *The Aventurous Gardener*, first published Allen Lane, 1983, Penguin edition 1985.

Lloyd, Christopher, *The Well-Chosen Garden*, Elm Tree Books, Hamish Hamilton, England, 1984.

Lubbock, Percy, *Gardens of Delight*, Miles and John Hadfield, Cassell & Co, England, 1964.

Lycett-Green, Candida , 'Mrs Rupert Lycett-Green's Garden', *The New English-woman's Garden*, by Rosemary Verey and Avilde Lees-Milne, Chatto & Windus, Random House, England, 1987.

McKay, Christine, and Peck, Wanda, *Quotes from the Garden*, Mills Publications, New Zealand, 1993.

Milnes, Richard Monckton, Lord Houghton, *Monographs*, England, 1873.

Mitford, Nancy, *Love in a Cold Climate*, Hamish Hamilton, England, 1977.

Moore, Sir Frederick, letter to the *Gardener's Chronicle*, 13 March 1937.

Nichols, Beverley, *Down the Garden Path*, Jonathan Cape, England, 1932. Reprinted by permission of Janet and Eric Glass, England.

Nichols, Beverley, *Garden Open Tomorrow*, Heinemann, England, 1968.

Nichols, Beverley, *The Englishman's Garden*
*New Zealand Rosarian*, Spring 1993.

Orwell, George, article in the *Tribune*, 21 January 1944.

Pack, Elizabeth, 'Cabbage White', publication unknown.

Paddison, Valda, 'Throwing Down the Gauntlet', *New Zealand Gardener*, September 1995.

Padmore, Diane, 'Delphinia', Australia, unpublished.

Perenyi, Eleanor, *Green Thoughts*, Allen Lane, England, 1982. Reprinted by permission of Random House Inc. and Penguin Books, England.

Phillips, Lesley, *The New Small Garden*.

Richardson, Justin, 'Parasite's Paradise', *Punch*, July 1947, England.

Sackville-West, Vita, *The Garden*, Michael Joseph, England, 1946. Reproduced by permission of Curtis Brown, London.

Sackville-West, Vita, *Vita Sackville-West's Garden Book*, Michael Joseph, England, 1968. Reproduced by permission of Curtis Brown, London.

Sackville-West, Vita, *In Your Garden*, Michael Joseph, England, 1951. Reproduced by permission of Curtis Brown, London.

Sellar, W.C., and Yeatman, R.J., *Garden Rubbish*, Methuen & Co, England, 1936.

Seton, Lady Frances Eveleen, *My Town Garden*, Nisbet and Co, England, 1927.

Simmons, Jean, 'Nurseryman's Lament', *New Zealand Gardener*, February 1996.

Sinclair Rohde, Eleanor, *The Scented Garden*, Medici Society, England, 1931. Reprinted 1948.

Sitwell, Sir George, *On the Making of Gardens*, reprinted by permission of David Higham & Associates and Frank Magro, England, c1942.

Sitwell, Osbert, *Laughter in the Next Room*, Macmillan, England, 1949. Reproduced by permission of David Higham Associates and Frank Magro.

Stevenson, Robert Louis, *Memories and Portraits*, Chatto & Windus, England, 1920.

Sutherland, Douglas, *The Art of Gentle Gardening*, Breslich and Foss, England, 1984.

Thaxter, Celia, *An Island Garden*, Houghton Mifflin Co., USA, 1894.

*The Gardener's Quotation Book*, Robert Hale, England, 1991.

Thomas, Dylan, *Under Milk Wood*, J.M. Dent & Sons, England.

Thompson, Flora, *Lark Rise to Candleford*, Oxford University Press, England, 1939.

Titchmarsh, Alan, *Avant-Gardening*, Souvenir Press, England, 1984.

Von Arnhim, Elizabeth, *Elizabeth and Her German Garden*, Macmillan & Co, England, 1898. Reproduced by permission of Virago Press, courtesy Little Brown & Co, England, 1996.

Wallace, Jan, 'The Gardener's Heaven', *New Zealand Gardener*, April 1996.

Walpole, Horace, Letter to the Earl of Harcourt, *Letters Vol. VI*, England, 1771.

Wenzel, Barbara, *Painting the Roses White*, first published McCulloch Publishing Pty, Australia, 1989. Revised edition Collins Angus & Robertson, division of Harper Collins, Australia, 1993.

White, Gilbert, *Garden Kalendar*, England, 1759.

White, Gilbert, *The Natural History of Selborne*, England, 1777.

Wightman, Ralph, *A Book of Gardens*, Cassell, England, 1963.

Wodehouse, P.G., *Leave it to Psmith*, reprinted by permission of Lady Wodehouse and the Hutchinson Group, England.